CMS Made Simple Development Cookbook

Over 70 simple but incredibly effective recipes for extending CMS Made Simple with detailed explanations – useful for beginners and experts alike!

Samuel Goldstein

[PACKT] PUBLISHING

open source*
community experience distilled

BIRMINGHAM - MUMBAI

CMS Made Simple Development Cookbook

Copyright © 2011 Packt Publishing

All rights reserved. No part of this book may be reproduced, stored in a retrieval system, or transmitted in any form or by any means, without the prior written permission of the publisher, except in the case of brief quotations embedded in critical articles or reviews.

Every effort has been made in the preparation of this book to ensure the accuracy of the information presented. However, the information contained in this book is sold without warranty, either express or implied. Neither the author, nor Packt Publishing, and its dealers and distributors will be held liable for any damages caused or alleged to be caused directly or indirectly by this book.

Packt Publishing has endeavored to provide trademark information about all of the companies and products mentioned in this book by the appropriate use of capitals. However, Packt Publishing cannot guarantee the accuracy of this information.

First published: April 2011

Production Reference: 1190411

Published by Packt Publishing Ltd.
32 Lincoln Road
Olton
Birmingham, B27 6PA, UK.

ISBN 978-1-849514-68-2

www.packtpub.com

Cover Image by Asher Wishkerman (a.wishkerman@mpic.de)

Credits

Author
Samuel Goldstein

Reviewers
Jeremy Bass
Robert Campbell
Nuno Costa
Ted Kulp

Acquisition Editor
Sarah Cullington

Development Editor
Hyacintha D'Souza

Technical Editor
Arun Nadar

Copy Editor
Laxmi Subramanian

Indexer
Tejal Daruwale

Editorial Team Leader
Vinodhan Nair

Project Team Leader
Priya Mukherji

Project Coordinator
Srimoyee Ghoshal

Proofreader
Mario Cecere

Graphics
Nilesh Mohite

Production Coordinator
Adline Swetha Jesuthas

Cover Work
Adline Swetha Jesuthas

About the Author

Samuel Goldstein received a TRS-80 computer for his 12th birthday, and has been programming ever since. Today, he is a principal at 1969 Communications (`http://www.1969web.com`), a Los Angeles-based web development firm. 1969 Communications builds and maintains web-based business tools for clients that include national brands like Isuzu Commercial Vehicles and Bioness Medical Inc. 1969 Communications specializes in e-commerce, integrating web applications with back-end/legacy systems, complex workflows, content management solutions, and troubleshooting complex issues.

Before coming to 1969 Communications, Samuel served as Vice President of Technology at Magnet Interactive in Los Angeles, Director of Engineering at COW, and Lead of the Programming Department at BoxTop Interactive. Projects at these companies included development of reusable frameworks, web-based applications, and data-driven systems. Clients ranged from dot-coms to well-known companies such as Nissan/Infiniti, Quiksilver, National Lampoon, Stanford University, Guess?, USC, Kahlúa (Allied Domecq), UPN, UCLA, Major League Soccer, and SegaSoft.

Prior to focusing on Internet technology, Samuel worked as a member of the technical staff at The Aerospace Corporation, where he researched distributed systems and database technologies. He holds a Bachelor of Arts in Physics from Pomona College in Claremont, California and a Master of Science in Computer Engineering from the University of Southern California.

> I thank Elizabeth for her love, support, and encouragement, without which I would be unable to carry on any meaningful endeavor. I also must acknowledge the many delicious soups she prepared for me during the writing of this book. I'd like to thank my colleagues Karl, Stacy, and Ron for their friendship, support, and for putting up with me. Of course, the book wouldn't have been possible without the help of many current and former CMS Made Simple core team members. I'd particularly like to thank Ted Kulp, Jeremy Bass, Robert Campbell, and Nuno Costa. I also am indebted to the many CMSMS community members who have attended the annual GeekMoot, sponsored modules, and offered advice and friendship. I'd also like to thank the team at Packt for making the book happen. Thanks to you all!

About the Reviewers

Jeremy Bass has been working with CMSMS for a few years now and has joined the development team. He aims to put out modules that will help his workflow and hopefully others will find it useful. One of his start modules is ScriptDeploy, which has the goal of handling severed scripts whether it's JavaScript, CSS, or HTML code. His prediction on his next hot module is one called FontIn, which lets you manage site fonts with previews and all the streamlining ScriptDeploy has for serving them.

Jeremy Bass is the Co-Founder and Chief Development Officer of the Philadelphia-based software firm Defined Clarity. His responsibilities include developing and managing quality assurance processes, management of the development team, along with leading the development strategy for the organization.

Defined Clarity provides business applications and frameworks for small and large organizations. Services provided include building, customizing, and supporting platform, web content management, enterprise content management, and database management applications.

He has also worked on a book—*CMSMS Beginners guide to 1.6.x*.

Jeremy currently resides in beautiful Idaho with his wife and son Corben.

I'm blessed to have a good family.

Nuno Costa began his career in new technologies by accident. When working on a business project in the transportation industry, Nuno realized he was actually building a web site and corporate image. At that moment he came to the conclusion that his real vocation was in technology, not in the transportation field as he had originally envisioned.

Nuno has held training courses in Designer and other multimedia technologies. He has worked as a web designer, mobile designer, and a specialist in User Interfaces and Web 2.0 technology, as well as working as a Unix system administrator. He has worked for companies in Portugal who were elected the best SMEs (small and medium enterprises), while developing work for both Portugal and international use. His preference in Open Source software includes CMS Made Simple, Drupal, WordPress, Magento, Roundcube, and Piwik.

Nuno spent three years as part of the core development team of CMS Made Simple, and served as the official translator for the Portuguese language. When Nuno Costa joined the CMS Made Simple team, he revolutionized the graphics and UI of both the default administration and front-end themes. He created the default themes that have shipped with the most recent versions of CMSMS.

Currently, Nuno Costa is developing applications for iPhone, Android, and Facebook.

Ted Kulp has more than 10 years of experience in professional software development, web development, software architecture, and open source project management. In 2004, he created the CMS Made Simple content management system, and has grown the project's use in countless production websites. In 2007 and 2008, the project received multiple awards in the Packt Publishing Open Source CMS awards, sharing ranks with CMSs much larger than itself. In 2010, the project's core reached a milestone of 1,000,000 downloads.

In 2008, he started Shift Refresh, a consultancy dedicated to the support, development and maintenance of the CMS Made Simple project. As both developer and manager, Shift Refresh helped Ted learn all aspects of business ownership beyond software development, including finances, customer relations, and project management.

Prior to Shift Refresh, Ted was a developer for Not Sold Separately, a local web development and marketing house. He worked directly with Fortune 500 clients and startups alike, developing on multiple languages, frameworks, and systems. He also played a large role in system administration, project management, and systems architecture.

A native of the Philadelphia area, Ted lives in Bucks County, Pennsylvania with his wife, two daughters, and beagle. He enjoys music, gaming, and travelling.

www.PacktPub.com

Support files, eBooks, discount offers and more

You might want to visit `www.PacktPub.com` for support files and downloads related to your book.

Did you know that Packt offers eBook versions of every book published, with PDF and ePub files available? You can upgrade to the eBook version at `www.PacktPub.com` and as a print book customer, you are entitled to a discount on the eBook copy. Get in touch with us at `service@packtpub.com` for more details.

At `www.PacktPub.com`, you can also read a collection of free technical articles, sign up for a range of free newsletters and receive exclusive discounts and offers on Packt books and eBooks.

PACKTLiB®

`http://PacktLib.PacktPub.com`

Do you need instant solutions to your IT questions? PacktLib is Packt's online digital book library. Here, you can access, read and search across Packt's entire library of books.

Why Subscribe?

- Fully searchable across every book published by Packt
- Copy and paste, print and bookmark content
- On demand and accessible via web browser

Free Access for Packt account holders

If you have an account with Packt at `www.PacktPub.com`, you can use this to access PacktLib today and view nine entirely free books. Simply use your login credentials for immediate access.

Table of Contents

Preface   1

Chapter 1: Understanding CMS Extensions   7
  Introduction   7
  Will a User-Defined Tag solve my problem?   8
  Will a Tag Solve My Problem?   11
  Will a Module solve my problem?   13
  Create a "Hello World" User-Defined Tag   14
  Create a "Hello World" Tag   17
  Create a "Hello World" Module   21
  Using CMS in Debug Mode   24

Chapter 2: Programming with Smarty and Core Modules   27
  Introduction   28
  Using Smarty to create a color set in your stylesheet   28
  Using Smarty to do the math in your stylesheet   32
  Renaming the "Extra Page Attributes" in the CMS Admin   36
  Creating a personnel directory using Menu Manage   39
  Creating a basic Google Sitemap with Menu Manager and mod_rewrite   46
  Embedding JavaScript in your template without causing Smarty to throw a fit   51
  Using Smarty loops to generate similar stylesheet constructs   53
  Displaying a block only for the Home page   56
  Using Smarty "Capture" and conditionals to hide empty content blocks   60
  Seeing what Smarty variables are available to your template   63

Table of Contents

Chapter 3: Getting the Most out of Tags and User-Defined Tags — 69
Introduction — 70
Displaying the User's IP address from a User-Defined Tag — 71
Using the CmsObject and the current content object in a User-Defined Tag — 73
Making a variable available to Smarty — 76
Displaying the number of pages in the CMS using a User-Defined Tag — 80
Using URL parameters safely in a User-Defined Tag — 83
Using Smarty values as inputs in a User-Defined Tag — 87
Displaying stock prices from Yahoo with a User-Defined Tag — 89
Displaying a translation of the current page using Babelfish with a User-Defined Tag — 95
Posting an article to the News Module when the Admin adds a new Group — 100
Reversing a string in two ways using a Smarty Modifier — 104
Adding registered trademark symbols to a name automatically — 107

Chapter 4: Getting Started with Modules — 113
Introduction — 113
Creating the file structure for a module — 114
Creating a new module stub using the Skeleton module — 118
Creating a new module stub using the ModuleMaker module — 121
Breaking a module into multiple files — 125
Making a module localizable — 128
Using Smarty variables and templates with a module — 132
Calling methods on other modules and specifying module dependencies — 136

Chapter 5: Using the Database API — 143
Introduction — 143
Creating a database table when a module gets installed — 144
Creating a database index when creating a table — 148
Making a database query from a module — 153
Creating and using a database sequence — 157
Altering a database table when a module gets upgraded — 161
Cleaning up when a module is uninstalled — 166

Chapter 6: Using the Module Form API — 171
Introduction — 171
Creating a basic form in a module — 172
Restricting and sanitizing parameters to a module — 179
Using debug_display or error_log to see what parameters your module is receiving — 183

Making your module display its output without disrupting the rest of the page	186
Embedding your module output in a different page after a form submission	191
Creating checkboxes that always submit a value	195

Chapter 7: Your Module and the Community — 199

Introduction	199
Creating an account on the CMS Made	200
Simple Developer's Forge	200
Adding your module to the Forge	202
Creating your Subversion Repository	204
Using Subversion while developing your module	206
Publishing a module release	211
Creating your Git repository	214
Using Git while developing your module	217
Deciding on Git versus Subversion	222

Chapter 8: Creating Useful Admin Panels — 225

Introduction	225
Creating an admin panel for your module	226
Creating multiple tabs for your admin module	228
Creating and enforcing new permissions for your module's administration	233
Displaying a page in the CMS Admin without the surrounding theme	238
Writing a line to the CMS Admin Log	242
Displaying a message after installation	244
Creating an admin-side input element from your module using a ContentModule block	246
Hiding your module from Administrators who don't have permission to use it	253
Creating a module-specific preference and admin panel to set it	257
Displaying an alert in the CMS Admin from a module	260

Chapter 9: Using Events — 265

Introduction	265
Attaching a User-Defined Tag to an event	266
Finding what parameters an event passes using a User Defined Tag	268
Generating an Event from a module	270
Handling an Event with a module	276
Use an event to send an e-mail when an Administrator Account is added or deleted	279

Table of Contents

Chapter 10: Advanced Module Tricks and SEO — 283
- Introduction — 283
- Overriding Module strings or layout — 284
- Making your module's data available to CMS Site Search — 287
- Outputting a downloadable CSV file from your module — 293
- Setting special diagnostic messages for debug mode — 298
- Using Pretty URLs in your module — 300
- Custom URLs for module records in CMS Made Simple version 1.9+ — 307

Index — 313

Preface

The CMS Made Simple Development Cookbook gets you started building feature-rich sites quickly, regardless of your experience level. It contains clear recipes that introduce the key concepts behind each approach to extending the CMS, while also providing examples of solutions to real-world problems.

CMS Made Simple has great capabilities "out of the box," but one of its great strengths is the ease of extending those capabilities. You can add a surprising amount of functionality just by customizing the core modules, but once you learn to write your own tags and modules, your ability to add features is virtually limitless.

What this book covers

Chapter 1, Understanding CMS Extensions, introduces the key differences between tags, user-defined tags, and modules, and teaches you to determine which is optimal for any given purpose. This chapter focuses on understanding the different approaches and deciding which to use to solve any particular problem.

Chapter 2, Programming with Smarty and Core Modules, demonstrates the use of Smarty and template logic to achieve complex functionality without installing anything beyond the CMS Made Simple core. You'll see how to do things you never thought were possible – all without writing any PHP code.

Chapter 3, Getting the Most out of Tags and User-Defined Tags, gives examples of Tags and User-Defined Tags, and shows how to create tags to handle such varied tasks as setting Smarty variables, filtering content, interfacing with modules, and interacting with web services. This chapter also includes information on some key CMS components, security pointers, and more.

Chapter 4, Getting Started with Modules, shows how you can use tools to jump start the module writing process, and demonstrates how to write fully-localizable modules in a maintainable and memory-efficient fashion. This chapter will give you a good basic understanding of how modules are organized and how they work.

Preface

Chapter 5, Using the Database API, shows how to interact with the underlying database using the Database API for safe, platform-independent access. This also includes discussion of updating database tables during module upgrades, getting better performance from your database with indexes, and generating unique IDs.

Chapter 6, Using the Module Form API, demonstrates how to render and process complex forms and user interfaces with the Form API. This chapter includes an example of a complete web form-handling application, along with tricks for debugging forms and sanitizing parameters.

Chapter 7, Your Module and the Community, gets you fully involved in the CMS Made Simple community. This chapter gives you a brief tour of the Developer's Forge, shows you how to use shared source-control repositories, and explains how to publish your modules.

Chapter 8, Creating Useful Admin Panels, teaches you how to build tabbed admin-side panels so site administrators can manage and configure your module. This chapter also covers custom content block types, admin permissions, setting preferences, and displaying messages to site administrators.

Chapter 9, Using Events, demonstrates handling events with User-Defined Tags, and both triggering and handling events with modules. This chapter explains how you can use events to enable complex interactions with tags and modules.

Chapter 10, Advanced Module Tricks and SEO, explains how to implement SEO-friendly URLs, making your module's content available to site search, override module strings, and export module data to desktop applications.

What you need for this book

The minimal requirements for this book would be a web server with PHP 5.2 (5.2.18 or later preferred) and a database server (MySQL version 4.1 or later, or PostgreSQL). Any web server should work, but one recipe uses Apache's `mod_rewrite`, so to test that one, an Apache-compatible web server would be needed. We will also need a modern web browser (IE 8+, Firefox 3.x+, Safari, or Chrome), some kind of text editor, and, of course, CMS Made Simple version 1.9.x.

CMS Made Simple's full requirements can be found at `http://wiki.cmsmadesimple.org/index.php/User_Handbook/Installation/Requirements` and the code can be downloaded at `http://dev.cmsmadesimple.org/project/files/6`.

Who this book is for

If you are a CMS Made Simple user wanting to expand your skill set, or a programmer who wants to develop for CMS Made Simple, this book is for you. You will need working knowledge of PHP, HTML, and SQL. Some experience with CMS Made Simple is recommended.

Conventions

In this book, you will find a number of styles of text that distinguish between different kinds of information. Here are some examples of these styles, and an explanation of their meaning.

Code words in text are shown as follows: "Custom URLs are accomplished entirely in your module's `SetParameters()` method, by creating new `CmsRoute` objects, and registering them with the CMS."

A block of code is set as follows:

```php
<?php
class Monsters extends CMSModule
  {
  function GetName()
    {
    return 'Monsters';
    }

  function GetVersion()
    {
    return '0.1';
    }
  }
?>
```

Any command-line input or output is written as follows:

mkdir MyModule/lang/ext

New terms and **important words** are shown in bold. Words that you see on the screen, in menus or dialog boxes for example, appear in the text like this: "Click on the **XML** button next to your module, and save the exported file in some easily accessible directory".

[Warnings or important notes appear in a box like this.]

[Tips and tricks appear like this.]

Reader feedback

Feedback from our readers is always welcome. Let us know what you think about this book—what you liked or may have disliked. Reader feedback is important for us to develop titles that you really get the most out of.

To send us general feedback, simply send an e-mail to feedback@packtpub.com, and mention the book title via the subject of your message.

If there is a book that you need and would like to see us publish, please send us a note in the **SUGGEST A TITLE** form on www.packtpub.com or e-mail suggest@packtpub.com.

If there is a topic that you have expertise in and you are interested in either writing or contributing to a book, see our author guide on www.packtpub.com/authors.

Customer support

Now that you are the proud owner of a Packt book, we have a number of things to help you to get the most from your purchase.

Downloading the example code

You can download the example code files for all Packt books you have purchased from your account at http://www.PacktPub.com. If you purchased this book elsewhere, you can visit http://www.PacktPub.com/support and register to have the files e-mailed directly to you.

Errata

Although we have taken every care to ensure the accuracy of our content, mistakes do happen. If you find a mistake in one of our books—maybe a mistake in the text or the code—we would be grateful if you would report this to us. By doing so, you can save other readers from frustration and help us improve subsequent versions of this book. If you find any errata, please report them by visiting http://www.packtpub.com/support, selecting your book, clicking on the **errata submission form** link, and entering the details of your errata. Once your errata are verified, your submission will be accepted and the errata will be uploaded on our website, or added to any list of existing errata, under the Errata section of that title. Any existing errata can be viewed by selecting your title from http://www.packtpub.com/support.

Piracy

Piracy of copyright material on the Internet is an ongoing problem across all media. At Packt, we take the protection of our copyright and licenses very seriously. If you come across any illegal copies of our works, in any form, on the Internet, please provide us with the location address or website name immediately so that we can pursue a remedy.

Please contact us at copyright@packtpub.com with a link to the suspected pirated material.

We appreciate your help in protecting our authors, and our ability to bring you valuable content.

Questions

You can contact us at questions@packtpub.com if you are having a problem with any aspect of the book, and we will do our best to address it.

1
Understanding CMS Extensions

This chapter covers:

- When to use User-Defined Tags
- When to use Tags
- When to use Modules
- How to create a User-Defined Tag
- How to create a Tag
- How to create a Module
- How to use CMS Debug Mode

Introduction

If you're reading this book, you already know that CMS Made Simple is a powerful system for creating websites. Even the base install enables you to easily produce sites with many sophisticated features. There are times, however, when you need to be able to do things that are beyond the basic capabilities. You can often find pre-made extensions on the official CMS Made Simple sites: Tags and Modules in the Developer's Forge (or directly through the Module Manager), and examples of User-Defined Tags on Wiki or posted in the forum.

Understanding CMS Extensions

What are these different kinds of extension? This chapter will answer that question in greater detail. However, we will define them briefly here. All three types of extension share some things in common: they are PHP code which can be embedded in site pages, templates, or Global Content Blocks, or may be called by other code. A User-Defined Tag is distinct in that you can create and edit it through the CMSMS admin area. A Tag is similar, but must be placed as a file on your server, and provides more information to the site administrator. A module has available to it the rich functionality of the Module API, and enables the creation of much more complex applications.

As mentioned before, there is a wealth of pre-made extensions which are available to you. But even if these pre-made extensions don't meet your needs, all is not lost. You can jump in and create your own extensions! You will discover that the power of CMS Made Simple is only limited by your imagination.

> In this chapter, we will learn how to approach the problem you're trying to solve. Is it something that can be solved without writing an extension? Would you be able to use or adapt an existing extension? If not, what conditions will the extension need to handle? The requirements that you think of will help you determine what kind of extension you should implement.

There are three recipes here that will help you to identify which kind of extension is appropriate for a given problem, and three recipes that go over the basics of creating each major type.

Will a User-Defined Tag solve my problem?

You have reached the point where you know you need to extend CMS Made Simple to solve some particular problem, but you may not yet know what approach to take. Your options are to create a Tag, a User-Defined Tag (UDT), or a Module, but which will be best to solve your specific problem?

This recipe will help you examine your problem and consider whether creating a UDT is the most appropriate solution.

How to do it...

First, we determine if the problem you want to solve is one that will require you to write some custom code. This is the easy part. You've already considered whether or not an existing solution will suffice and have decided that it will not. So the next step is to figure out whether or not a User-Defined Tag is the correct approach to solving the problem.

Go through the following list, and for each item, determine if it applies to the problem you are trying to solve. Feel free to write down a list of your answers (yes/no).

1. Can your problem be solved with Smarty logic or standard CMS authoring practices like using Global Content Blocks in your page template?
2. Are you trying to solve a problem that requires multiple actions? An example of multiple actions would be both displaying a form and processing its results.
3. Will you need to support localization and internationalization to solve your problem? For example, if your code will be displaying messages, will the messages need to be translated into multiple languages?
4. Will your solution require an Administration panel?
5. Will you want to share this solution with other people so that they can install it into their own CMS Made Simple sites?
6. Do you need to create new database tables or set up new preferences to solve your problem?
7. Do you want your code to display help text in the Admin area, so site administrators understand what parameters are available and what the code does?
8. Will your solution serve as a Smarty modifier (a modifier in Smarty is a function that does something to convert a variable for display)? An example of a Smarty modifier would be {$variable|uppercase} where the modifier ("uppercase") serves to transform the variable ("$variable").

If you answered "no" to all of the above questions, a User-Defined Tag is a good candidate!

How it works...

A User-Defined Tag is a way to connect a tag, that will be recognized by Smarty, to an arbitrary bit of PHP code. That PHP code can do anything. While there are very few things that cannot be done in CMS Made Simple using UDTs, it doesn't necessarily mean that a UDT is the best approach for everything. Because User-Defined Tags are so versatile, the best way to determine if they are the ideal approach is by disqualification. We ask questions about the few things for which UDTs are less optimal, to see if any of those things match our requirements. If none of them match, then a User-Defined Tag is probably the best approach.

If we do find that our requirements include functionality for which UDTs are not ideally suited, we should consider using a Tag or a module instead. We will explore these options in greater detail elsewhere in this chapter.

For now, let's look at those qualifying questions again and examine why they would encourage us to use a different approach.

Understanding CMS Extensions

Disqualifying Question	If you answered "Yes"
Can the problem be solved by simply using Smarty?	We don't need to write any PHP code at all! For some great examples, please see *Chapter 2, Programming with Smarty and Core Modules*.
Does your problem require multiple actions?	It is, in fact, possible to handle multiple actions using a User-Defined Tag, but it is not elegant. If you need to support multiple actions, the CMS Made Simple Module API has extensive support for doing so, as well as conventions that will help keep the code separated nicely into maintainable chunks.
Do you need localization or internationalization?	Again, this would be possible to do in a User-Defined Tag, but you would have to do all the work. The Module API provides utilities for simplifying this enormously.
Will you need an Administration Panel?	There is no easy way to implement an Administration panel in a UDT, so this would strongly push you in the direction of using a Module, where a rich set of functions make the task easier.
Will you want to share your code?	While nothing would stop you from sharing the code you write as a User-Defined Tag, there are neither facilities for making the process simple nor standards for documenting the UDT. Furthermore, UDTs exist only in the database, as contrasted with Tags and Modules that exist as files, so they are not as easy to simply package up and share.
Do you need to create database tables or preferences?	You could write logic into your UDT to check on the existence and conditionally create database tables or preferences, but it would be easier to use the Module API that has specific support and standards for doing those operations.
Do you want your code to display help text in the Admin area?	As mentioned before, User-Defined Tags offer no facility for displaying help text to the Admin. Both Tags and Modules, on the other hand, have standard methods for doing so.
Will your solution serve as a Smarty modifier?	User-Defined Tags cannot natively work as Smarty modifiers, while Tags can do so easily.

See also

- *Will a Tag Solve my Problem* recipe?
- *Will a Module Solve my Problem* recipe?
- *Create a "Hello World" User-Defined Tag* recipe.

Will a Tag Solve My Problem?

As in the previous recipe, you know that we have three different possibilities for extending CMS Made Simple and solving a problem: User-Defined Tag, Tags, and Modules. Deciding which of these is the best approach, however, requires additional knowledge about the strengths and weaknesses of each technique.

This recipe will help you examine your problem and consider whether creating a Tag is the most appropriate solution.

How to do it...

The criteria for deciding to use a Tag to extend CMS Made Simple are quite similar to the criteria for a User-Defined Tag.

To figure this out, consult the following list, and determine if each item applies to the problem you are trying to solve. Feel free to write down a list of your answers (yes/no).

1. Can your problem be solved with Smarty logic in your page template?
2. Are you trying to solve a problem that requires multiple actions? An example of multiple actions would be both displaying a form and processing its results.
3. Will you need to support localization and internationalization to solve your problem? For example, if your code will be displaying messages, will the messages need to be translated into multiple languages?
4. Will your solution require an Administration panel?
5. Do you need to create new database tables or set up new preferences to solve your problem?

If you answered "no" to all of the above questions, either a Tag or a User-Defined Tag would be a viable approach. To decide whether a Tag would be better than a UDT, consider the following questions:

1. Will you want to share this solution with other people so they can install it into their own CMS Made Simple sites, or will you want to reuse this code yourself on other sites?
2. Do you want your code to display help text in the Admin area, so site administrators understand what parameters are available and what the code does?
3. Will your solution serve as a Smarty modifier? A Smarty modifier is a function that reformats a variable for display, for example, {$variable|uppercase} where the modifier ("uppercase") serves to transform the variable ("$variable").

If you answer "yes" to any of these three questions, you should write a Tag instead of a User-Defined Tag.

Understanding CMS Extensions

How it works...

A Tag is a way to connect a Smarty tag to some PHP code. The PHP code can do anything. Like in the case of User-Defined Tags, there are very few things that cannot be done in CMS Made Simple using Tags.

Because Tags are so versatile, the best way to determine if they are the ideal approach is by disqualification. We ask questions about the few things for which Tags are not ideal, to see if any of those things match our requirements. If none of them match, then the problem could be solved by either a Tag or a User-Defined Tag. To make the decision between those two approaches, we consider a few other criteria that will steer us in the right direction.

Let's consider the disqualifying questions again and examine why they would encourage us to use a different approach. The first five questions are the same as they were for User-Defined Tags.

Disqualifying Question	If you answered "Yes"
Can the problem be solved simply using Smarty?	If this is the case, we don't need to extend CMS Made Simple at all! For some great examples, please see *Chapter 2, Programming with Smarty and Core Modules*.
Does your problem require multiple actions?	It is, in fact, possible to handle multiple actions using a Tag, but the CMS Made Simple Module API has extensive support to simplify multiple actions, as well as conventions that will help keep the code separated nicely into maintainable chunks. Thus a Module would be a much better choice.
Do you need localization or internationalization?	These features could theoretically be implemented using a Tag, but there is no built-in support for either. The Module API, on the other hand, has facilities specifically to simplify those tasks.
Will you need an Administration Panel?	There is no easy way to implement an Administration panel in a Tag, while the Module API has numerous methods specifically for this purpose.
Do you need to create database tables or preferences?	You could write logic into your Tag to check on the existence and conditionally create database tables or preferences, but it would be easier to use the Module API which has specific support and standards for doing those operations.

Now, let's consider the three things that differentiate a Tag from a User-Defined Tag:

Tag Qualifying Question	If you answered "Yes"
Will you be sharing this solution with other people?	A Tag is stored as a file on the server, which makes it easier to share with other CMS Made Simple users, since they can simply place the file in their own installation. A User-Defined Tag, on the other hand, is stored in the database, that adds extra steps if you want to share it.
Do you want your code to display help text in the Admin area?	The structure of a Tag has a special method for presenting information to the site administrator, while a User-Defined Tag has no such mechanism.
Will your solution serve as a Smarty modifier?	There are several kinds of Tags, including Smarty modifier tags. There is only one kind of User-Defined Tag, and it will not work as a Smarty modifier.

See also

- *Will a User-Defined Tag Solve My Problem* recipe?
- *Will a Module Solve My Problem* recipe?
- *Create a "Hello World" Tag* recipe

Will a Module solve my problem?

The previous two recipes have shown you how to assess two possible types of CMS extension, and to see if they are optimal for any specific problem. This recipe rounds out the analysis and shows you how to determine whether creating a Module is the most appropriate solution.

How to do it...

By examining your requirements, and comparing them to the strengths of the Module API, we can figure out whether or not a Module is the best way to implement your extension.

To do so, consult the following list, and determine if each item applies to the problem you are trying to solve. Feel free to write down a list of your answers (yes/no).

1. Are you trying to solve a problem that requires multiple actions? An example of multiple actions would be both displaying a form and processing its results.
2. Will you need to support localization and internationalization to solve your problem? For example, if your code will be displaying messages, will the messages need to be translated into multiple languages?
3. Will your solution require an Administration panel?

Understanding CMS Extensions

4. Will you want to share this solution with other people so they can install it into their own CMS Made Simple sites?
5. Do you need to create new database tables or set up new preferences to solve your problem?
6. Do you want your code to display help text in the Admin area, so site administrators understand what parameters are available and what the code does?

If you answered "yes" to any of the above questions, a Module is going to be the best way to implement your extension—with one possible exception. If you want to write an extension that you can apply to Smarty variables within a template to reformat their output (that is, a Smarty modifier), you will need to use a Tag. However, outside of that one case, a Module will be your best bet. If you answered "no" to all of the above questions, you could still use a module, but you might want to consider using a Tag or User-Defined Tag, as you will still be able to solve your problem with less complexity and overhead.

How it works...

A Module is PHP code that extends the CMSModule Class, which means that you start with a rich API that will save you a great deal of work. Module code can do virtually anything that PHP can do. The only thing that Modules cannot do (and which Tags can do) is act directly as Smarty modifiers.

Modules are extremely powerful and versatile, but that power comes with additional complexity. If you find that it would be possible to solve your problem with a Tag or User-Defined Tag, you should opt for the simpler approach. If, however, your requirements go beyond the capabilities of those extensions, there are very few limits to what you can accomplish with a Module!

See also

- *Will a User-Defined Tag solve my problem* recipe?
- *Will a Tag solve my problem* recipe?
- *Create a "Hello World" module* recipe

Create a "Hello World" User-Defined Tag

If you have decided to create a User-Defined Tag to solve a problem, you might want to know what a UDT looks like.

This recipe shows you how to make a simple User-Defined Tag.

Getting ready

Like most of the recipes in this book, you will need to have CMS Made Simple installed and working. You will need login access to the site's Administration area as a member of the "admin" group (or as a member of a group with "Modify User-defined Tags" and "Add Pages" permission settings).

How to do it...

1. Log in to the Administration panel of your CMS.
2. On the top menu, select "**Extensions**" and click on "**User-Defined Tags**".
3. Click on the "**Add User Defined Tag**" button.
4. Enter the name "**helloworld**" in the "Name" field for your new User-Defined Tag.
5. Enter the following code snippet into the "Code" field, and click on "Submit".

    echo "Hello World, Welcome to CMS Made Simple version ".CMS_VERSION;

```
*Name:
helloworld

*Code
echo "Hello World, Welcome to CMS Made Simple version ".CMS_VERSION;
```

6. On the top level menu, select "**Content**" and click on "**Pages**".
7. Click on the "**Add New Content**" button.
8. Fill in the name of the new page as "**Hello World**".
9. Enter "**Hello World**" as the menu text.
10. For the page content, put in your new tag {helloworld}, and then hit "**Submit**".
11. View your site from the user side. Click on the new "**Hello World**" page.

12. Admire the output from your User-Defined Tag!

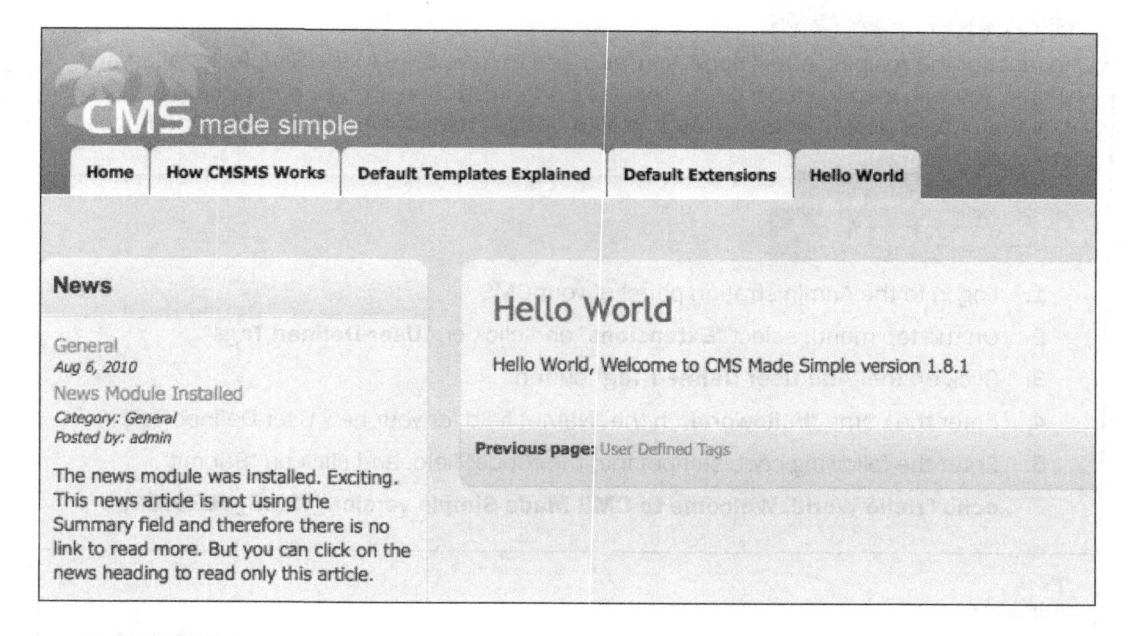

How it works...

A User-Defined Tag is a way of attaching arbitrary PHP code to a Smarty tag. When the CMS Made Simple templates get parsed, Smarty will call the User-Defined Tag and execute the code. Any output from the code will be substituted into the template at the point of the tag.

Our basic example creates a Smarty tag which is called "helloworld." The code for the tag simply outputs a string of text, in this case, the welcome message. To add a bit of interest, we also have it output some useful information: the version of CMS Made Simple that you're running. That value is available in CMS Made Simple via a PHP define, and it can be used in any code run by the CMS.

There's more...

Keep in mind that CMS Made Simple page content is also sent to Smarty for processing—even though we consider it "content", Smarty regards it as a template. This means that you can place your User-Defined Tag in your underlying page template or in your page content, and it will work just the same either way.

We've seen that any output from a User-Defined Tag gets substituted for that tag in the final rendering of the page. It may not be obvious at first, but UDTs aren't required to produce output at all! A User-Defined Tag may do invisible things behind the scenes: set a flag in the PHP session object, update a counter, and even generate an e-mail. If a UDT does not create any visible output, its Smarty tag will simply be removed from the finally rendered page.

Caching

CMS Made Simple has mechanisms built-in for caching pages in order to improve performance. Under normal circumstances, a User-Defined Tag is not cached—if the UDT creates output, that output is not cached. Similarly, if a UDT does not create any output, it will be called even if the page itself is cached.

See also

- *Will a User-Defined Tag solve my problem* recipe?
- *Create a "Hello World" tag* recipe

Create a "Hello World" Tag

You have decided that you want to create a Tag to add some functionality to your site, but you don't yet know what this entails. This recipe shows you how to make a simple Tag.

Getting ready

For this recipe, you will need login access to the site's Administration area as a member of the "admin" group (or as a member of a group with "Add Pages" permission settings). You will also need permissions to create a file on the server, whether via FTP or some other means.

How to do it...

1. Open your favorite text editing program, and create a new file.
2. Type the following code:

```
<?php
function smarty_cms_function_helloworld($params, &$smarty)
{
return "Howdy, World! You're visiting a site made with CMS Made Simple version ".CMS_VERSION;
}

function smarty_cms_help_function_helloworld()
{
```

Understanding CMS Extensions

```
echo "Put the tag {helloworld} in your page or template for a
special message.";
}
function smarty_cms_about_function_helloworld()
{
echo "Hello World version 1.0, written by your_name<you@
yourdomain.com>";
}
?>
```

> **Downloading the example code**
> You can download the example code files for all Packt books you have purchased from your account at http://www.PacktPub.com. If you purchased this book elsewhere, you can visit http://www.PacktPub.com/support and register to have the files e-mailed directly to you.

3. Substitute "your_name" with your name, and "you@yourdomain.com" with your e-mail address.
4. Save this file as "function.helloworld.php" in your CMS Made Simple base install's "plugins" directory.
5. Log in to the Administration panel of your CMS.
6. Verify that the CMS sees your Tag: using the top menu, go to "**Extensions**" and click on "**Tags**".

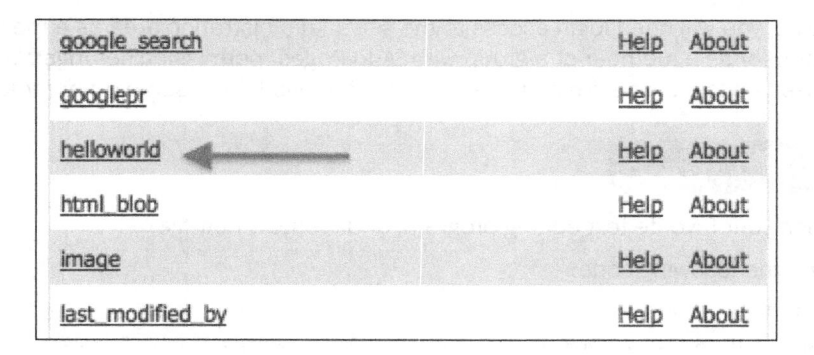

google_search	Help	About
googlepr	Help	About
helloworld ←	Help	About
html_blob	Help	About
image	Help	About
last_modified_by	Help	About

7. Next to your new tag name, click on the "**Help**" link to view the help text, or on the "**About**" link to view the about text.
8. On the top level menu, select "**Content**" and click on "**Pages**".
9. Click on the "**Add New Content**" button.
10. Fill in the name of the new page as "**Hello World**".

11. Enter "**Hello World**" as the menu text.
12. For the page content, put in your new tag {**helloworld**}, then hit "**Submit**".
13. View your site from the user side. Click on the new "**Hello World**" page.
14. Admire the output from your Tag!

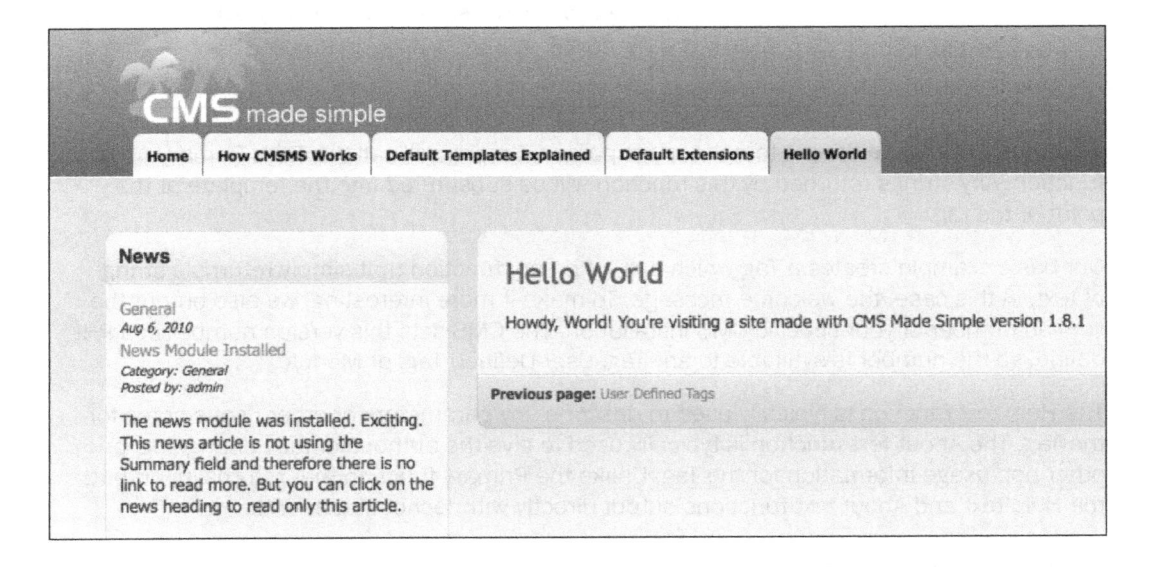

How it works...

A Tag is a way of attaching PHP code to a Smarty tag, modifier, pre-compile function, or post-compile function. This recipe is an example of a Smarty tag.

A Tag has three functions it must declare:

- the Primary function
- a "Help" text function
- an "About" text function

Understanding CMS Extensions

These functions are defined using a naming convention that tells CMS Made Simple what they do. For a given Tag named "`helloworld`," the functions are named as follows:

Function	Naming Convention
Primary function	`smarty_cms_function_helloworld` (or `smarty_function_helloworld`—see note on caching below)
Help text function	`smarty_cms_help_function_helloworld`
About text function	`smarty_cms_about_function_helloworld`

When the CMS Made Simple templates get parsed, Smarty will call the Tag's Primary function. Any strings returned by this function will be substituted into the template at the point of the tag.

Our basic example creates a Tag which has a Primary function that simply returns a string of text, in this case, the welcome message. To make it more interesting, we also output the version number of your specific CMS installation. The CMS sets this version number in a PHP define, so the number is available to any Tag, User-Defined Tag, or Module.

The Help text function is typically used to describe any parameters or other usage notes for the Tag. The About text function is typically used to give the author, contact, changelog, or other non-usage information for the Tag. Unlike the Primary function that returns its output, the Help text and About text functions output directly with "echo" statements.

There's more...

You can place your Tag into the content of a CMS page, into a CMS template, or even in a Global Content Block (GCB). CMS Made Simple passes all of these through the Smarty templating engine, so your tag will get interpreted the same way in any of those cases.

We've seen that any string returned from a Tag gets substituted for that tag in the final rendering of the page. It may not be obvious at first, but Tags aren't required to produce output at all! A Tag may do invisible things behind the scenes: set a flag in the PHP session object, update a counter, and even generate an e-mail. If a Tag does not create any visible output, its Smarty tag will simply be removed from the finally rendered page.

Caching

As mentioned previously, CMS Made Simple has mechanisms built-in for caching pages in order to improve performance. If your Tag implementation is not a modifier, pre-compile function, or post-compile function, you can control whether or not your tag will be cached.

If you want your Tag's output to be cached, you need to simply alter the naming convention for the Primary function from `smarty_cms_function_helloworld` to `smarty_function_helloworld`.

Tag Names and Namespaces

Tags and User-Defined Tags both establish a Smarty tag that can be embedded in your templates or pages. The Smarty syntax for both is identical. It turns out that the namespace is also shared. So what happens if you have a Hello World Tag and a Hello World User-Defined Tag and they're both known to Smarty by the tag {helloworld}? It turns out that User-Defined Tags have precedence, so in this situation, the output will be from the UDT.

See also

- *Will a Tag solve my problem* recipe?
- *Create a "Hello World" User-Defined Tag* recipe

Create a "Hello World" Module

So far in this chapter, we have seen examples of simple Tags and User-Defined Tags. The last remaining type of extension to explore is the Module.

This recipe will show you how to create a simple Module for CMS Made Simple.

Getting ready

This recipe requires access to your site's Administration area with "Add Pages" and "Modify Modules" permissions, and permissions to create a file on the server.

How to do it...

1. Find your CMS Made Simple base install directory. Within that directory will be a "modules" directory.
2. Inside the "modules" directory create a new directory, and name it "HelloWorld" (keeping in mind that the directory name is case-sensitive in most operating systems).
3. Open your favorite text editor, and type in the following code:

```php
<?php
class HelloWorld extends CMSModule
  {
  functionGetName()
    {
    return 'HelloWorld';
    }

  functionIsPluginModule()
```

Understanding CMS Extensions

```
    {
    return true;
    }
    functionDoAction($action, $id, $params, $returnid=-1)
    {
    echo 'Hello World.  Welcome to the '.$this->GetName().' module
(version '.$this->GetVersion();
    echo ') running in CMS Made Simple version '.CMS_VERSION;
    }
    }
?>
```

4. Save this file in your new "`HelloWorld`" directory with the filename "`HelloWorld.module.php`" (again, keeping in mind that most operating systems are case-sensitive).
5. Log in to your CMS Made Simple admin area.
6. Using the top menu, go to "**Extensions**" and click on "**Modules**".
7. Click on "**Install**" next to the **HelloWorld** module.

Modules

Name	Version	Status	Active	Action
CMSMailer	2.0	Installed	✓	Uninstall
FileManager	1.0.2	Installed	✓	Uninstall
HelloWorld	0.0.0.1	Not Installed		Install Remove
MenuManager	1.6.5	Installed	✓	Uninstall

8. On the top level menu, select "**Content**" and click on "**Pages**".
9. Click on the "**Add New Content**" button.
10. Fill in the name of the new page as "Hello World."
11. Enter "Hello World" as the menu text.
12. For the page content, put in the tag for your new Module {cms_module module='HelloWorld'}, then hit "**Submit**".
13. View your site from the user side. Click on the new "**Hello World**" page.
14. Admire the output from your Module!

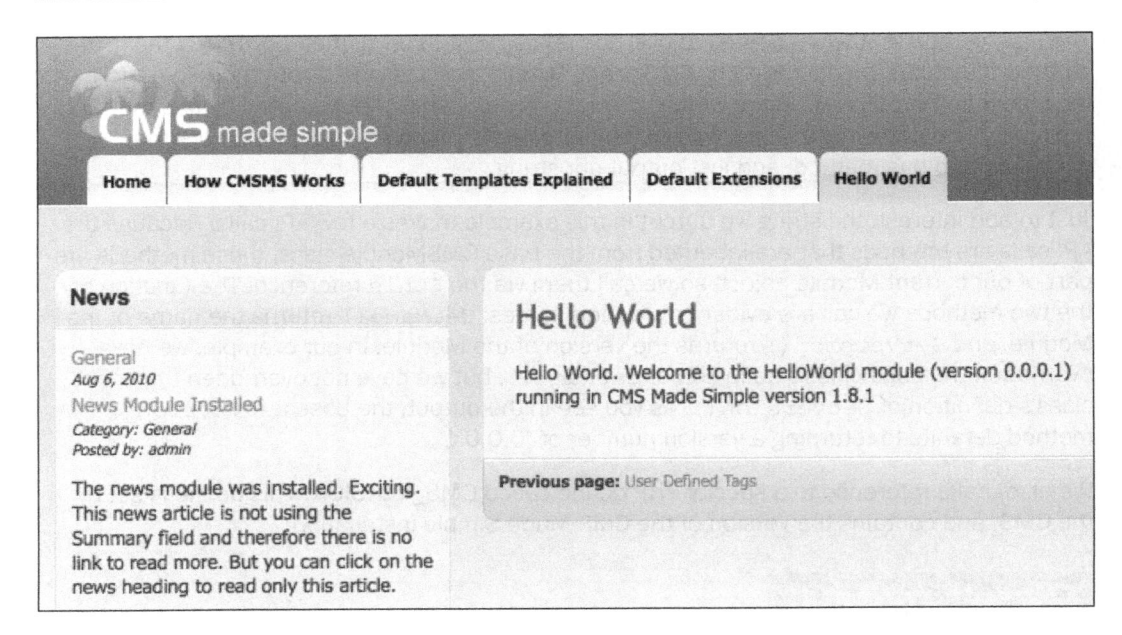

How it works...

When you install CMS Made Simple, one piece of the core library that gets installed is the CMSModule base class. This class includes a vast collection of useful methods for simplifying all kinds of module-related tasks; we refer to this collection as the **CMS Made Simple Module API** (or, more briefly, the **Module API**).

When you implement a module, you do it by extending the CMSModule base class. By extending the CMSModule class, your code automatically inherits all of the methods of the Module API. As you can see in the previous code, the first thing you do is declare the Hello World Module's class as an extension of the CMSModule class.

Next, your job as a module developer is to identify which methods of the CMSModule class you will be calling or overriding in order to solve your particular programming problem. The Module API has in excess of 225 methods. Fortunately, there are only a few dozen you'll ever need to override. In fact, as this recipe shows, you can implement a Module by overriding only three methods!

The first method you override needs to be the `GetName()` method. This method must return the class name of your module. Be careful here, since it is case-sensitive and must match both the name of the class and the name of the primary Module file!

The second method you need to override is the `IsPluginModule()`. This returns a true or false value, depending on whether your module will be inserted into your site using a Smarty tag. The base method in the CMSModule class returns false. In our case, we are writing a Plugin module, so we return true.

Understanding CMS Extensions

The last method that you will need to override is the `DoAction()` method. This is the method that actually gets called by CMS Made Simple, and it's where your module performs its appointed purposes. If you're writing a Plugin module, any output created by this method replaces the module tag in your page or template. In this simplest case, we ignore the parameters to this method, and just output our string.

Just to add interest, the string we output in this example makes a few API calls. Because the API calls are methods that are inherited from the base CMSModule class, these methods are part of our current Module object, so we call them via the `$this` reference. The function of the two methods we call are evident from their names: `GetName()` returns the name of the Module, and `GetVersion()` returns the version of the Module. In our example, we have overridden the base class's definition of `GetName()`, but we have not overridden the base class's definition of `GetVersion()`. As you see in the output, the base `GetVersion()` method defaults to returning a version number of "0.0.0.1".

We also make reference to a special PHP define called CMS_VERSION. This define is set by the CMS, and contains the version of the CMS Made Simple installation.

There's more...

Don't let the simplicity of this example deceive you! The majority of the recipes in this book involve different aspects of the Module API, and some of its powerful capabilities.

See also

- *Chapter 4, Creating a new module stub using the Skeleton module* recipe
- *Chapter 4, Creating a new module stub using the ModuleMaker module* recipe

Using CMS in Debug Mode

When you start developing extensions of any kind for CMS Made Simple, a certain amount of your development time will involve tracking down things that aren't working the way you expect them to. Happily, CMS Made Simple has some built-in tools for helping in the debugging process.

This recipe shows you how to run CMS Made Simple in debug mode, and gives you some idea of what to look for in debug output.

How to do it...

1. Find your CMS Made Simple base install directory. Within that directory will be your install's `config.php` file.
2. Edit `config.php` and locate the following section

   ```
   # CMSMS Debug Mode?  Turn it on to get a better error when you
   # see {nocache} errors, or to allow seeing php notices, warnings,
   and errors in the html output.
   # This setting will also disable browser css caching.
   $config['debug'] = false;
   ```
3. Change the "`false`" to "`true`" and save the file.
4. Browse through your site. At the bottom of each page will be the debug information:

```
Generated in 0.673676 seconds by CMS Made Simple using 72 SQL queries and 9376980 bytes of memory (peak memory usage was 9968524)

Debug: (0.092426) - (853588)
loading smarty
Debug: (0.099413) - (1197936)
loading adodb
Debug: (0.102607) - (1308872)
loading page functions
Debug: (0.130382) - (1588948)
loading content functions
Debug: (0.135053) - (1855444)
loading pageinfo functions
Debug: (0.135566) - (1899268)
loading translation functions
Debug: (0.136409) - (1985576)
loading events functions
Debug: (0.137906) - (2105528)
loading php4 entity decode functions
Debug: (0.141959) - (2413448)
done loading files
Debug: (0.172441) - (3245944)
(mysql): SET NAMES 'utf8'
Debug: (0.17336) - (3264236)
(mysql): SELECT sitepref_name, sitepref_value from cms_siteprefs
Debug: (0.190421) - (3349784)
(mysql): SELECT * FROM cms_userplugins
Debug: (0.196009) - (3884472)
(mysql): SELECT * FROM cms_modules WHERE admin_only = 0 AND active = 1 ORDER by module_name
Debug display of 'End of include':(0.222017) - (5734768)
Debug: (0.255702) - (5934252)
(mysql): SELECT sitepref_value from cms_siteprefs WHERE sitepref_name = 'pseudocron_lastrun'
Debug: (0.256066) - (5935732)
(mysql): UPDATE cms_siteprefs SET sitepref_value = '1282086455' WHERE sitepref_name = 'pseudocron_lastrun'
Debug display of 'Load Content Operations':(0.256212) - (5884376)
Debug display of 'End Load Content Operations':(0.26194) - (6644928)
Debug: (0.262285) - (6652392)
(mysql): SELECT content_id FROM cms_content WHERE default_content = 1
Debug: (0.262802) - (6649992)
(mysql): SELECT c.content_id, c.content_name, c.content_alias, c.menu_text, c.titleattribute, c.hierarchy, c.metadata, c.id_hierarchy, c.p
Debug: (0.263188) - (6652424)
(mysql): SELECT MAX(modified_date) AS thedate FROM cms_content c
Debug display of 'Start Loading Hierarchy Manager':(0.263603) - (6642000)
Debug display of 'starting tree':(0.26365) - (6644268)
Debug: (0.265334) - (6830064)
file needs loading
Debug display of 'ending tree':(0.282383) - (6886744)
Debug display of 'End Loading Hierarchy Manager':(0.282437) - (6874336)
Debug: (0.282481) - (6874568)
start findNodeByTag
```

Understanding CMS Extensions

How it works...

Debug mode causes CMS Made Simple to do a number of things differently than in normal production mode:

1. PHP error reporting is changed to `E_ALL`, so warnings and errors will all be displayed.
2. Page and CSS caching is disabled.
3. Page redirecting via the API is disabled; instead, a link is displayed that will lead to the original destination.
4. All database interactions are displayed.
5. Select core functions display diagnostic information

Often, the display of otherwise hidden warnings or errors will be sufficient for you to track down issues by revealing problems like typos in variable names, missing parentheses, or other syntax errors.

The display of database interactions is useful for diagnosing query problems. Ideally, of course, all extension code we write has proper error checking and reporting. If, however, our code isn't that robust (or if we're still in early development, when such error handling has not yet been added), debug mode helps us identify problems.

```
Debug: (0.321418) - (9535724)
(mysql): select * from cms_content where content_type='content'
Error (1054): Unknown column 'content_type' in 'where clause'
```

See also

- *Chapter 10, Setting Special Diagnostic Messages for Debug Mode* recipe

2
Programming with Smarty and Core Modules

In this chapter, we will cover:

- Using Smarty to create color sets in your stylesheet
- Using Smarty to do the math in your stylesheet
- Renaming the "Extra Page Attribute" fields in the CMS Admin
- Creating a personnel directory using Menu Manager
- Creating a basic Google Sitemap with Menu Manager and `mod_rewrite`
- Embedding JavaScript in your template without causing Smarty to throw a fit
- Using Smarty loops to generate similar stylesheet constructs
- Displaying a block only for the Home page
- Using Smarty "Capture" and conditionals to hide empty content blocks
- Seeing what Smarty variables are available to your template

Introduction

When implementing new features for their CMS Made Simple sites, people's first thought is often some kind of PHP extension: a User-Defined Tag or a Module. It turns out, though, that there is a whole class of problems that can be solved using Smarty or the Core modules.

This chapter will show you a number of tricks which may not be obvious at first, but that will open up a whole new world of possibilities.

There are many advantages to using the built-in approaches when you can. You save the overhead of installing Modules or Tags, and you don't have to worry as much about upgrades.

Most of the recipes that are presented here will serve to simplify the maintenance of your sites, or at least add useful capabilities without adding too much complexity. Several recipes are oriented towards simplifying tasks for the person or people who will be administering the site as editors or writers. It's important to remember that any time you reduce complexity for the people creating content for a site, you're reducing the opportunity for error.

As a web developer, one of the primary reasons for using CMS Made Simple is to allow your customer to take over a website once you've worked your magic. By simplifying the task for them, you're saving yourself support calls—and saving your customer's budget, so they can hire you for enhancing site capabilities in the future. By building a site in an easy-to-maintain way, you are essentially guaranteeing yourself more interesting jobs rather than tedious jobs like fixing broken formatting.

Using Smarty to create a color set in your stylesheet

This recipe will show you how to use Smarty variables in your stylesheet to create a color set. By using variables for colors, we make it much easier to change the entire color scheme of a site by updating just a few lines at the top of our stylesheet.

Getting ready

For this recipe, you will need to have CMS Made Simple installed and working. You will need login access to the site's Administration area as a member of the "admin" group, or as a member of a group with a fair number of permissions: "Add Stylesheets", "Add Stylesheet Associations", and "Manage All Content".

How to do it...

- Log in to your CMS Administration area.
- Using the top menu, go to "**Layout**" and click on "**Stylesheets**".
- Click on the "**Add a Stylesheet**" button.
- Enter "**colors**" into the "**name**" field.
- Enter the following stylesheet into the "**content**" area:

```
[[assign var='dark_color' value='#2634cf']]
[[assign var='main_color' value='#4a76ef']]
[[assign var='background_color' value='#e0e4ef']]
[[assign var='highlight_color' value='#5fb7ff']]
body
   {
   color: [[$main_color]];
   background: [[$background_color]];
   }
h1, h2, h3 { color: [[$dark_color]]; }
a { color: [[$main_color]]; }
.currentpage
   {
   background: [[$dark_color]];
   color: [[$highlight_color]];
   }
```

- Under "**Media Types**", click the checkbox for "**all: Suitable for all devices**" and then click "**Submit**".
- Next to your stylesheet in the list, click on the CSS icon.

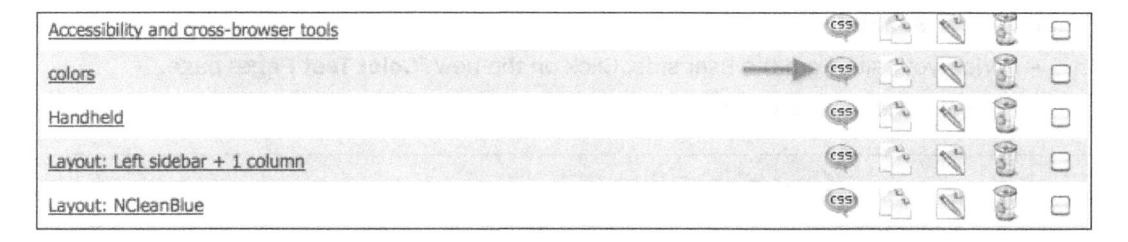

Accessibility and cross-browser tools		CSS			□
colors	→	CSS			□
Handheld		CSS			□
Layout: Left sidebar + 1 column		CSS			□
Layout: NCleanBlue		CSS			□

- In the drop-down menu, select "**Minimal Template**" and click on the "**Attach to this Template**" button.
- Using the top menu, go to "**Content**" and select "**Pages**".
- Click on the "**Add New Content**" button.

Programming with Smarty and Core Modules

- Fill in the name of the new page as "**Color Test Page**".
- Enter "**Color Test Page**" as the menu text.
- For the page content, type in some sample text.
- Click on the "**Options**" tab.
- Select "**Minimal Template**" with the "**Template**" drop-down.
- Hit the "**Submit**" button.
- View your site from the user side. Click on the new "**Color Test Page**" page.
- Admire the page!

> **Color Test Page**
> - Home
> - How CMSMS Works
> - Default Templates Explained
> - Default Extensions
> - Hello World
> - Color Test Page
>
> This is an example of content in the test page. We will change color variables in the stylesheet to transform it!

- Now, imagine that your client called, and wanted a red palette instead of a blue palette. In the Administration area, use the top menu to go to "**Layout**" and click on "**Stylesheets**".
- Click on "**colors**" to edit your stylesheet.
- Change only the first four lines to read:
  ```
  [[assign var='dark_color' value='#9f1326']]
  [[assign var='main_color' value='#ff3f59']]
  [[assign var='background_color' value='#efe0e2']]
  [[assign var='highlight_color' value='#ff8f9e']]
  ```
- Click "**Submit**".
- View your site from the user side. Click on the new "**Color Test Page**" page.
- Admire the changes to the page.

> **Color Test Page**
> - Home
> - How CMSMS Works
> - Default Templates Explained
> - Default Extensions
> - Color Test Page
>
> This is an example of content in the test page. We will change color variables in the stylesheet to transform it!

How it works...

This recipe is an example of using variables to simplify your CSS. Instead of specifying colors directly in each style definition, we create variables for commonly used colors.

The first four lines of the stylesheet are where we create those variable definitions. For example, in the first line, we're creating a variable named "`dark_color`" and assigning it the value "`#2634cf`"—a value which represents a darkish blue color.

In the stylesheet below, whenever we wish to use that shade, instead of repeating the specific hex code for the color, we use the Smarty variable (as shown when we changed the color palette from blue to red). This approach minimizes the number of changes necessary to update the colors for an entire stylesheet.

> If you have worked with Smarty elsewhere in your site, for example, in page templates, it might surprise you that the Smarty commands are set off by the double bracket delimiters instead of the more commonly used curly braces. This decision was made because of the prevalence of curly braces in CSS definitions. If the delimiters had been left as curly braces, the CSS would have been so filled with Smarty {literal} and {/literal} tags that it would have been completely unreadable.

There's more...

While this recipe demonstrates using variables for colors, you can use Smarty variables for any string that might show up in your stylesheet. If there is anything that recurs throughout your stylesheet that you might want to change in a single place, this is a good way to do it. Some other interesting possibilities you might explore:

- Font faces
- Font sizes
- List item bullet styles
- Images

See also

- *Using Smarty to do the math in your stylesheet* recipe
- *Using Smarty loops to generate similar stylesheet constructs* recipe

Using Smarty to do the math in your stylesheet

This recipe shows you how you can use Smarty to compute sizes in your stylesheet. By setting a few key sizes and computing other dimensions from those values, we make it much easier to change the layout of a site while preserving the proportions.

Getting ready

For this recipe, you will need login access to the site's Administration area as a member of the "admin" group or as a member of a group with a fair number of permissions: "Add Stylesheets", "Add Stylesheet Associations", and "Manage All Content".

How to do it...

- Log in to your CMS Administration area.
- Using the top menu, go to "**Layout**" and click on "**Stylesheets**".
- Click on the "**Add a Stylesheet**" button.
- Enter "**width_calculator**" into the "**name**" field.
- Enter the following stylesheet into the "content" area:

```
[[assign var='box_width' value='300']]
[[assign var='middle_width' value='10']]
[[assign var='left_percent' value='20']]

[[math assign='left_size' equation='(box_width - middle_width) *
left_percent/100' box_width=$box_width middle_width=$middle_width
left_percent=$left_percent]]

#wrapper {
  border: 1px solid black;
  width: [[$box_width]]px;
  min-height: 80px;
  }
#middle_portion{
  float: left;
  width: [[$middle_width]]px;
  min-height:80px;
  }
#left_portion {
  float: left;
  width: [[$left_size]]px;
```

```
    background: #ffbfc9;
    min-height: 80px;
  }
#right_portion {
    float: right;
    width: [[$box_width-$left_size-$middle_width]]px;
    background: #bfc4ff;
    min-height: 80px;
  }
```

- Under "**Media Types**", click the checkbox for "**screen : Intended primarily for color computer screens**" and then click "**Submit**".
- Find "**width_calculator**" in the stylesheet list, and click its CSS icon.
- In the drop-down menu, select "**NCleanBlue**" and click on the "**Attach to this Template**" button.
- Using the top menu, go to "**Content**" and select "**Pages**".
- Click on the "**Add New Content**" button.
- Fill in the name of the new page as "**Width Test**".
- Enter "**Width Test**" as the menu text.
- If you are using a WYSIWYG editor for the content area, uncheck the checkbox labeled "**Turn WYSIWYG on/off**".

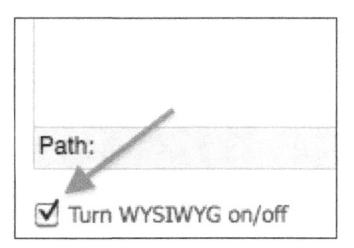

- Enter the following HTML code into the content area:

```
<div id="wrapper">
  <div id="left_portion">
    This is the left portion.
  </div>
  <div id="middle_portion">
  .<br/>.<br/>.<br/>.
  </div>
  <div id="right_portion">
    This is the right portion.
  </div>
</div>
```

Programming with Smarty and Core Modules

- Click "**Submit**".
- View your site from the user side. Click on the new "**Width Test**" page.

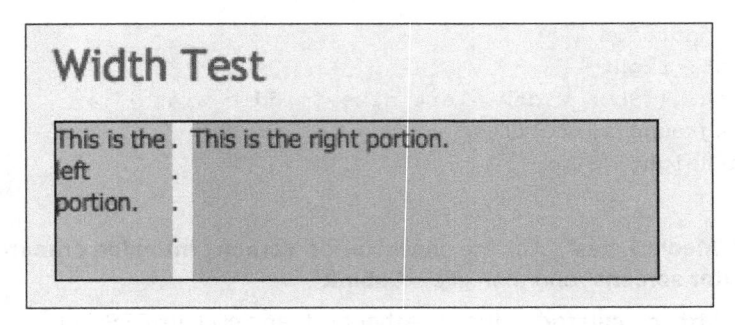

Width Test

This is the left portion. This is the right portion.

- Use Web Developer tools or other browser capabilities to view the generated CSS:

```css
#wrapper {
  border: 1px solid black;
  width: 300px;
  min-height: 80px;
  }
#middle_portion{
   float: left;
   width: 10px;
   min-height:80px;
   }

#left_portion {
   float: left;
   width: 58px;
   background: #ffbfc9;
   min-height: 80px;
   }

#right_portion {
   float: right;
   width: 232px;
   background: #bfc4ff;
   min-height: 80px;
   }
```

How it works...

In this recipe, we are exploring the mathematical capabilities of Smarty, and how we can use them in our stylesheets. To demonstrate this, we will create a box that is divided into two portions with a fixed divider between them. The box, the two portions, and the divider are all defined using simple HTML div tags with IDs that we can use to target them with our CSS rules.

We begin by setting a few basic variables using Smarty "assign" statements. First, we set our outer box dimension to the unitless value of 300. We omit the units since we will be performing arithmetic on the value and can assign the units later when we substitute in the variable in the CSS itself. You can see that below in the CSS in the rules for `#wrapper`, where there is the width specification:

```
#wrapper {
  border: 1px solid black;
  width: [[$box_width]]px;
```

Next, we assign the other values that will define our geometry. We set the width of the division, which we call `middle_width`, as ten units. Then we set `left_percent`, that will determine the percentage of the total box occupied by the left portion, and we use the value 20 (for twenty percent).

Once the basic geometrical description is set, we use Smarty to compute the size of the left portion. In this case, since we will be doing more complex math than addition and subtraction, we use the Smarty "math" command to specify an equation and to assign the computed value to a variable named `left_size`. As you can see, the Smarty math command binds the variables in the equation template to Smarty variables. For simplicity, we used our existing variable names in the equation, but we still have to bind the equation template variables to our defined variables, which is why we have the seemingly redundant assignments like `box_width=$box_width`.

The output of the Smarty computation, stored in `left_size`, is still unitless. When we substitute the value into our CSS, you can see that we put the units of `px` (for pixels) after the variable instantiation.

The manual page for Smarty recommends avoiding the use of the math command when performance is an issue, for example, like in a loop. It turns out that for simple arithmetic, it's easy to avoid. As you will see where we compute the width of the `right_portion` div, you can put subtraction into an ordinary Smarty variable instantiation. In this case, we subtract our left portion and middle portion from the overall width.

Programming with Smarty and Core Modules

Now that you have the dimensions determined mathematically, you can play around to see how it functions. Try changing the percentage of the div that the `left_portion` occupies, or modifying the overall box width. From this, you can see that if your entire layout was done using Smarty math, it takes only a single variable change to alter your design—all without affecting proportions.

There's more...

One thing to look out for when using Smarty logic in your stylesheet is caching. People are occasionally surprised by the results they get when they put Smarty logic in their CSS that is supposed to do something conditionally, based upon the current page name or Smarty variables set in the "Smarty data or logic that is specific to this page" field of the Page admin. The symptom is that the logic doesn't work at all, or alternatively works the first time, but then triggers on pages where it shouldn't. The reason for this is stylesheet caching. For performance reasons, CMS Made Simple generates stylesheets the first time they're needed, and uses caches thereafter. Until you change the stylesheet source, the same CSS will be served up to all pages.

The solution to this problem is to move any page-specific logic to your page template. If you want a different style for H1 tags on your home page, put the class into a conditional rather than putting the condition in the stylesheet:

```
<h1 class="{if
  $special_condition==true}special_class{else}normal_class{/if}">
```

This will work as you expect.

See also

- *Using Smarty to create a color set in your stylesheet* recipe
- *Using Smarty loops to generate similar stylesheet constructs* recipe

Renaming the "Extra Page Attributes" in the CMS Admin

When editing a page in the CMS Admin area, there are three fields under the "Options" tab called "Extra Page Attribute 1", "Extra Page Attribute 2", and "Extra Page Attribute 3". You can use these in your page template for a variety of purposes, but those uses may not be obvious to the Administrator. This recipe shows you how you can change the names of these attributes to clarify how they're used.

Getting ready

This recipe requires that you have login access to the site's Administration area as a member of the "admin" group (or as a member of a group with "Modify Any Page" permission settings). You will also need permissions to create a file on the server, either via FTP or some other means.

How to do it...

- Using your FTP client or a login shell, find your base installation directory.
- Inside the "admin" directory, create a directory named "custom".
- Inside your new "custom" directory, create a directory named "lang".
- Inside the new "lang" directory, create a new directory called "en_US".
- Using your favorite text editor, create a file containing the following:

```php
<?php
$lang['admin']['extra1'] = 'Make';
$lang['admin']['extra2'] = 'Model Year';
$lang['admin']['extra3'] = 'Mileage';
?>
```

- Save this file as "admin.inc.php" in your newly created custom/lang/en_US directory.
- Log in to your CMS Administration area.
- Using the top menu, go to "**Content**" and click on "**Pages**."
- Click to edit any page, and then click on the "**Options**" tab.
- Scroll down and see your new labels:

Disable WYSIWYG editor on this page (regardless of template or user settings):
☐

Make:
[   ]

Model Year:
[   ]

Mileage:
[   ]

Programming with Smarty and Core Modules

How it works...

The CMS Made Simple Administration area has built-in localization support. The way localization works is that the text strings that are displayed by the Admin area are abstracted: within the code, a string name is used instead of the string itself, and that name is used in conjunction with files of translated strings. For example, the string that is expressed in English as "Extra Page Attribute 1" is labeled in the code using a tag "extra1".

If you have the Admin set to "US English", the translation subsystem reads in the `en_US` version of the `admin.inc.php` file where the tag "extra1" is translated to "Extra Page Attribute 1". Similarly, if your Admin is set to German, the translation subsystem reads in the `de_DE` version of `admin.inc.php`, and the tag "extra1" is translated to "Zusätzliches Seiten-Attribut 1".

[One advantage of this system of localization is that the CMS allows you to override the translation of these tags. In the Admin area, the CMS translation functions look for the special directory "`custom/lang/LANG`", where LANG is the current Admin user's language code, and if it exists, the translation system will read in the "`admin.inc.php`" file within.

Since this custom file is read in after the translations, any tag that you override here will then reflect your changes in the Admin area.]

As shown in this recipe, you simply put a list of tag definitions into your custom "`admin.inc.php`" file to change how the tags are displayed.

There's more...

In this recipe, we only overrode the names of the extra page attribute tags in English. If your site has multiple administrators who use different languages, you'll want to override the names of the attributes in all of those languages.

The process for doing this is equally simple. Inside of the "`custom/lang`" directory, you'll need to create a directory for each language that needs to be overridden. The naming convention for these directories is the two-letter ISO 639-1 language code (in lowercase) followed by an underscore, followed by the two-letter ISO 3166-1 country code. For an easy way to find the list of the languages supported by CMS Made Simple, take a look in the "`admin/lang/ext`" directory under your base installation.

Once you have created the language directory, create an "`admin.inc.php`" file within it, and add your translations to that file.

Chapter 2

What else can I rename?

You can change the text for any string displayed by the Administration area code. To find the names of the tags to override, look at "admin.inc.php" in the "admin/lang/en_US" directory within your CMS base installation.

While it is true that all of the text displayed by the Administration area may be overridden in a Custom file, this statement could be considered misleading because of the tight integration between the Administration area and modules. Technically, many strings are displayed by modules, not by the Administration area itself. For example, if you look through the "admin.inc.php" file, you won't find any of the strings for MenuManager or other core modules.

It turns out that overriding strings from Modules is done in a different way, which is detailed in a later recipe.

See also

- *Chapter 4, Making a module localizable* recipe
- *Chapter 10, Overriding Module strings* recipe

Creating a personnel directory using Menu Manage

This recipe shows the power of the standard Core modules when used in conjunction with a simple naming convention. We create a personnel directory where a top-level directory page links to individual biographical pages for employees. It is designed to minimize the difficulty for the person maintaining the directory: it automates much of the formatting, and avoids any requirement to enter redundant data.

Getting ready

This recipe requires that you have login access to your site's Administration area with permission to "Add Pages", "Add Global Content Blocks", "Manage Menu", and "Modify Any Content". You will also need permissions to create a file on the server.

How to do it...

- Using your FTP client or a login shell, find your base installation directory.
- Inside the "admin" directory, create a directory named "custom".
- Inside your new "custom" directory, create a directory named "lang".
- Inside the new "lang" directory, create a new directory called "en_US".

39

Programming with Smarty and Core Modules

- Using your favorite text editor, create a file containing the following:
  ```php
  <?php
  $lang['admin']['extra1'] = 'Title';
  $lang['admin']['extra2'] = 'Phone Number';
  $lang['admin']['extra3'] = 'Email Address';
  ?>
  ```
- Save this file as "`admin.inc.php`" in your newly created `custom/lang/en_US` directory.
- Log in to your CMS Administration area.
- Using the top menu, go to "**Content**" and click on "**Global Content Blocks**".
- Click on the "**Add Global Content Block**" button.
- In the "**Name**" field, type "**personnel**".
- If you are using a WYSIWYG editor for the content area, uncheck the checkbox labeled "**Turn WYSIWYG on/off**".

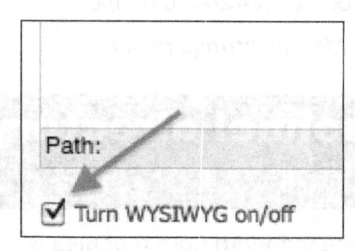

- Type the following code into the "**Content**" text area:
  ```
  <div class="person">
    <img src="uploads/images/personnel/{$page_alias}.jpg" alt="{title}" /><br />
    <strong>{title}, {$content_obj->GetPropertyValue('extra1')}</strong><br />
    Phone: {$content_obj->GetPropertyValue('extra2')}<br />
    Email: {$content_obj->GetPropertyValue('extra3')}
  </div>
  ```
- Click on "**Submit**".
- Using the top menu, go to "**Layout**" and click on "**Menu Manager**".
- Click on the "**Add Template**" button.
- In the "**New Template Name**" field, type "**personnel**".
- In the "**Template Content**" field, type the following code:
  ```
  {foreach from=$nodelist item=node}
    <div style="float:left; padding:10px;">
      <img src="/uploads/images/personnel/thumb_{$node->alias}.jpg"
  ```

```
    alt="{$node->menutext}" />
        <br />
        <a href="{$node->url}">{$node->menutext}</a>, {$node->extra1}
    </div>
{/foreach}
```

- Click on "**Submit**".
- Using the top menu, go to "**Content**" and click on "**Image Manager**".
- Type "**personnel**" into the field labeled "**Create New Folder**" and click on "**Create**".
- Click on the folder icon labeled "**personnel**".
- Using the "**Upload**" field, upload a picture. It should be in JPEG format, and should have dimensions of 150 by 200 pixels. It should be named "`sierra.jpg`".
- Using the "**Upload**" field, upload another picture. It should be in JPEG format, and should have dimensions of 150 by 200 pixels. It should be named "`javier.jpg`".
- Using the top menu, go to "**Content**" and click on "**Pages**".
- Click on the "**Add New Content**" button.
- In the "**Title**" and "**Menu Text**" fields, type "**Personnel**".
- In the "**Content**" text area, type the following code:

  ```
  {menu loadprops='1' childrenof=$page_alias template='personnel'}
  ```

- Click on the "**Options**" tab, and type "**personnel**" in the "**Page Alias**" field.
- Click "**Submit**".
- Click on the "**Add New Content**" button.
- In the "**Title**" field, type "**Sierra S. Maxwell**".
- In the "**Menu Text**" field, type "**Sierra**".
- With the "**Parent**" drop-down, select the "**Personnel**" page you just created.
- In the "**Content**" area, type in the following:

  ```
  {global_content name='personnel'}
  Sierra has led the CMS Module Factory for ten years, following a
  long career in industrial welding.
  ```

- Click on the "**Options**" tab, and type "**sierra**" into the "**Page Alias**" field.
- Scroll down to "**Title**" and type in "**CEO**".
- Enter some imaginary values for the "**Phone Number**" and "**Email Address**" fields.
- Click on "**Submit**".
- Click on the "**Add New Content**" button.
- In the "**Title**" field, type "**Javier Sullivan**".
- In the "**Menu Text**" field, type "**Javier**".

Programming with Smarty and Core Modules

- With the "**Parent**" drop-down, select the "**Personnel**" page.
- In the "**Content**" area, type in the following:
  ```
  {global_content name='personnel'}
  Javier has been our hard-working President since inventing the
  Miraculous Module Maker.
  ```
- Click on the "**Options**" tab, and type "**Javier**" into the "**Page Alias**" field.
- Scroll down to "**Title**" and type in "**President**".
- Enter some imaginary values for the "**Phone Number**" and "**Email Address**" fields.
- Click on "**Submit**".
- View your site from the user side. Click on the new "**Personnel**" page:

> **Personnel**
>
> Sierra, CEO   Javier, President
>
> **Previous page:** User Defined Tags
> **Next page:** Sierra S. Maxwell

- Click on "**Sierra**" to view the CEO's bio page:

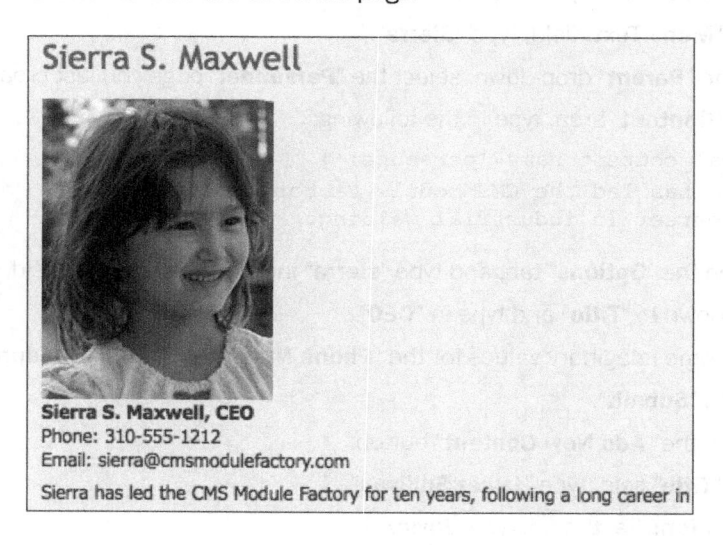

> **Sierra S. Maxwell**
>
> **Sierra S. Maxwell, CEO**
> Phone: 310-555-1212
> Email: sierra@cmsmodulefactory.com
> Sierra has led the CMS Module Factory for ten years, following a long career in

How it works...

This recipe takes advantage of several built-in CMS Made Simple features and several tricks:

- Overriding Extra Page Attribute names
- Accessing page variables in a Global Content Block
- Using the page alias as part of a naming convention
- Creating custom MenuManager templates
- Relying on the ImageManager's thumbnailing feature

The first of these tricks, changing Extra Page Attribute names, is described in detail in another recipe in this chapter, so it won't be described here.

Let's start by looking at the "personnel" Global Content Block (GCB) we defined. It is used to present structured information: in this case, the people in our imaginary company. It guarantees a standardized presentation. The data-entry person who fills in the user pages doesn't have to remember any particular format. To achieve that end, you'll notice that the entire GCB is generic—it makes no reference to any specific person. Each piece of information it presents comes from page variables or is based on the page alias.

First, the "personnel" GCB presents an image of the person. The image name is simply the page alias (followed by the ".jpg" extension). It assumes a subdirectory of the usual image upload directory, which helps in keeping the personnel pictures separate and organized. The "alt" tag for the image uses the standard {title} tag, that is available to all CMS Made Simple pages. When we create pages for people, we will use their names for the page titles, so the image will be their picture and the "alt" tag will contain their name. The "personnel" GCB then includes the three Extra Page Attributes, and labels them according to how we use them.

When the Global Content Block is included in a page, all of the data fields that are referred to generically will be filled in with the appropriate value for the containing page. So when we create Sierra and Javier's biographical pages, we start by including the "personnel" GCB to present their information in a consistent, structured fashion.

At this point, we have consistent biographical pages for our personnel, but if we were to just leave it at that, someone would need to make the top-level directory, that links to the individual bio pages. Instead, we use the Menu Manager to do the work for us.

In our main personnel directory page, we add a tag to call Menu Manager. While Menu Manager is typically used to create menus (as its name suggests), what it does under the hood is generate a data structure of hierarchical page information, which it then formats according to a template. Menus often format the data structure into unordered lists, but we're not limited to that kind of markup. In this case, we're specifying our "personnel" Menu Manager template, that formats the lists into separate divs for each page. We'll describe that in more detail below.

Programming with Smarty and Core Modules

Before we examine our Menu Manager template, we need to look at a few parameters that we use that aren't generally used in site menus. These parameters are quite handy, and once you use them a few times, you'll find yourself discovering other uses. The first of these is "`loadprops`." By default, Menu Manager loads only a limited set of information about the pages: name, menu text, link, and so on. By specifying "`loadprops=1`", we're saying that we want Menu Manager to load the extended properties of the page, which include such useful things as the Extra Page Attributes.

The next interesting parameter to Menu Manager is "`childrenof`." By passing a page alias, this parameter limits the information it returns to the children of the specified page in the content hierarchy. If you want to limit a menu to a site section, this is one way of doing that. In this case, we're being sneaky, and passing "`childrenof`" a variable: the page alias for the current page. In other words, we're telling Menu Manager to return a hierarchical list of pages that are the children of the page containing this tag. We'll be assigning all our biographical pages this personnel directory page as their parent, so this tag will bring in a list of all of these bio pages.

Now that we know we're processing a list of all the bio pages, complete with Extra Page Attributes, let's look at our Menu Manager template. For each entry in the list, we're given a "node" variable that has the specific page details as attributes. Each directory entry is going to start with a picture. Remember our naming convention where the people's pictures are named after their page alias? We use that same convention here, except we prepend the name with "`thumb_`" to retrieve the thumbnail image that is automatically generated by the Image Manager when we upload JPEG images. For the "alt" tag in the images, we use the menu text attribute for the bio page; if we wanted to be more formal and use the person's full name, we could use the page title instead. We then specify the person's name again, and wrap it in a link to their page. You'll notice that accessing the Extra Page Attributes in Menu Manager templates is even easier than in a standard page template, since it's a direct attribute of the node (`$node->extra1`).

There's more...

Much of this recipe is designed to simplify the creation of a personnel section for a site without requiring the person to do the data entry to key in redundant information or worry too much about formatting. This is not done just to make the job of the data entry person easier—long experience has shown that forcing someone to enter the same data in multiple places results in errors, and counting on someone to use consistent formatting on multiple pages rarely works out.

There is one place where we could improve this recipe and minimize the opportunity for error even further: we could obviate the necessity for the data entry person to include the Global Content Block tag for each biography page. The way we do this is to make a copy of our main template, put the GCB tag into this template before the {content} tag, and then save it as the "personnel" template. Then, when the data entry person creates a new biographical page, they simply select the "personnel" template when they are keying information into the "Options" tab.

Using other page attributes

When generating a custom directory or another collection using pages and the Menu Manager, there are a number of page attributes you can use. The entire set is listed in the module help for Menu Manager, but some of the more interesting ones include:

- hierarchy: This is a outline-type representation of the page's position in the site hierarchy, (for example "1.2")
- haschildren: This is true if there are pages below this specific node in the site hierarchy.
- image: If a page has been assigned an image, this will be the image's name (without any path information). This is only available if you tell Menu Manager to load all properties.
- thumbnail: If a page has been assigned a thumbnail, this will be the thumbnail image's name (without any path information). This is only available if you tell Menu Manager to load all properties.
- created: The date the page was created.
- modified: The date the page was last modified.

Why use a naming convention for images?

You probably already knew that you could assign an image and thumbnail to a content page. As you can see in the list of attributes above, the names of those files are available to the Menu Manager template. Given this, why would we use a naming convention based on the page alias rather than these attributes?

Programming with Smarty and Core Modules

There are a few tradeoffs for each approach:

Built-in Attributes	Naming Convention
Requires Menu Manager to load all properties (decreased performance).	Menu Manager may be able to load only basic attributes (increased performance).
User can select image and thumbnail independently on content page.	Images may be organized more logically in subdirectories of uploads/images.
Images must be in uploads/images directory.	User doesn't need to remember to assign images to page.
No need to remember exact names or follow exact convention.	User must remember and follow exacting naming convention.

In our recipe we're already telling Menu Manager to load extended properties for each page, so there's not much of an advantage to using a naming convention. If, however, we were not using the Extra Page Attributes in our directory, we could improve performance by loading only standard content attributes.

In the end, you should select the approach that you think will be simplest for the person or people who will maintain the site.

See also

- *Renaming the "Extra Page Attribute" fields in the CMS Admin* recipe
- *Creating a basic Google Sitemap with Menu Manager and mod_rewrite* recipe

Creating a basic Google Sitemap with Menu Manager and mod_rewrite

This recipe uses the Module Manager to create an XML site map according to Google's sitemap standard. Since all of the major search engines have adopted this format, the sitemap should work well for all indexes.

Getting ready

This recipe requires login access to your site's Administration area as a member of a group with permissions to "Add Pages", "Manage Menu", and "Modify Any Content". For the recipe to work completely, you need to be running Apache web server or a web server that has some `mod_rewrite` compatible capability. You will need to be able to update the Apache configuration, either directly or via `.htaccess` files. You will also need permissions to create files on the server.

How to do it...

- Log in to your CMS Administration area.
- Using the top menu, go to "**Layout**" and click on "**Menu Manager**".
- Click on the "**Add Template**" button.
- In the "**New Template Name**" field, type "**sitemap**".
- In the "**Template Content**" field, type the following code:

```
<?xml version="1.0" encoding="UTF-8"?>
<urlset xmlns="http://www.sitemaps.org/schemas/sitemap/0.9">
{if $count > 0}
{assign var='now' value=$smarty.now|strtotime}
{foreach from=$nodelist item=node}
  <url>
    <loc>{$node->url|escape:'html'}</loc>
    <lastmod>{$node->modified|date_format:'%Y-%m-%dT%T-08:00'}</lastmod>
    <changefreq>{assign var='mod' value=$node->modified|strtotime}
{math assign='age' equation="(n-m)/86400" n=$smarty.now m=$mod}
{if $age < 2}hourly{elseif $age< 14}daily{elseif $age < 30}weekly{else}monthly{/if}</changefreq>
    <priority>{math equation='1/depth' depth=$node->depth}</priority>
  </url>
{/foreach}
{/if}
</urlset>
```

- Click on "**Submit**".
- Using the top menu, go to "**Content**" and click on "**Pages**".
- Click on the "**Add New Content**" button.
- In the "**Title**" and "**Menu Text**" fields, type "**sitemap**".
- In the "**Content**" text area, type the following code:

```
{menu template='sitemap' show_all='1' collapse='0'}
```

- Click on the "**Options**" tab.
- Uncheck the "**Show in Menu**" checkbox.
- Type "**sitemap**" in the "**Page Alias**" field.
- Click "**Submit**".

Programming with Smarty and Core Modules

▶ If you are already using the standard `.htaccess` file to do `mod_rewrite` pretty URLs, add the following after the "RewriteBase" line:

```
RewriteCond %{REQUEST_FILENAME} !-f
RewriteCond %{REQUEST_FILENAME} !-d
RewriteRule ^sitemap.xml$ index.php?page=sitemap&showtemplate=false [L]
```

▶ If you are not using `mod_rewrite` pretty URLs, use your favorite text editor to create a file containing the following:

```
<IfModule mod_rewrite.c>
RewriteEngine on
#
#Sub-dir e.g: /cmsms
RewriteBase /

RewriteCond %{REQUEST_FILENAME} !-f
RewriteCond %{REQUEST_FILENAME} !-d
RewriteRule ^sitemap.xml$ index.php?page=sitemap&showtemplate=false [L]

</IfModule>
```

▶ Save this file as ".htaccess" in the base CMS Made Simple root directory.

▶ You can test your site map with any web browser: go to `http://www.yoursite.com/sitemap.xml`

How it works...

This recipe uses Menu Manager to output a list of all the pages on the site, and a custom template to format that list as XML according to the Google sitemap standard. The structure of the XML file is elementary: an XML declaration and a "urlset" tag that contains a collection of site-specific URLs, each with a few descriptive attributes.

Let's examine the Menu Manager template. It starts by declaring that the file is an XML file and the characters are encoded in UTF-8. Next, it outputs the main container, which is the `urlset` tag. This `urlset` attribute specifies an XML name space (`xmlns`) from the `sitemaps.org` website; in this case, we're specifying that we'll be using the namespace for the sitemap 0.9 schema.

Next, the template sets a variable containing the current time. This will be used when describing the currency of each URL.

The next part is the main substance of the template: we loop through the site pages (in the nodelist variable), and for each page, we output an URL tag. Each URL tag contains several attributes:

- a "`loc`" attribute that contains the actual URL. We use Smarty's HTML escaping modifier in case the URL has characters like ampersands in it. This prevents the creation of invalid XML.
- a "`lastmod`" attribute, that is the "modified" date of the page reformatted into a date string according to the W3C date standard.
- a "`changefreq`" attribute, that designates how frequently the content is expected to change. The allowable values are strings: always, hourly, daily, weekly, monthly, yearly, or never. We use the amount of time since the last modification, and output the appropriate string.
- a "`priority`" attribute, which is a value between 0 and 1. We compute a value based on the depth in the site hierarchy, on the assumption that the most important pages are the top-level pages.

Once we have the Menu Manager template, we place the menu tag into a page. The page is set to be active, but not to show up in the site navigation.

The last step is to link this page to a standardized URL—according to the sitemap standard, search engines look for a filename "`sitemap.xml`" in the site root (although many search engines allow you to register a different location, if you choose to).

We use the magic of Apache's `mod_rewrite` module to map the filename "`sitemap.xml`" to our page containing the sitemap tag. Specifically, the `mod_rewrite` rules check to see if the incoming request is not for a directory or an existing filesystem file. If those tests pass, it checks to see that "`sitemap.xml`" was requested. If so, it rewrites the URL and drops out of further rewrite tests.

The rewritten URL has one special feature—it calls the page containing the sitemap, but also passes the parameter "`showtemplate=false`". This noteworthy parameter tells CMS Made Simple to output the page but suppress the page template that surrounds the page's {`content`} tag output. This allows us to output the unadorned XML of the sitemap.

There's more...

The sitemap generated by this recipe includes all active pages in your site, whether or not they show up in the menu. In some cases, you may want to use the menu visibility to determine what is included in the site map. It is easy to change this recipe to include only pages that are in the menu. In your "sitemap" page, change the "`show_all='1'`" to "`show_all='0'`".

The changefreq and priority attributes

There are two sitemap attributes that we're computing, and which might bear some further examination.

If you look at how we generate the "changefreq" attribute, we're looking at how long it's been since the page was last updated, and glibly asserting that that's the average time between updates. This, of course, is not necessarily accurate. CMS Made Simple doesn't track the number of updates to any one page, so it seemed like a reasonable compromise number, but you may wish to be more accurate for Search Engine Optimization (SEO) purposes. One way of doing that would be to use an Extra Page Attribute to store update frequency. If you do this, be sure to add "loadprops='1'" to your menu tag, so that Menu Manager knows to load the extra page attributes.

Similarly, we're computing page priority based upon the page's depth in the site hierarchy. We're saying page priority is inversely proportional to the page depth: top level pages get a priority 1, next level get a priority of 0.5, third level get 0.33, and so on. You may have a different formula for rating page priority, or you may wish to specify on a page-by-page basis using an Extra Page Attribute.

One thing to keep in mind about priority—this number represents relative importance on your site. You'll encounter overly enthusiastic people who think that rating all of their pages with a priority of 1 will improve their site's overall search engine performance. Unfortunately, this is not true; the number is relative to your own pages, not anybody else's.

For more information on the sitemap standard, visit the site Google set up to document it at https://www.sitemaps.org.

What if my site is not UTF-8?

Character encoding is one of the more confusing and troublesome problems of programming for the internet.

The sitemap standard requires the XML file to be encoded as UTF-8. In most cases, you'll want your CMS Made Simple site to create UTF-8 encoded output anyway.

However, in the event that your site is not using UTF-8 encoding, you may still be able to use this recipe. In fact, as long as your site don't use characters outside of the old ASCII alpha-numeric range in any URLs, the encoding won't matter. If, however, your URLs use extended characters and you are using a non-UTF-8 encoding, your sitemaps won't be handled properly by search engine indexers.

See also

- *Creating a personnel directory using Menu Manager* recipe
- *Renaming the "Extra Page Attribute" fields in the CMS Admin* recipe

Embedding JavaScript in your template without causing Smarty to throw a fit

Embedding JavaScript directly in a page is usually discouraged, but is also sometimes unavoidable. In a CMS Made Simple site, you may see errors when adding JavaScript to a page because Smarty confuses the JavaScript curly braces with its own delimiters. Embedding JavaScript is not impossible, though!

This recipe demonstrates adding JavaScript to a template that is parsed by Smarty. It also discusses incorporating Smarty variables within JavaScript.

Getting ready

For this recipe, you will need to access the site's Administration area with "**Modify Templates**" permissions. This recipe assumes you are using NCleanBlue as your default site template.

How to do it...

- Log in to your CMS Administration area.
- Using the top menu, go to "**Layout**" and click on "**Templates**".
- Click on "**NCleanBlue**" in the template list to edit the page.
- Find the line that reads "**{* This is how all the stylesheets attached to this template are linked to *}**", and paste the following code after it:

```
{literal}
<script type="text/javascript">
function hi() {
alert('hi');
}

hi();
</script>
{/literal}
```

- Load your site's home page in your browser. You will see a JavaScript alert pop up saying "**hi**".

How it works...

This recipe is a contrived example to illustrate the use of Smarty's {literal} tag. In the version of Smarty used in CMS Made Simple, curly braces are reserved for template directives. The fact that they are syntactically important in JavaScript becomes a problem: Smarty thinks that your curly braces are meant for it, so it throws template errors when it attempts to render the page containing JavaScript.

The {literal} and {/literal} tags tell Smarty to ignore curly braces within an area. This allows you to include your JavaScript without confusing Smarty.

An alternative approach

Smarty has an alternative to {literal}{/literal} tags. Instead of marking off the boundaries of your JavaScript, you replace all of your curly braces in your JavaScript with one of two Smarty-friendly tags: either {ldelim} or {rdelim}. These stand for "left delimiter" and "right delimiter," respectively, and will render into your template as a left curly brace and a right curly brace.

Since this approach is verbose, it is not frequently used.

Using Smarty Variables in your JavaScript

As we've seen, setting off JavaScript with {literal}{/literal} tags prevents Smarty from generating parse errors. But what about the cases when you want to pass a variable to your JavaScript from Smarty? This turns out to just be a matter of ending one literal block and starting another.

Here's an example of a script that will pop up an annoying confirmation box any time someone wants to leave a page. It uses the "title" Smarty tag to customize the message for the current page, even if the script lives in the page template.

```
{literal}
<script type="text/javascript">
function confirm_exit(e) {
  if(!e) e = window.event;
  e.cancelBubble = true;
  e.returnValue = 'You will be leaving the page "{/literal}{title}{literal}"?';
  if (e.stopPropagation) {
    e.stopPropagation();
    e.preventDefault();
  }
}
window.onbeforeunload=confirm_exit;
```

```
</script>
{/literal}
```

Using Smarty loops to generate similar stylesheet constructs

You can use Smarty in your stylesheets for more than just setting up named variables, or computing sizes. With creative use, you can make Smarty do drudge-work for you!

This recipe shows you how you can use Smarty's built-in looping capabilities to create groups of similar CSS rules.

Getting ready

This recipe requires that you have access to the site's Administration area with permission to "Add Stylesheets", "Add Stylesheet Associations", and "Manage All Content".

How to do it...

- Log in to your CMS Administration area.
- Using the top menu, go to "**Layout**" and click on "**Stylesheets**".
- Click on the "**Add a Stylesheet**" button.
- Enter "**color_boxes**" into the "**name**" field.
- Enter the following stylesheet into the "**content**" area:
  ```
  [[setlist var=boxes value='"red":"#df0000","green":"#00df00","blue":"#0000df"']]
  [[foreach from=$boxes key=current_box item=box_color]]
  #[[$current_box]] {
    background: #fff;
    color: [[$box_color]];
    border: 1px solid [[$box_color]];
    width: 200px;
  }
  #[[$current_box]] h1 {
    background: [[$box_color]];
    color: #fff;
    font-weight: bold;
    text-align: center;
  }
  [[/foreach]]
  ```

Programming with Smarty and Core Modules

- Under "**Media Types**", click the checkbox for "**all: Suitable for all devices**" and then click "**Submit**".
- Find "**color_boxes**" in the stylesheet list, and click on the CSS icon.
- In the drop-down, select "**NCleanBlue**" and click on the "**Attach to this Template**" button.
- Using the top menu, go to "**Content**" and select "**Pages**".
- Click on the "**Add New Content**" button.
- Fill in the name of the new page as "**Boxes**".
- Enter "**Boxes**" as the menu text.
- If you are using a WYSIWYG editor for the content area, uncheck the checkbox labeled "**Turn WYSIWYG on/off**".

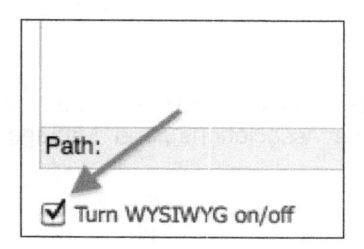

- Enter the following HTML code into the content area:

```
<div id="red">
  <h1>Red Box</h1>
  <p>This is a red box</p>
</div>
<div id="green">
  <h1>Green Box</h1>
  <p>This is a green box</p>
</div>
<div id="blue">
  <h1>Blue Box</h1>
  <p>This is a blue box</p>
</div>
```

- Click "**Submit**".
- View your site from the user side. Click on the new "**Boxes**" page.

Boxes

Red Box
This is a red box

Green Box
This is a green box

Blue Box
This is a blue box

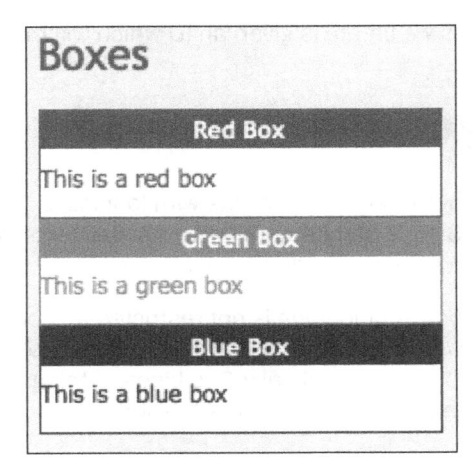

How it works...

This recipe uses built-in Smarty looping to generate separate, but related, CSS rule sets.

It starts with a CMS Made Simple-specific Smarty tag called "`setlist`", which allows you to create a Smarty variable that is an associative array. The tag takes two parameters: "`var`", that specifies the name of variable to use, and "`value`", that specifies the array to be stored. The syntax for the "`value`" parameter is similar to a JSON format, with colon-delimited name-value pairs in a comma-separated list.

So the first line creates an associative array named "boxes" with the color names as the keys and the color hex triplet as the value.

The next line is where we tell Smarty that we want it to loop through the array we just created. The `foreach` command takes a number of parameters:

- from—what array to loop through
- key—what variable to use to refer to the key for the current item
- item—what variable to use to refer to for the current item's value

Our command says to loop through the array stored in the "boxes" variable. That means that for each element in the array, we'll be interpreting all of the code between the [[foreach]] and [[/foreach]], and within that scope, we will have a variable called "`current_box`", that will be the current array element's key, and a variable called "`box_color`", that will be the current array element's value.

From there, we have a set of CSS rules, where we substitute in our values. In this case, we're using our "`current_box`" for a CSS ID, and we're using the "`box_color`" to set the color attributes. In our template, we only need to write out the rules once, and the loop will generate one set of rules for each box in our array.

Programming with Smarty and Core Modules

In our HTML, each of the divs we create is given an ID which will match the IDs generated in the CSS.

There's more...

You might worry that the generation of stylesheets with looping is computationally expensive. Never fear! The CMS Made Simple architecture caches stylesheets, so the computation will only happen once after each source change.

Also, keep in mind that the power of looping is not restricted to looping through sets of colors. You could use a loop along with some Smarty arithmetic to generate a set of header tags (H1 – H10, say) and set the sizes programmatically. The kinds of things you can do with Smarty logic in your stylesheets is only limited by your imagination.

See also

- *Using Smarty to create color sets in your stylesheet* recipe
- *Using Smarty to do the math in your stylesheet* recipe

Displaying a block only for the Home page

Site designs often use identical or near-identical designs for all pages, with one or more extra elements on the Home page. It would be ideal if we could avoid duplicating templates to achieve this, as each duplicate increases the difficulty of maintenance and making changes. In this case, it would be best if we could use a single template for all pages and, fortunately, we can! This recipe shows you how to place conditional logic in your page template that will show some content only on certain pages.

Getting ready

This recipe requires access to the Admin area with "Add Global Content Blocks", "Modify Templates", and "Manage All Content" permissions. We also assume you are using the default NCleanBlue template.

How to do it...

- Log in to your CMS Administration area.
- Using the top menu, go to "**Content**" and click on "**Global Content Blocks**".
- Click on the "**Add Global Content Block**" button.

- Enter "**welcome**" into the "**name**" field.

  ```
  Enter the welcome message into the "content" text area:<div class="sbar-top">
     <h2 class="sbar-title">Welcome!</h2>
  </div>
  <div class="sbar-main">Welcome to {sitename}!</div>
  ```

- Click the "**Submit**" button.
- Using the top menu, go to "**Layout**" and click on "**Templates**".
- Click on "**NCleanBlue**" to edit the template.
- Find the end of the left column definition in the template, which will look like:

  ```
  {* Start left side *}
          <div id="left" class="core-float-left">
  ```

- After the start of the div, insert the conditional code so it looks like:

  ```
  {* Start left side *}
          <div id="left" class="core-float-left">
  {if $page_alias eq 'home'}
      {global_content name='welcome'}
  {/if}
  ```

- Then click on the "**Submit**" button.

Programming with Smarty and Core Modules

▶ View your site from the user side. Click on the "**Home**" page, and you will see your "**Welcome**" block:

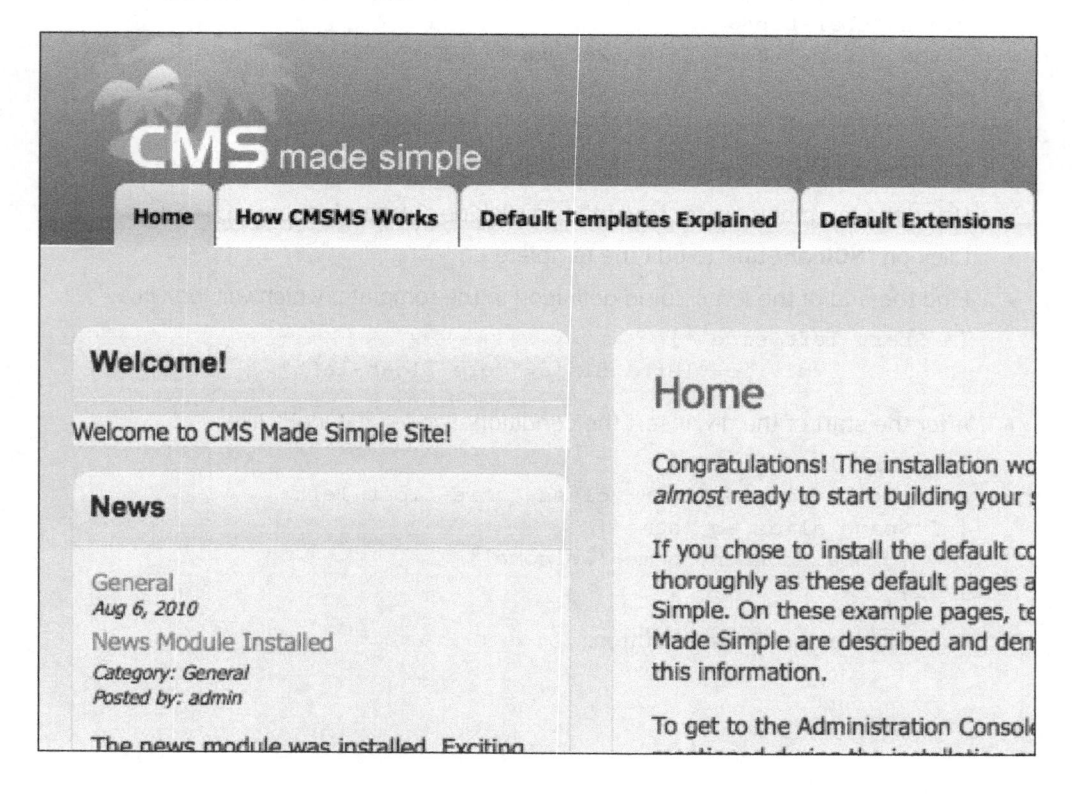

▶ View any other page that uses the same template, and the "**Welcome**" block will not appear.

How it works...

This recipe uses Smarty logic in the template to display a block of content only on the Home page of the site. The comparison takes place in the template, with the condition comparing the variable $page_alias to the string 'home'. If there is a match, everything within the conditional clause is rendered into the template.

In this example, we place our "welcome" content into a Global Content Block. You would typically do it this way so that an admin user would not need to edit the template to update the welcome block. This works out well, since users are usually more comfortable editing a Global Content Block than a template, and you as the site developer don't have to worry about someone accidentally messing up the entire site template by removing the {/if} tag or something similar.

You'll note that this example assumes that the Home page of the site has the alias "home." In the default content distributed with CMS Made Simple, this will be true. If your site is set up differently, you will need to compare the $page_alias to whatever is appropriate for your site.

There's more...

There are several other Smarty variables that are set for each CMS Made Simple page. You could choose to compare with any of those variables when creating a conditional, including:

- $page_id—the internal ID of the current page
- $position or $friendly_position—the numerical representations of where the page is in the site menu hierarchy.

This is also a good place to use the Extra Page Attributes, although they're a little harder to get to. Extra Page Attributes can be found on the **"Options"** tab when editing content. They are stored in a Smarty variable called $content_obj and you refer to them using a function called GetPropertyValue. So, for example, if you wanted to use the Extra Page Attribute 2 to flag whether or not to show your "welcome" content, you could use:

```
{if {if $content_obj->GetPropertyValue('extra2') eq 'true'}
    {global_content name='welcome'}
{/if}
```

Then, for any page where you typed the word "true" into Extra Page Attribute 2, your "welcome" content would be displayed.

More complex comparisons

Smarty supports not only simple "if" conditions, but also "if-else" conditions. You can use this to show one specific piece of content on the Home page and a different piece of content on all other pages:

```
{if $page_alias eq 'home'}
    {global_content name='welcome'}
{else}
    {global_content name='something_else'}
{/if}
```

It's a short step from doing page comparisons to doing comparisons based on other Smarty variables. For example, perhaps you would want your logo to have special decorations on special dates. With Smarty comparisons, this is easy:

```
{if $smarty.now|date_format:"%m%d" == '0101'}
  <img src="logo_newyears.jpg" />
{elseif $smarty.now|date_format:"%m%d" == '0314'}
  <img src="logo_einstein_birthday.jpg" />
```

Programming with Smarty and Core Modules

```
{else}
  <img src="logo.jpg" />
{/if}
```

This example uses the built-in Smarty date variable ($smarty.now) and the built-in Smarty date format modifier to create a four-digit string representing the month and day of the month.

It compares the month to January ("01") and the day to the 1st ("01"), and if there is a match, outputs the New Year's version of the logo. If there isn't a match, it compares the date to March 14th, and, if it matches, it outputs the version of the logo for Einstein's Birthday. If neither condition matches, the everyday version of the logo is output.

See also

- *Using Smarty "Capture" and conditionals to hide empty content blocks* recipe
- *Seeing what Smarty variables are available to your template* recipe
- *Renaming the "Extra" Page Attributes in the CMS Admin* recipe

Using Smarty "Capture" and conditionals to hide empty content blocks

This recipe shows you how you can create multiple content blocks on a page, and have the site design automatically adapt when a content block is empty.

Getting ready

You will need to access your site Administration area with "Modify Templates" and "Manage All Content" permissions. This recipe assumes you are using the default NCleanBlue template, but will work with any template.

How to do it...

- Log in to your CMS Administration area.
- Using the top menu, go to "**Layout**" and click on "**Templates**".
- Click on "**NCleanBlue**" to edit the template.
- Find the end of the left column definition in the template, which will look like:
  ```
  {* Start left side *}
          <div id="left" class="core-float-left">
  ```
- After the start of the div, insert the capture and conditional code so it looks like:

```
{* Start left side *}
        <div id="left" class="core-float-left">
        {capture assign="special"}{content
          block="special"}{/capture}
        {if $special != ''}
          <div class="sbar-top">
            <h2 class="sbar-title">Special!</h2>
          </div>
          <div class="sbar-main">{$special}</div>
        {/if}
```

- Then click on the "**Submit**" button.
- Using the top menu, go to "**Content**" and select "**Pages**".
- Click on the "**Add New Content**" button.
- Enter "**Offer**" into both the "**Title**" and "**Menu Text**" fields.
- Enter a short line of text into the "**Special**" text area, for example, "Tour the Pleiades in your Own Spaceship!" and add formatting if you'd like.
- Enter more content into the main "**Content**" text area.
- Click on the "**Options**" tab and make sure that the selected template is "**NCleanBlue**".
- Hit the "**Submit**" button.
- View your site from the user side. Click on the "**Offer**" page, and you will see your "**Special**" block displayed:

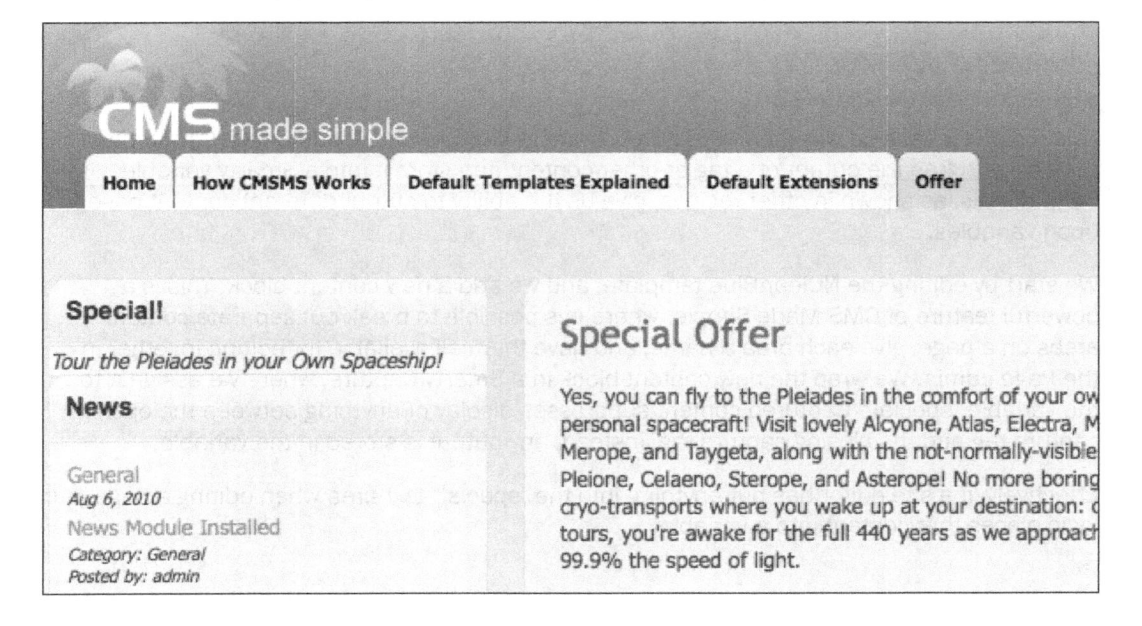

▶ Now click on the link to the Home page, where you have not entered any information into the "**Special**" content block. Note that it appears as you would expect:

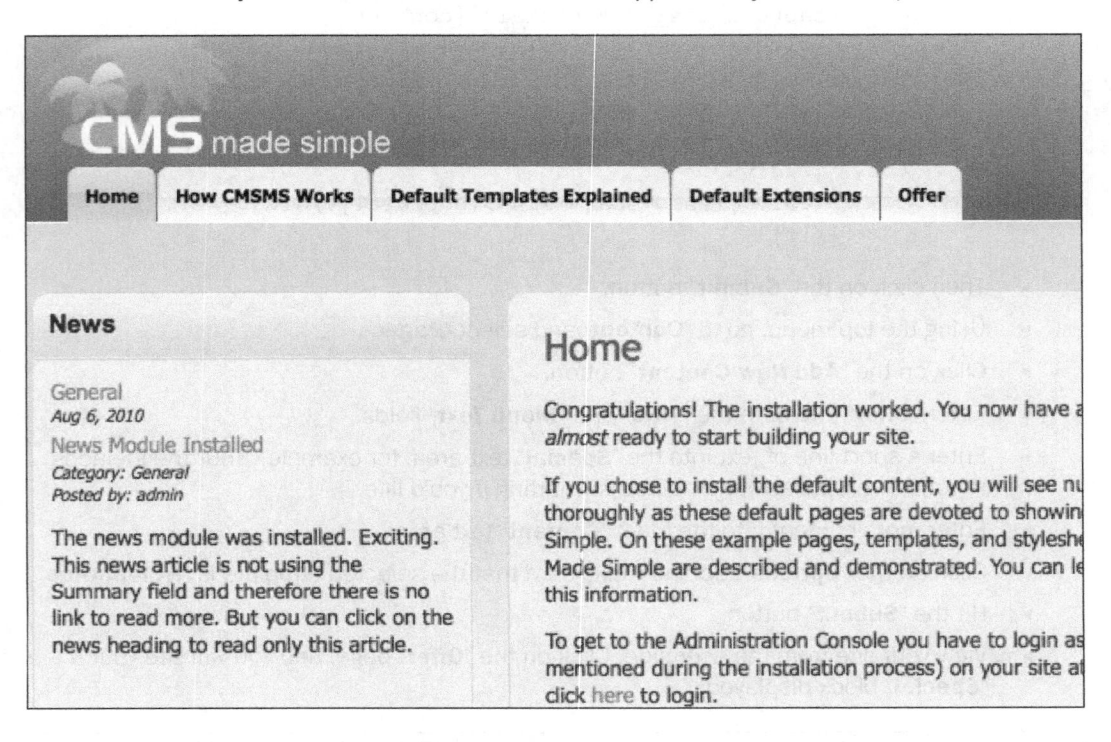

How it works...

This recipe focuses on two Smarty features, namely, capture and conditionals. Capture is the ability to trap the output of a tag or other content and store it into a Smarty variable. Conditionals, as shown in other recipes, give us the ability to output different content based upon variables.

We start by editing the NCleanBlue template, and we add a new content block. This is a powerful feature of CMS Made Simple, where it is possible to break out separate content areas on a page, give each area a name, and have them all available for editing together in the Page admin. We wrap the new content block in a Smarty Capture, where we assign it to the variable "special." Captured content suppresses display of anything between the opening capture tag and the closing capture tag. Instead, any output is stored in the variable.

Effectively, if a site editor has put anything into the "special" text area when editing a page, our logic places that content into a variable.

In our next line, we test the "special" variable to see if it does, in fact, contain anything. If it does, we wrap it in some formatting, and display it. If it is empty, however, we skip that.

There's more...

Once you have captured site content into a variable, you can do all kinds of creative things. You can run Smarty modifiers against it for all kinds of effects like capitalizing the first letter of each word, converting to upper or lowercase, running replacements with regular expressions, and so on.

There are other Smarty features that could be used for altering the layout of the page, such as the `count_words` modifier. For example, if you want to alter the layout when there is a lot of text, you could do something like the following:

```
{capture assign="my_content"}{content}{/capture}
<div class="{if $my_content|word_count < 10}narrow{else}wide{/
if}">{$my_content}</div>
```

This little snippet will display the content block in a div with a class of "narrow", if there are fewer than ten words of content, or in a div with a class of "wide" if there are ten or more words.

See also

- *Displaying a block only for the Home page* recipe

Seeing what Smarty variables are available to your template

During development, it's sometimes useful to find out which Smarty variables are in scope and available for your use in a template. This recipe shows you how to do that.

Getting ready

This recipe requires you have Administration area access with "Modify Templates", "Modify News", and "Manage All Content" permissions. This recipe assumes you are using all of the default content and templates from a basic installation, but the principles will work regardless.

How to do it...

- Log in to your CMS Administration area.
- Using the top menu, go to "**Content**" and click on "**Pages**".

Programming with Smarty and Core Modules

- Click on the edit icon for your home page.
- In the "**Content**" text area, place the following before any content:
  `{get_template_vars}`
- Click on "**Submit**".
- View your site from the user side. Click to your home page, and observe the output in your main content area:

```
Home

SCRIPT_NAME = /index.php
app_name = CMS
sitename = CMS Made Simple Site
lang =
encoding = utf-8
gCms = Object
content_obj = Object
content_id = 15
page = 15
page_id = 15
page_name = home
page_alias = home
position = 00001
friendly_position = 1
search_actionid = cntnt01
hogan = onfocus="if(this.value==this.defaultValue) this.value='';" onblur="if(this.
searchtext = Enter Search...
startform = <form id="cntnt01moduleform_1" method="post" action="http://cms
<div class="hidden">
<input type="hidden" name="mact" value="Search,cntnt01,dosearch,0" />
```

- Return to the Admin area of your site. Using the top menu, go to "**Content**" and click on "**Pages**".
- Click on the edit icon for your home page.
- In the "**Content**" text area, remove the `{get_template_vars}` tag.
- Click on the "**Submit**" button.
- Using the top menu, go to "**Content**" and click on "**News**".
- Click on the "**Details Template**" tab.
- Click on the edit icon for the "**Sample**" template.

Chapter 2

- In the "**Template Source**" text area, place the following before any other template text:
  {get_template_vars}
- Click on the "**Submit**" button.
- View your site from the user side. Go to your home page.
- In the "**News**" column on the left, click on the link to read more of the article "**News Module Installed**".
- Examine the output:

```
SCRIPT_NAME = /index.php
app_name = CMS
sitename = CMS Made Simple Site
lang =
encoding = utf-8
gCms = Object
content_obj = Object
content_id = 39
page = 39
page_id = 39
page_name = news
page_alias = news
position = 00004.00001.00001
friendly_position = 4.1.1
search_actionid = cntnt01
hogan =
onfocus="if(this.value==this.defaultValu
e) this.value='';"
onblur="if(this.value=='')
this.value=this.defaultValue;"
searchtext = Enter Search...
startform = <form
id="cntnt01moduleform_1" method="get"
action="http://cmsbook.samuel
/index.php?page=news" class="cms_form">
<div class="hidden">
<input type="hidden" name="mact"
value="Search,cntnt01,dosearch,0" />
<input type="hidden"
name="cntnt01returnid" value="39" />
```

News

```
SCRIPT_NAME = /index.php
app_name = CMS
sitename = CMS Made Simple Site
lang =
encoding = utf-8
gCms = Object
content_obj = Object
content_id = 39
page = 39
page_id = 39
page_name = news
page_alias = news
position = 00004.00001.00001
friendly_position = 4.1.1
search_actionid = cntnt01
hogan = onfocus="if(this.value==this.defau
this.value=this.defaultValue;"
searchtext = Enter Search...
startform = <form id="cntnt01moduleform_1"
class="cms_form">
<div class="hidden">
<input type="hidden" name="mact" value="Sea
<input type="hidden" name="cntnt01returnid
</div>
label = <label for="cntnt01searchinput">Sea
searchprompt = Search
submittext = Submit
endform = </form>
```

How it works...

The {get_template_vars} tag is a CMS Made Simple-specific wrapper to an underlying Smarty function that, as its name suggests, returns the entire set of template variables assigned to Smarty. The tag does some minimal formatting to give some idea if a variable contains an array (and if so, how many elements it comprises) or whether a variable contains an object.

Programming with Smarty and Core Modules

The information presented may appear somewhat trivial, but it can save an enormous amount of time when working with a module that doesn't provide strong documentation on the variables it makes available to various templates.

There's more...

As you can see in the sample output, the {get_template_vars} tag provides only superficial insight into more complex variables. Sometimes, it's enough to know that something is an object or array, but sometimes you want to know the specifics.

One way of displaying this kind of detail is using the "print_r" Smarty modifier. For example, you may see a variable "$items" exists in your page, and contains an object. From experience, you may have an idea that it's defined by the News module, but you may be uncertain or you may want to know exactly which attributes it possesses. To get this information, you could put the following tag into a page or template:

```
{$items|print_r}
```

Then when you view the page, you will see output like the following:

Home

stdClass Object ([author_id] => 1 [author] => admin [authorname] => [id] => 1 [title] => News Module Installed [content] => The news module was installed. Exciting. This news article is not using the Summary field and therefore there is no link to read more. But you can click on the news heading to read only this article. [summary] => [postdate] => 2010-08-06 10:32:57 [startdate] => [enddate] => [create_date] => 2010-08-06 10:32:57 [modified_date] => 2010-08-06 10:32:57 [category] => General [fieldsbyname] => Array ( ) [fields] => Array ( ) [file_location] => http://cmsbook.samuel/uploads/news/id1 [link] => http://cmsbook.samuel/index.php?mact=News,cntnt01,detail,0&cntnt01articleid=1&cntnt01origid=15&cntnt01returnid=39 [titlelink] => News Module Installed [morelink] => More [moreurl] => http://cmsbook.samuel/index.php?mact=News,cntnt01,detail,0&cntnt01articleid=1&cntnt01origid=15&cntnt01returnid=39 [printlink] => Print [printurl] => http://cmsbook.samuel/index.php?mact=News,cntnt01,print,0&cntnt01articleid=1&cntnt01showtemplate=false&cntnt01returnid=15) Array

---

As this demonstrates, the print_r modifier is the same as the PHP function of the same name.

Risky recursion

The {get_template_vars} tag avoids running into termination problems by providing a shallow view of the variables that are available to the template. The print_r modifier, on the other hand, delves much deeper into the contents of variables, and follows object pointers to try to provide a full description of the specified variable.

Like the underlying PHP function, `print_r` has some protection against objects or variables that have pointers to themselves. Depending upon the data structures in question, however, an inopportune `print_r` can create enormous amounts of output. Using, say, {$gCms|print_r} may well exhaust the memory PHP has allocated, and will not give you the information you desire.

Often, you will run into this problem via unexpected references. You may think that {$gCms->modules|print_r} would output less content than {$gCms|print_r}, but each module has a pointer to $gCms, so the command gamely tries to show the entire data structure.

In a case where you are unable to display data structures using the `print_r` modifier, adding specificity to your output statement can help. Instead of dumping out all of $gCms, dump out the exact portion that interests you, for example, {$gCms->db|print_r}.

See also

- *Chapter 1, How to use CMS in Debug Mode* recipe

3
Getting the Most out of Tags and User-Defined Tags

In this chapter, we will cover:

- Displaying the User's IP address from a User-Defined Tag
- Using the current content object in a User-Defined Tag
- Making a variable available to Smarty from a User-Defined Tag
- Displaying the number of pages in the CMS using a User-Defined Tag
- Using URL parameters in a User-Defined Tag
- Using Smarty values as inputs in a User-Defined Tag
- Display a stock price from Yahoo with a User-Defined Tag
- Displaying a translation of the current page using Babelfish with a User-Defined Tag
- Posting an article to the News Module using a User-Defined Tag
- Reversing a string in two ways using a Smarty Modifier
- Adding Registered Trademark symbols to a name automatically

Getting the Most out of Tags and User-Defined Tags

Introduction

One of the most popular uses of CMS Made Simple involves an administrator who creates a basic site structure and template, and one or more editors who maintain page content without having to worry about the site layout. In this configuration, you can think of the CMS essentially as a big template engine with some utilities to add content.

Each page of the site comprises a page template with areas that get populated with various kinds of content. These areas are either tags or variables, where the distinction is that a tag involves the execution of code, while a variable is a simple substitution of values. The CMS comes with a large assortment of built-in tags, including the fundamental `content` tag and a variety of useful supporting tags for building navigation, links, including images, and so forth.

Because CMS Made Simple can be seen as being built around tags, it is not surprising that there are facilities for creating your own tags. You can create tags directly through the Admin panel—these are called User-Defined Tags or UDTs. If you want even more extensive capabilities in your tag, you can have those capabilities by creating a file that follows a few basic conventions.

The template engine used by CMS Made Simple comes from the Smarty project. Pages are Smarty templates, and the built-in CMS tag types are all Smarty tags. Behind the scenes, both UDTs and file-based tags also become Smarty tags.

[For additional information on Smarty, the documentation provided by the Smarty project is invaluable. You can read more at `http://www.smarty.net/docsv2/en/`]

In this chapter, we will explore a few applications of tags. Most of these recipes are User-Defined Tags, because the capabilities of the User-Defined Tags are nearly identical to the file type of a tag. However, there are two recipes that show off using tags as Smarty filters or variable modifiers.

These recipes have been specially selected to demonstrate capabilities. While they may be useful as provided, they are designed to show the range of what can be done with tags, and to provide examples of useful operations such as setting Smarty variables, interfacing with the database, interacting with modules, and consuming data from remote web services. You are encouraged to use these recipes as starting points for your own projects.

Displaying the User's IP address from a User-Defined Tag

This recipe demonstrates creating a very simple User-Defined Tag, and using it to display information, that it gets from PHP globally-defined variables.

Getting ready

For this recipe, you will need to have CMS Made Simple installed and working. You will need login access to the site's Administration area as a member of the "admin" group, or as a member of a group with permissions to "Modify User-Defined Tags" and "Manage All Content".

How to do it...

1. Log in to your CMS Administration area.
2. Using the top menu, go to "**Extensions**" and click on "**User Defined Tags**".
3. Click on the "**Add User Defined Tag**" button.
4. In the "**Name**" field type "**user_ip**".
5. In the "**Code**" text area, type the following code:
   ```
   echo 'Welcome user from '.$_SERVER['REMOTE_ADDR'].' -- enjoy your visit!';
   ```
6. Click on the "**Submit**" button.
7. Using the top menu, go to "**Content**" and click on "**Pages**".
8. Click on the "**Add New Content**" button.
9. In the "**Title**" and "**Menu Text**" fields, type "**Tag Test**".
10. In the "**Content**" text area, type the following code:
    ```
    {user_ip}
    ```
11. Click on the "**Submit**" button.

Getting the Most out of Tags and User-Defined Tags

12. View your site from the user side. Click on the new "**Tag Test**" page.

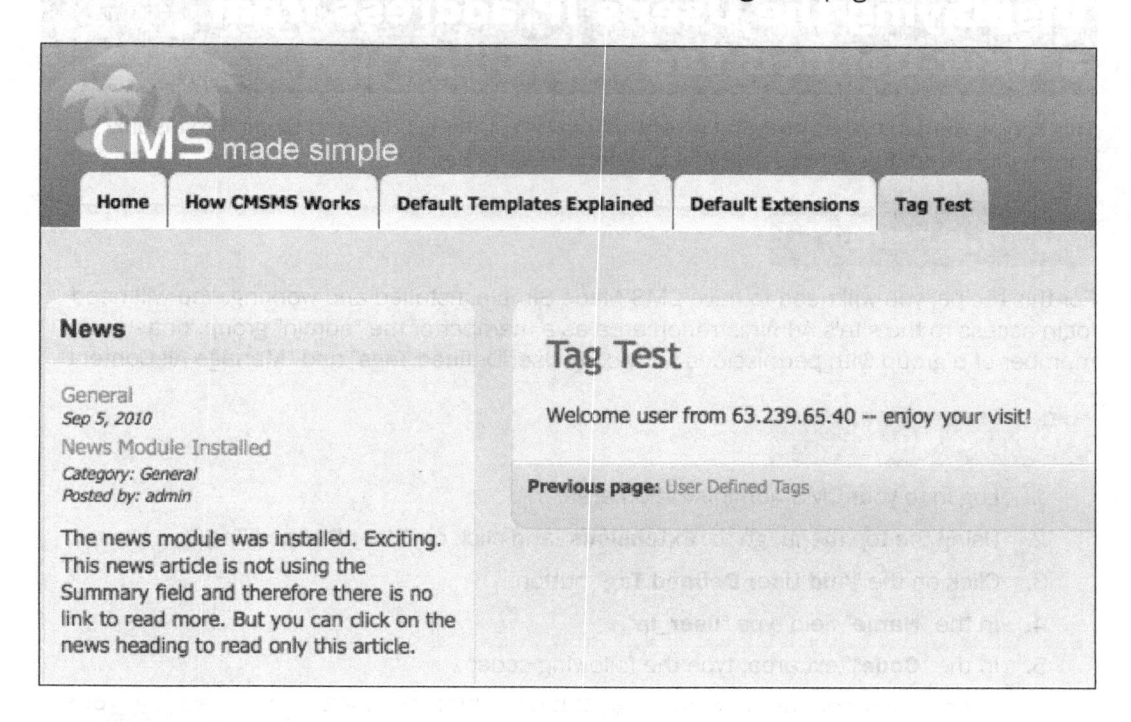

How it works...

User-Defined Tags work by linking a piece of PHP code to a tag which is recognized by Smarty. When Smarty parses a template and encounters that tag, it executes the code in question, and substitutes the tag markup with any output from that PHP code.

When we create a UDT in the CMS Made Simple admin area, the name we enter into the text field becomes the tag which Smarty will look for, and the code we enter into the text area is the PHP associated with the tag.

This recipe is an example of outputting text directly from a User-Defined Tag. It works by echoing a string, that then replaces the {user_ip} tag in the content. This substitution of the tag can take place either in a page template or in the page content, which might seem a little confusing since it's stated earlier that Smarty processes tags that it finds in templates. The confusion, though, is mostly due to terminology; CMS Made Simple processes both layout templates and page content through Smarty, so while it is being processed, page content serves as a template from Smarty's perspective.

The User-Defined Tag we create accesses one of the PHP "superglobals"—the $_SERVER variable. This variable contains information about the HTTP request and some environmental information about the PHP server. In this case, we're getting the user's IP address information to display.

See also

- *Chapter 1, Create a "Hello World" User-Defined Tag* recipe

Using the CmsObject and the current content object in a User-Defined Tag

This recipe shows you how to access the Page Content object via the CmsObject in a User-Defined Tag.

The primary technique that it demonstrates—getting a reference to the CmsObject and using the CmsObject to get a reference to other important CMS runtime objects—is one that you will use to solve many different kinds of problems.

In this recipe, we use the CmsObject to get a reference to the Page Content object. Once we have a reference to this object, we can call upon its methods to report all kinds of interesting information about the current page content.

Getting ready

For this recipe, you will need login access to your site's Administration area with permission to "Modify User-Defined Tags" and "Manage All Content".

How to do it...

1. Log in to your CMS Administration area.
2. Using the top menu, go to "**Extensions**" and click on "**User Defined Tags**".
3. Click on the "**Add User Defined Tag**" icon.
4. In the "**Name**" field, type "**content_description**".
5. In the "**Code**" field, type the following code:

   ```
   $gCms = cmsms();
   $contentops = $gCms->GetContentOperations();
   $content_obj = $contentops->getContentObject();
   echo 'Current content object is "'.$content_obj->Name().'"<br />';
   echo 'which was created on '.$content_obj->GetCreationDate().'<br />';
   ```

Getting the Most out of Tags and User-Defined Tags

```
echo 'its alias is "'.$content_obj->Alias().'"<br />';
echo 'and its URL is "'.$content_obj->GetURL().'"<br />';
```

6. Click on the "**Submit**" button.
7. Using the top menu, select "**Content**" and click on "**Pages**".
8. Click on the "**Add New Content**" button.
9. Enter "**New Content Page**" into the "**Title**" and "**Menu Text**" fields.
10. In the "**Content**" field, enter:

    ```
    {content_description}
    ```

11. Click on the "**Submit**" button.
12. View your site from the user side. Click on the new "**Content Page**" page.

Sample Content Page

Current content object is "Sample Content Page"
which was created on 2010-09-09 16:15:41
its alias is "sample-content-page"
and its URL is "http://cmsbook.samuel/index.php?page=sample-content-page"

Previous page: User Defined Tags

How it works...

CMS Made Simple uses an internal object called "CmsObject" to keep track of a great deal of what it needs to serve content. This information includes the site hierarchy, the installed and active modules, references to the database, and more. The CmsObject is available to Modules, Tags, and User-Defined Tags via the cmsms() function.

In this recipe, we want to display information from the current Content object. However, this object is not directly accessible. To get access to this object, we need to make a static call to the ContentOperations object, but this object is also not directly accessible from our code. To get access to these objects, we need to get references to them.

We start by gaining access to the CmsObject by calling the global cmsms() function. From our reference to the CmsObject, we request a reference to the ContentOperations object, that we then use to request a reference to the current content object.

Once we have the current content object, we can call assorted methods on it to retrieve information about the current content. In this recipe, we get the content's name, when it was last modified, its alias, and its URL. Since this recipe is an example, we don't format these various pieces of information or use a template, but simply echo them. In a production UDT or one in which there's any complexity to what is being displayed, it would be more advisable to use the values to populate Smarty variables for later display, or use a template for formatting them.

There's more...

There are a number of interesting objects, that `CmsObject` manages. References can be requested to:

- `BookmarkOperations`—used in the Admin area
- `ContentOperations`—which has methods to handle Content and content metadata
- `Db`—which wraps the ADODB database API
- `GlobalContentOperations`—which has methods to handle Global Content Blocks
- `GroupOperations`—which has methods to handle Admin Groups
- `HierarchyManager`—which has methods for handling site content hierarchies
- `ModuleOperations`—which has methods for managing Modules
- `Smarty`—which wraps the Smarty template engine
- `StylesheetOperations`—which has methods for handling
- `TemplateOperations`—which has methods for handling Smarty templates
- `UserOperations`—which has methods for handling Admin Users
- `UserTagOperations`—which has methods for handling User-Defined Tags

Examples of many of these can be found in other recipes in this book.

Getting attributes using page_attr

If you're looking to display information about the current content object, CMS Made Simple has a custom Smarty tag that provides some attributes: {page_attr}. You can use this tag to display page attribute information—simply by specifying a key to the information you're requesting. For example, to get the page's "image" attribute, you could use the tag {page_attr key="image"}. Other keys that are supported include:

- target
- image
- thumbnail
- extra1
- extra2

- extra3
- searchable
- pagedata
- disable_wysiwyg
- content_en

As you can see, this is not as rich a collection of information as you can get from the content object directly using your own UDT.

Old code and the use of globals

If you look at old modules or User-Defined Tags that have been posted in the CMS Made Simple forum, you may see the following code:

```
global $gCms;
```

instead of the `$gCms = cmsms()` used here. For a long time, the use of the global declaration was the preferred way to access the `CmsObject`. This approach is now deprecated for a number of reasons, most important of which is a security issue and also including portability of code between CMS Made Simple 1.x and the upcoming 2.x versions.

While use of the global declaration to access the `CmsObject` will likely still work, it is strongly discouraged.

Making a variable available to Smarty

Sometimes you will have tag-generated content that you want to show in multiple areas on a page, or that you will want to manipulate in some way, or even use the value in some kind of conditional logic. Instead of having your tag display its output directly in the template, you can have it set a Smarty variable.

This recipe demonstrates getting a reference to the Smarty engine within a User-Defined Tag, and exporting variables for use in Smarty.

Getting ready

For this recipe, you will need login access to your site's Administration area with permission to "Modify User-Defined Tags", "Modify Templates", and "Manage All Content".

How to do it...

1. Log in to your CMS Administration area.
2. Using the top menu, go to "**Extensions**" and click on "**User Defined Tags**".
3. Click on the "**Add User Defined Tag**" icon.
4. In the "**Name**" field, type "**assorted_variables**".
5. In the "**Code**" field, type the following:

   ```
   $gCms = cmsms();

   $smarty = $gCms->GetSmarty();

   $smarty->assign('quotation','A computer lets you make more mistakes faster than any invention in human history, with the possible exceptions of handguns and tequila. -- Mitch Ratcliffe');

   $items = array('Brandt','Bunny','Donny','Dude','Jeffrey','Maude','Smokey','Walter');

   $smarty->assign_by_ref('characters',$items);
   ```

6. Click on the "**Submit**" button.
7. Using the top menu, select "**Layout**" and click on "**Template**".
8. Click to edit the current default template.
9. Near the top after the `<body>` tag, add your `{assorted_variables}` tag and click the "**Submit**" button.
10. Using the top menu, select "**Content**" and click on "**Pages**".
11. Click on the "**Add New Content**" button.
12. Enter "**Smarty Test**" into the "**Title**" and "**Menu Text**" fields.
13. If you are using a WYSIWYG editor for the content area, uncheck the checkbox labeled "**Turn WYSIWYG on/off**".

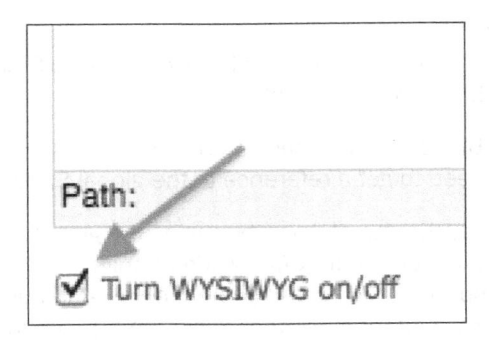

Getting the Most out of Tags and User-Defined Tags

14. In the content area, type the following:

    ```
    <ul>
    {foreach from=$characters item=who}
      <li>{$who}</li>
    {/foreach}
    </ul>
    <p>{$quotation}</p>
    ```

15. Then click the "**Submit**" button.
16. View your site from the user side. Click on the new "**Smarty Test**" page.

Smarty Test

- Brandt
- Bunny
- Donny
- Dude
- Jeffrey
- Maude
- Smokey
- Walter

A computer lets you make more mistakes faster than any invention in human history, with the possible exceptions of handguns and tequila. -- Mitch Ratcliffe

Previous page: User Defined Tags

How it works...

This recipe shows how you can export variables from your UDT to Smarty, so that the variables can be used in page templates and page content.

The first step is giving the UDT a way to access Smarty, since it is not directly in scope. To get this access to Smarty, we need to get a reference to the global Smarty object.

We start by gaining access to the `CmsObject` by calling the global `cmsms()` function. The `CmsObject` is a key internal structure for CMS Made Simple, and serves as a central resource for getting references to important CMS management objects. In this case, we retrieve a reference to the `CmsObject`, and then use that to get a reference to the global Smarty object.

Once we can talk to Smarty, we tell it how we want to map variables. Smarty variables are like associative arrays, in that they assign some value, object, or data structure to a static key. The `assign()` method is used to make this kind of mapping, as you can see when we assign our quotation string to a Smarty variable "`quotation`".

In this recipe, we assign an array of strings to a Smarty variable named "`characters`", where we use Smarty's `assign_by_ref()` method instead of the simple `assign()` method. This method instructs Smarty to use references to the source variable instead of making a copy. This guarantees that if you change the value of the Smarty variable, the change will be reflected in the source data as well. If you are using PHP 4, it also has the potential for saving memory. However, the PHP manual recommends against second-guessing how to pass variables; by specifying how to do it, you may actually have a deleterious effect on PHP's own optimizations. Furthermore, PHP 5 passes variables by reference by default. In other words, while the use of `assign_by_ref()` is included in this recipe for pedagogical reasons, don't use it in your code unless you have a specific need to do so.

Once our UDT is defined, we place it in the page template. Now when Smarty parses the page, the variables will be assigned to Smarty and will be made available to the rest of the template, to page content, and so on.

There's more...

Order is relevant when you export variables from a User-Defined Tag. Variables exported to Smarty by the UDT will be in scope after the inclusion of the tag. In a page template, that translates to the variables being available in the page template below the tag itself—with one caveat. CMS Made Simple processes the template `<head></head>` and `<body></body>` areas of a page template in reverse order.

The reverse order processing of `<head>` and `<body>` enables modules to export information to the page metadata, among other advantages. While you can override this behavior by the CMS configuration variable `process_whole_template` in general, it is better to expect that `<body>` gets processed first.

What this means practically, is that if you create a UDT that assigns Smarty variables, and place the tag immediately after the `<body>` start tag, those Smarty variables will be available to nearly everything in your page: template, content, module templates, and global content blocks. If you place your UDT in the `<head>` area of your page template, the variables that it exports to Smarty will be only available below the tag in the `<head>` area (and any `cms_stylesheets` included).

See also

- Chapter 2, *Seeing what Smarty variables are available to your template* recipe
- *Using Smarty values as inputs in a User-Defined Tag* recipe

Displaying the number of pages in the CMS using a User-Defined Tag

Virtually, all of the content that CMS Made Simple displays or uses to display pages is stored in a database; therefore, it's not at all unexpected that you might want to access the database from a User-Defined Tag. Fortunately, this is not a difficult thing to do.

This recipe shows you how to get a reference to the database abstraction layer and how to issue and process a query from within your User-Defined Tag.

Getting ready

For this recipe, you will need access to your site's Administration area with permission to "Modify User-Defined Tags" and "Modify Templates". It assumes that you are using the default NCleanBlue template, but will work for any template.

How to do it...

1. Log in to your CMS Administration area.
2. Using the top menu, go to "**Extensions**" and click on "**User Defined Tags**".
3. Click on the "**Add User Defined Tag**" icon.
4. In the "**Name**" field, type "**page_counter**".
5. In the "**Code**" field, type the following:

    ```
    $gCms=cmsms();
    $db = $gCms->GetDb();
    $count = $db->GetOne('select count(*) from '.cms_db_prefix().'content where active=1');
    echo 'Total pages: '.$count;
    ```

6. Click on the "**Submit**" button.
7. Using the top menu, go to "**Layout**" and click on "**Templates**".
8. Click on "**NCleanBlue**" in the template list to edit the template.

9. Find the lines where the print button tag is included, and add the `page_counter` tag. It will look something like:

   ```
   {* main top, holds top image and print image *}
           <div class="main-top">
              <div class="print core-float-right">
                 {print showbutton=true}
           <br />
           {page_counter}
              </div>
           </div>
   ```

10. Click on "**Submit**".

11. View your site from the user side.

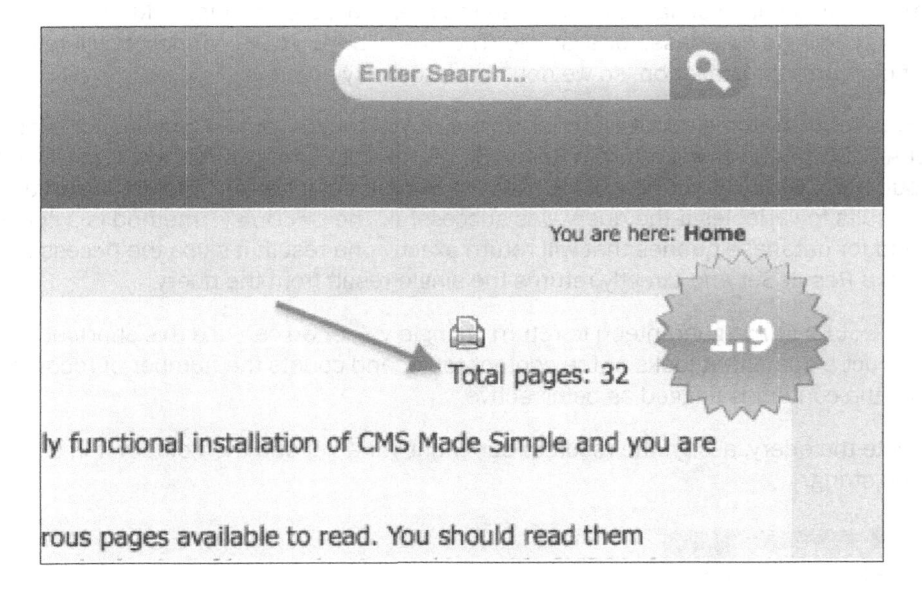

How it works...

This recipe shows how to execute a database query from a User-Defined Tag. CMS Made Simple uses ADODB Lite as a database abstraction layer, that makes it easier to write code that will work with a variety of databases (rather than tying you to one specific database management system or even a specific DBMS version). The database layer is accessed via method calls to the ADODB object.

The first step in this recipe is giving the UDT a way to access the database abstraction object, since it is not directly in scope. To get this access, we need to get a reference to the ADODB object.

Getting the Most out of Tags and User-Defined Tags

We start by gaining access to the `CmsObject` by calling the global `cmsms()` function. The `CmsObject` is a key internal structure for CMS Made Simple, and serves as a central resource for getting references to important CMS management objects. In this case, we retrieve a reference to the `CmsObject`, and then use that to get a reference to the `Db` object (which is really an ADODB connection object).

Once we have this reference to the database abstraction layer, we can make database queries. In this case, we construct a query that counts the number of active content pages in our site. This query is quite straightforward, but it does have some notable features.

The first noteworthy aspect of the query is the call to `cms_db_prefix()`. When you install CMS Made Simple, one step in the installation asks you for a database prefix. This defaults to `"cms_"` and very few sites deviate from this default. It is not safe, however, to assume that every site uses the default. Some people who have a limited number of databases available to them in their hosting configuration will use the prefix to install multiple CMS Made Simple instances in a single database, for example. The `cms_db_prefix()` function will return the prefix of our current installation, so we don't have to worry about it.

The next noteworthy thing about our query is the use of the `GetOne()` method for executing it. Most ADODB methods will return a Result Set, from which you can retrieve error conditions and result data. Typically, your code will check the result set for error conditions, and then assign results to variables if the query was successful. The `GetOne()` method is a special shorthand for database queries that will return exactly one result; it skips the necessity to get data from a Result Set and directly returns the single result from the query.

Since the `count(*)` is guaranteed to return a single value, we can use this shortcut. We construct a query that looks at the content table, and counts the number of records for which the content is flagged as being active.

We execute the query, assign the result to our count variable, and then output it in a formatted string.

There's more...

We used the `GetOne()` method for accessing the database as described previously. This is safe to do when you are guaranteed a single result from the database query. However, it's always wise to consider what is meant by "guaranteed". An SQL `count(*)` command will always return a result if the query is valid, meaning it refers to an extant table and any conditions in the `"where"` clause are against extant fields.

In the event we're using some dynamic element to our query, and there's a chance that the query generated will not be guaranteed to return a single result, it would be preferable to use the more verbose approach of using the `Execute()` method instead of the `GetOne()` method. The `Execute()` method returns a Result Set, which can be checked for error conditions before retrieving result values themselves.

Chapter 3

See also

- Chapter 5, *Making a database query from a module* recipe

Using URL parameters safely in a User-Defined Tag

When people started writing code for website forms and data input, security was not much of a consideration—after all, websites were mostly run by researchers to share their research. It was fine to have code that made assumptions about incoming data, even for sites that faced the open Internet. Those innocent days are long gone, of course. Websites are subjected to continuous threats by automated attack scripts and malicious users looking to deface, hijack, or abuse accounts. Spammers, Phishers, Crackers, and other unsavory types can be expected to look for vulnerabilities in your code.

Today, securing web applications is a vital part of the development process.

As you can see in the "Restricting and sanitizing parameters to a module" recipe, the CMS Made Simple Module API has a collection of utilities to help guarantee that incoming parameters are safe to use. User-Defined Tags, however, don't have a similar facility, so it's imperative that you use safe practices when it comes to user input.

This recipe shows you how to safely handle incoming parameters in your User-Defined Tag.

Getting ready

For this recipe, you will need to have access to your site's Administration area with permission to "Modify User-Defined Tags" and "Manage All Content". This recipe also assumes that you have the standard default content installed; if you don't, you will need to adapt a few of the example URLs to see results.

How to do it...

1. Log in to your CMS Administration area.
2. Using the top menu, go to "**Extensions**" and click on "**User Defined Tags**".
3. Click on the "**Add User Defined Tag**" icon.
4. In the "**Name**" field, type "**get_page**".
5. In the "**Code**" field, type the following:
   ```
   $gCms = cmsms();
   $db = $gCms->GetDb();
   $content_name='';
   ```

83

```
            if (isset($_GET['alias']) && !empty($_GET['alias']))
              {
              $res = $db->Execute('select content_name from '.cms_db_prefix().
                'content where content_alias=?',array($_GET['alias']));
              if ($res)
                {
                $row = $res->FetchRow();
                $content_name = 'Alias '.htmlspecialchars($_GET['alias']).
                  ' maps to "'.$row['content_name'].'"';
                }
              else
                {
                $content_name = 'Alias '.htmlspecialchars($_GET['alias']).
                  ' is not in the database.';
                }
              }

            if (!empty($content_name))
              {
              echo $content_name;
              }
```

6. Click on the "**Submit**" button.
7. Using the top menu, select "**Content**" and click on "**Pages**".
8. Click on the "**Add New Content**" button.
9. Enter "**URL Test**" into the "**Title**" and "**Menu Text**" fields.
10. In the "**Content**" text area, enter the **{get_page}** tag.
11. Click on the "**Submit**" button.
12. Check the page on the user side.

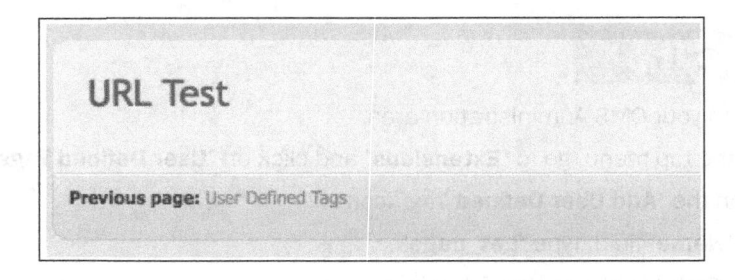

URL Test

Previous page: User Defined Tags

13. Now test by adding "`&alias=default_templates`" to the end of the URL in your browser's address bar.

> **URL Test**
>
> Alias default_templates maps to Default Templates Explained
>
> **Previous page:** User Defined Tags

14. Now, try to use a sneaky SQL-Injection attack by adding `"&alias=';delete from cms_content;"` to the end of the URL in your browser's address bar.

> **URL Test**
>
> Alias ';delete from cms_content; is not in the database.
>
> **Previous page:** User Defined Tags

15. Lastly, we try to use a sneaky Cross-Site Scripting attack (XSS) by adding `"&alias=<script>alert("hi")</script>"` to the end of the URL in your browser's address bar.

> **URL Test**
>
> Alias alert("hi") is not in the database.
>
> **Previous page:** User Defined Tags

How it works...

This recipe shows how to utilize user-supplied parameters to retrieve information from the database and for display, without putting the security of your server or your users at risk.

To execute a database query from a User-Defined Tag, we need to get access to the ADODB object. As described in greater detail in the previous recipe, we start by gaining access to the `CmsObject` by calling the global `cmsms()` function. From the `CmsObject`, we get a reference to the `Db` object, which we use for our actual queries.

Getting the Most out of Tags and User-Defined Tags

User-Defined Tags in CMS Made Simple don't have any special mechanism for handling incoming parameters. They use the standard PHP superglobals for accessing information from the HTTP request: `$_GET`, `$_POST`, and/or `$_REQUEST`. So for our recipe, we will be looking to see if there is a parameter called "`alias`" passed in on the URL, that would then be found in the `$_GET` supervariable.

We start by testing to see if `$_GET['alias']` is defined and has a non-blank value. If it does, we will query the database for any pages that have the provided string as their alias. The query we construct bears some examination.

As in the previous recipe, we construct our query using the `cms_db_prefix()` function, so that we get the correct table names. However, in the "`where`" clause, you can see that we don't simply substitute in the parameter that we are seeking—instead, we place a single, unquoted question mark. In the `Execute()` method, we pass our query and an array containing our parameter. What we're doing here is making sure we're sanitizing our parameters for the database, using a technique called "parameterized query".

Consider the case that we tested earlier, where we passed in the parameter "`&alias=';delete from cms_content;`". If we simply substituted `$_GET['alias']` into our query string, the resulting query would be:

```
select content_name from cms_content where content_alias=';delete from cms_content;
```

This would be interpreted by some databases as two separate queries—the first would be syntactically incorrect, and would do nothing, the second would delete all of the content in the `cms_content` table!

By using the parameterized query, the actual command that gets issued to the database is the harmless.

```
select content_name from cms_content where content_alias='\';delete from cms_content;'
```

(in the case of MySQL. Other databases may use a different escaping syntax, but ADODB handles that transparently for you).

While some databases (like MySQL) protect against this particular form of query stacking automatically, there are other insidious ways of tricking the database into retrieving additional information. Some of these SQL-injection attacks cannot be automatically prevented, and can only be averted by sanitizing parameters.

After issuing our query to the database, we get returned a Result Set. We check to see if it is valid and if it contains any records. If either of those tests fail, we return a string to the user saying that the alias does not exist in the database. If the Result Set is valid, and contains more than zero records, we retrieve the results into an associative array using the `FetchRow()` method. We then use this to display the title of the page to which the alias maps.

Chapter 3

In either the successful or unsuccessful case, we don't display the original parameter to the user directly. Instead, we pass it through the `htmlspecialchars()` function. This is to disarm any attempted cross-site scripting (XSS) attacks, as we demonstrate with the attempt to pass "`&alias=<script>alert("hi")</script>`" as a parameter. The `htmlspecialchars()` function converts a few key characters into HTML entities instead of raw characters, thereby defusing script attacks.

If we were to simply echo the parameter back to the user, a cleverly crafted URL could cause a script to send off cookie information or other data to an arbitrary site. Then an attacker could post the sneaky link on a forum or other popular site, and use it for nefarious purposes.

See also

> *Chapter 6, Restricting and sanitizing parameters to a module* recipe

Using Smarty values as inputs in a User-Defined Tag

You may find yourself in a situation where you need to access data that a module or the CMS Made Simple core has set a variable for use in Smarty, but has not made it available via a function call.

This recipe shows you how your User-Defined Tag can access variables that have been assigned to Smarty, but which may not be easily available via other means.

Getting ready

For this recipe, you will need access to your site's Administration area with permission to "Modify User-Defined Tags" and "Manage All Content". This recipe also assumes that you have the News module installed and used by your page template. It will help if you have a few News articles published.

How to do it...

1. Log in to your CMS Administration area.
2. Using the top menu, go to "**Extensions**" and click on "**User Defined Tags**".
3. Click on the "**Add User Defined Tag**" icon.
4. In the "**Name**" field, type "**get_news_items**".
5. In the "**Code**" field, type the following:

    ```
    $gCms = cmsms();
    ```

Getting the Most out of Tags and User-Defined Tags

```
$smarty = $gCms->GetSmarty();

$newsitems = $smarty->get_template_vars('items');
foreach ($newsitems as $item)
  {
  echo $item->titlelink.'<br />';
  echo $item->summary.'<br />';
  }
```

6. Click the "**Submit**" button.
7. Using the top menu, select "**Content**" and click on "**Pages**".
8. Click on the "**Add New Content**" button.
9. Enter "**Smarty Read Test**" into the "**Title**" and "**Menu Text**" fields.
10. In the "**Content**" text area, enter the **{get_news_info}** tag.
11. Click on the "**Submit**" button.
12. View your site from the user side. Click on the new "**Smarty Read Test**" page.

Smarty Read Test

Charlie bit me!
It really hurt.
Double Rainbows??
Sighted in Yosemite National Park. What does it MEAN?
News Module Installed
The news module was installed. Exciting.

Previous page: User Defined Tags

How it works...

This recipe shows how you can import variables to your User-Defined Tag from Smarty without having to process a template.

The first step is giving the UDT access to Smarty, since it is not directly in scope. We start by creating a reference to the `CmsObject` by calling the global `cmsms()` function. The `CmsObject` provides us a method to retrieve a reference to the Smarty object.

Once we can talk to Smarty, we can call the `get_template_vars()` method to retrieve any Smarty variables that have been assigned. Smarty assignments are like associative arrays, in that the variable names are bound to some value, object, or data structure. The `get_template_vars()` method is the inverse of the `assign()` method; when a module or UDT sets a Smarty variable using `assign()`, we can use the `get_template_vars()` method to get that value back.

In this recipe, we retrieve the "`items`" array that the News module assigned. Since we know it's an array of `StdClass` objects, we can iterate through using a `foreach` statement, and display the specific information that we want. Obviously, we are not limited to simply displaying this data—depending upon what we're trying to achieve, we may end up using values we retrieved for database queries, calculations, or other purposes.

There's more...

The Smarty variables that are used by templates and content in CMS Made Simple have a flat namespace, like an associative array. If two modules assign arrays to the Smarty variable "`items`", the values will clobber one another. The last to do the assignment will determine the value that gets seen subsequently by templates. This is not normally a problem, even in the case of multiple modules using the same variable name because modules typically assign Smarty variables and process their templates in one atomic operation, so their own particular version of those variables is used in their own particular output.

The example shown in this recipe, however, makes the assumption that the only module assigning values to the variable named "`items`" is the News module. Therefore, this approach should be used with a little bit of caution.

See also

- *Chapter 2, Seeing what Smarty variables are available to your template* recipe
- *Making a variable available to Smarty from a User-Defined Tag* recipe

Displaying stock prices from Yahoo with a User-Defined Tag

The promise of the World Wide Web of pervasive information availability is realized through countless websites publishing information that they synthesize, compute, or gather from the outside world. Because of the wide availability of information, the phenomenon of "mashups"—the combining of data from multiple sources in order to provide deeper insight into a situation—has become commonplace. Sometimes, the mashup is complex, and involves displaying combined data on maps, while sometimes the mashup is simple, and involves displaying external information about the primary subject of the website.

Getting the Most out of Tags and User-Defined Tags

In order to create a mashup, you need to be able to gather data from disparate sources. Some sources are designed specifically for data reuse, and provide interfaces for retrieving selected data. This recipe makes use of such a service to create a very simple mashup: the display of stock information.

Companies often want to display their financial data on their website, as a way of conveying a richer profile of their operations. Services such as Yahoo Financials make such information available for investors. This recipe shows you how you can access a remote data source using a UDT for display within a CMS Made Simple web page.

Getting ready

For this recipe, you will need login access to your site's Administration area with permission to "Modify User-Defined Tags", "Add Stylesheets", "Add Stylesheet Associations", and "Manage All Content". For this particular implementation, your PHP installation will need to have fopen wrappers enabled—please see the PHP manual pages on this topic: http://www.php.net/manual/en/filesystem.configuration.php#ini.allow-url-fopen

Before deploying this recipe, please make sure you are in compliance with Yahoo's terms of service, documented at http://info.yahoo.com/legal/us/yahoo/utos/

How to do it...

1. Log in to your CMS Administration area.
2. Using the top menu, go to "**Extensions**" and click on "**User Defined Tags**".
3. Click on the "**Add User Defined Tag**" icon.
4. In the "**Name**" field, type "**stocks**".
5. In the "**Code**" field, type the following:

    ```
    $symbols = array('aapl','goog','ibm','gknt','msft','orcl');
    $columns = array('Symbol','Last Trade','Last Trade Date',
       'Last Trade Time','Change','Open','High','Low','Volume');

    $stock = file('http://download.finance.yahoo.com/d/quotes.
    csv?f=sl1d1t1c1ohgv&s='.
       implode('+',$symbols));

    echo '<table class="stocktable"><tr>';
    foreach ($columns as $thisCol)
      {
      echo '<th>'.$thisCol.'</th>';
      }
    echo '</tr>';

    foreach ($stock as $thisStock)
    ```

```
        {
        $details = explode(',',$thisStock);
        echo '<tr>';
        foreach ($details as $thisDetail)
          {
          echo '<td>'.str_replace('"','',$thisDetail).'</td>';
          }  echo '</tr>';
        }
     echo '</table>';
```

6. Click on the "**Submit**" button.
7. Using the top menu, go to "**Layout**" and select "**Stylesheets**".
8. Click on the "**Add a Stylesheet**" button.
9. In the "**Name**" field enter "**stocktable**".
10. In the "**Content**" text area, enter the following:

    ```
    .stocktable th { font-weight: bold; padding-right: 0.5em; }

    .stocktable td { padding: 0.25em; border: 1px solid black; }
    ```
11. Click on the "**Submit**" button.
12. Find "**stocktable**" in the list of stylesheets, and click on the "**CSS**" button next to it.
13. Select "**NCleanBlue**" in the dropdown menu, and click "**Attach to this Template**".
14. Using the top menu, go to "**Content**" and select "**Pages**"
15. Click on the "**Add New Content**" button.
16. Enter "**Stocks**" into the "**Title**" and "**Menu Text**" fields.
17. In the "**Content**" text area, enter the {stocks} tag.
18. Click on the "**Submit**" button.
19. View your site from the user side. Click on the new "**Stocks**" page.

Stocks

Symbol	Last Trade	Last Trade Date	Last Trade Time	Change	Open	High	Low	Volume
AAPL	292.32	9/24/2010	4:00pm	+3.40	292.00	293.53	290.55	23195972
GOOG	527.29	9/24/2010	4:00pm	+13.81	521.40	527.829	518.26	3363247
IBM	134.11	9/24/2010	4:00pm	+2.44	132.42	134.15	132.34	7122325
GKNT	1.56	9/24/2010	3:59pm	-0.04	1.56	1.57	1.51	90288
MSFT	24.775	9/24/2010	4:00pm	+0.345	24.65	24.80	24.58	51948788
ORCL	26.96	9/24/2010	4:00pm	-0.16	27.45	27.50	26.74	58136208

Previous page: User Defined Tags

Getting the Most out of Tags and User-Defined Tags

How it works...

This recipe shows how you can use PHP's built-in functions to request data from services on the Internet, and reformat the data to present to the user.

This UDT starts by creating a few utility arrays: a list of stock symbols, and a list of column headers. It then uses PHP's built-in "file" command to make a web-service request to Yahoo's Finance site.

This request is a standard HTTP GET—you can copy the link into your web browser's address bar, and see the results. Unless your PHP installation has disabled open wrappers or you are in a restricted network environment, the `"file"` command will work identically when provided the name of a file on the local filesystem or a properly formatted URL. In this case, the command fetches the stock trade details from Yahoo, and adds each line that is returned into the `$stock` array.

The rest of the User-Defined Tag is simply formatting the output. It uses our column definitions and outputs them as table header elements, and then for each row of the `$stock` array, outputs the details. Since Yahoo returns the details to us in a comma-separated value string, we explode the string on the commas and then output each element into a table cell. The `str_replace()` call removes any quotation marks from the details to make it look a little cleaner.

This recipe also created a stylesheet to make the stock display nicer.

There's more...

As Leslie Lamport said, "A distributed system is one in which the failure of a computer you didn't even know existed can render your own computer unusable." What happens if Yahoo's server is down, or there is a network outage between your CMS Made Simple site and Yahoo? With the code as presented earlier, your website will stall until PHP times out (a default time of 30 seconds). This could cause unacceptable performance on your website, and cause your visitors to go elsewhere.

If your PHP installation has the cURL library installed, you have a great way to deal with this kind of situation. In the following code sample, we use cURL to fetch the data from Yahoo, but we set a one second timeout. If the fetch has not succeeded in that one second window, we tell the user that the stock data is unavailable.

```
$symbols = array('aapl','goog','ibm','gknt','msft','orcl');
$columns = array('Symbol','Last Trade','Last Trade Date','Last Trade Time',
'Change','Open','High','Low','Volume');

$curl = curl_init('http://download.finance.yahoo.com/d/quotes.csv?f=sl1d1t1c1ohgv&s='.
  implode('+',$symbols));
```

```
    curl_setopt($curl, CURLOPT_RETURNTRANSFER, true);
    curl_setopt($curl, CURLOPT_HEADER, false);
    curl_setopt($curl, CURLOPT_CONNECTTIMEOUT, 1);

    $results = curl_exec($curl);
    curl_close($curl);
    if ($results === false)
       {
        echo 'Stock information temporarily unavailable.';
       }
    else
       {
      $stock = explode("\n",$results);

      echo '<table class="stocktable"><tr>';
      foreach ($columns as $thisCol)
         {
         echo '<th>'.$thisCol.'</th>';
         }
      echo '</tr>';

      foreach ($stock as $thisStock)
         {
            $details = explode(',',$thisStock);
            echo '<tr>';
            foreach ($details as $thisDetail)
          {
          echo '<td>'.str_replace('"','',$thisDetail).'</td>';
          }
        echo '</tr>';
        }
     echo '</table>';
     }
```

To use cURL, you must first initialize a cURL object with the URL that you wish to retrieve. You can then set the options. In this case, we set CURLOPT_RETURNTRANSFER to true, which tells cURL that when we issue the `curl_exec()` next, we want it to return the contents of the fetched information as a string rather than output it directly. Next, we set CURLOPT_HEADER to false, so our return content doesn't include the raw HTTP headers. We set our timeout to one second using CURLOPT_CONNECTTIMEOUT. Later versions of cURL allow for millisecond precision for timeouts using the CURLOPT_CONNECTTIMEOUT_MS header, if you need that degree of control.

Getting the Most out of Tags and User-Defined Tags

After we have set all the options, we issue the `curl_exec()`, which actually performs the operation. This will either return a string containing the remote content, or it will return a Boolean `"false"` if it was unsuccessful. So we display an error in the latter case, or use our original code in the former.

Stocks

Stock information temporarily unavailable.

Previous page: User Defined Tags

Understanding Yahoo's stock quote URL format

Let's look a little closer at the actual request we make to Yahoo. Yahoo documents their web service interface to Stock Quotes at `http://help.yahoo.com/l/us/yahoo/finance/basics/fitaquoteweb.html`

Essentially, we're sending a request to their quote service. We specify that we want the results as a comma-separated value string, and we pass a format string to describe what details we want. To decode that string:

- s—the stock symbol
- s1—the last trade
- d1—the last trade date
- t1—the last trade time
- c1—the change in value
- o—the opening price
- h—the day's highest trade price
- g—the day's lowest trade price
- v—volume traded

The query is finished by passing a list of stock symbols for which we want data.

An example of the raw results from such a query looks like this:

```
"IBM",134.11,"9/24/2010","4:00pm",+2.44,132.42,134.15,132.34,7122325
```

See also

▶ *Displaying a translation of the current page using Babelfish with a User-Defined Tag* recipe

Displaying a translation of the current page using Babelfish with a User-Defined Tag

As its name suggests, the World Wide Web makes web pages available all over the world. While you may be building your site in English, or Dutch, or Korean, the people who end up visiting the site may speak an entirely different language. Fortunately, there are services that will provide approximate translations of web pages, that enable people to get information from sites that are in languages they wouldn't otherwise understand.

In the previous recipe, we demonstrated interacting with a web service that is designed to work with other programmatic services. This recipe provides an example of working with a web service that is designed to be human-readable rather than oriented for data exchange. In doing so, this recipe gives a complex example of using a web service in a User-Defined Tag. It takes the first hundred words of the main content block of a page and posts it to Yahoo's Babelfish service for translation. It then finds the relevant portion of Babelfish's output, and reformats the translated content for the end user.

Getting ready

For this recipe, you will need login access to your site's Administration area with permission to "Modify User-Defined Tags" and "Modify Templates". For this particular implementation, your PHP installation will need to have the cURL library installed—please see the PHP manual pages on this topic: http://www.php.net/manual/en/book.curl.php

Before deploying this recipe, please make sure your uses would be in compliance with Yahoo's terms of service, documented at http://info.yahoo.com/legal/us/yahoo/utos/

How to do it...

1. Log in to your CMS Administration area.
2. Using the top menu, go to "**Extensions**" and click on "**User Defined Tags**".
3. Click on the "**Add User Defined Tag**" icon.
4. In the "**Name**" field, type "**translator**".
5. In the "**Code**" field, type the following:

   ```
   $gCms = cmsms();
   ```

```
      $contentops = $gCms->GetContentOperations();
      $content_obj = $contentops->getContentObject();
      $page_cont = $content_obj->GetPropertyValue('content_en');
      $arr = preg_split("/[\s]+/", $page_cont);
      $arr = array_slice($arr,0,100);
      $page_cont = join(' ',$arr);
      $url = 'http://babelfish.yahoo.com/translate_txt';
      $headers = array('Accept-Charset: utf-8');
      $fields = array(
        'trtext='.urlencode($page_cont),
        'lp=en_de',
        'ei=UTF-8'
        );
      $ch = curl_init($url);
      curl_setopt($ch, CURLOPT_POST, count($fields));
      curl_setopt($ch, CURLOPT_POSTFIELDS, implode('&',$fields));
      curl_setopt($ch, CURLOPT_RETURNTRANSFER, true);
      curl_setopt($ch, CURLOPT_HTTPHEADER, $headers);
      $result = curl_exec($ch);
      if ($result!==false)
        {
        $count = preg_match('/\<div\sid\=\"result\"(.*?)\<\/div/',$result,$matches);
        if ($count > 0)
          {
          echo strip_tags($matches[0]);
          }
        }
      curl_close($ch);
```

6. Click on the "**Submit**" button.

7. Using the top menu, go to "**Layout**" and select "**Templates**".

8. Click on the default template's name to edit it.

9. Find the {content} tag, and place the {translator} tag after it with some simple code to set it off visually:

    ```
    {content}
        <div style="border-top: 1px solid black">
        {translator}
        </div>
    ```

10. Click on the "**Submit**" button.

11. View your site from the user side. Click on your "**Home**" page.

Home

Congratulations! The installation worked. You now have a fully functional installation of CMS Made Simple and you are *almost* ready to start building your site.

If you chose to install the default content, you will see numerous pages available to read. You should read them thoroughly as these default pages are devoted to showing you the basics of how to begin working with CMS Made Simple. On these example pages, templates, and stylesheets many of the features of the default installation of CMS Made Simple are described and demonstrated. You can learn much about the power of CMS Made Simple by absorbing this information.

To get to the Administration Console you have to login as the administrator (with the username/password you mentioned during the installation process) on your site at http://yourwebsite.com/cmsmspath/admin. If this is your site click here to login.

Read about how to use CMS Made Simple in the documentation. In case you need any help the community is always at your service, in the forum or the IRC.

License

CMS Made Simple is released under the GPL license and as such you don't have to leave a link back to us in these templates or on your site as much as we would like it.

Some third party add-on modules may include additional license restrictions.

Glückwünsche! Die Installation bearbeitet. Sie haben jetzt a völlig - die Funktionsinstallation von CMS gebildet einfach und Sie sind fast bereit Ihren, Aufstellungsort zu errichten zu beginnen. Wenn Sie beschlossen, den Rückstellungsinhalt anzubringen, sehen Sie die zahlreichen Seiten, die, um zu lesen vorhanden sind. Sie sollten sie gänzlich lesen, während diese Rückstellungsseiten dem Zeigen Ihnen der Grundlagen gewidmet werden von, wie man anfängt zu arbeiten mit CMS hergestellt einfach. Auf diesen Beispiel Seiten, Schablonen und stylesheets werden viele der Eigenschaften der Rückstellungsinstallation von CMS gebildet einfach beschrieben und demonstriert. Sie können viel über die Energie von CMS erlernen gebildet einfach

12. Click on another page to see that the translator tag is getting the correct page content.

How CMSMS Works

So how is a web-site created with CMS Made Simple? There are a couple of terms that are central to understanding this.

You first need to have templates, which is the HTML code for your pages. This is styled with CSS in one or more style sheets that are attached to each template. You then create pages that contain your websites content using one of these templates.

That doesn't sound too hard, does it? Basically you don't need to know any HTML or CSS to get a site up with CMS Made Simple. But if you want to customize it to your liking, consider learning some CSS.

In the menu to the left you can read more about this, as well as more advanced features like the Menu Manager, additional extensions for adding many kinds of functionality to your site and the Event Manager for managing work flow. Last is a summary of the basic work flow when creating a site with CMS Made Simple.

So wie wird eine Web site, die mit CMS einfach verursacht wird gebildet? Es gibt ein paar Ausdrücke, die zum Verständnis dieses zentral sind. Sie müssen zuerst Schablonen haben, das der HTML-Code für Ihre Seiten ist. Dieses wird mit CSS in einen oder mehreren Artblättern angeredet, die zu jeder Schablone angebracht werden. Sie stellen dann Seiten her, die Ihren siteinhalt unter Verwendung ein dieser Schablonen enthalten. Dieses doesn' t-Ton zu stark, tut er? Im Allgemeinen Sie don' t-Notwendigkeit, jedes mögliches HTML oder CSS zu kennen, um einen Aufstellungsort mit CMS zu erhalten bildete einfach. Aber wenn Sie sie besonders anfertigen möchten

Getting the Most out of Tags and User-Defined Tags

How it works...

This recipe has three major portions: using the CMS Made Simple facility for retrieving content information, issuing an HTTP POST to the Yahoo Babelfish translation service, and finding the relevant information in the output to present to the end user.

The tag starts by using the `cmsms()` function to get a reference to the `CmsObject`. The `CmsObject` provides us with, among other things, a method to retrieve a reference to the `ContentOperations` object. This important object is used by CMS Made Simple for managing various content functions, such as accessing, loading, and saving content blocks.

We use the `ContentOperations` object to retrieve the current content object, which is the primary content block of the current page, along with its metadata. From this object, we finally get the string, which is stored as its `content_en` property. In an English-language site, this will be what the end-user will think of as the content of the primary content block.

Since the Babelfish translation service is limited to chunks of text 150 words or less, we need to truncate this content down to a manageable length before translating it. The next three lines of the UDT accomplish this by splitting the string at each occurrence of whitespace, and storing this in an array. The array is then truncated at the hundredth element (we're being conservative—this could be increased to the whole 150 words), and joined again into a string.

The tag then uses the cURL library to POST this string and some additional control variables to Babelfish. After the URL is established in a string, a minimal array of HTTP headers is added to the `$headers` array. It turns out that the Bablefish service doesn't require any special headers, but we do pass an "Accept-charset" header, so that the string that is returned will be in the same encoding as the rest of our page (assuming that our site, like most CMS Made Simple sites, is in UTF-8 encoding).

For the variables that need to be sent to Babelfish, we create an array where the fields are defined. The string that is to be submitted for translation must be URL-encoded, and we do that when we assign it to the "`trtext`" parameter. We also set our translation language pair "`lp`"—the format for this parameter is the two-letter ISO 639-1 language code (in lower case) of the source language followed by an underscore followed by the two-letter language code of the destination language. In our implementation, we're translating from English to German, so we assign it the value "`en_de`". Lastly, we set the "`ei`" parameter, that specifies the incoming text character formatting as UTF-8.

Once we have the parameters all set up in our array, we initialize cURL by passing it the destination URL, and set some options:

- CURLOPT_POST—the number of fields being POSTed.
- CURLOPT_POSTFIELDS—the URL-encoded payload. We join our parameters into a string with ampersands (as per the standard for application/x-www-form-urlencoded data).

- CURLOPT_RETURNTRANSFER—we want cURL to return the results as a string, rather than display them.
- CURLOPT_HTTPHEADER—our HTTP headers, which in this case is only our "Accept-Charset" header.

Once cURL has been set up and configured, we execute the request.

If the operation is successful, we'll end up with a full web page source in our `$result` variable. From examining this source, we find that the translation we're looking for is set off in the code that looks like:

```
<div id="result"><div style="padding:0.6em;">translated text</div></div>
```

So, using a regular expression, we try to match the div with an id="result" through the first close div tag. If `preg_match()` gets a match, the resulting string will be placed into the `$matches` array. We run that matching string through a `strip_tags()` call to remove any extraneous formatting, such as that first styling div.

Finally, we have our translated content! We output it to the user, and then make sure to clean up by closing our cURL connection.

There's more...

The technique used in this recipe, sometimes referred to as "screen scraping" since we're processing HTML that's intended for display, is fraught with danger. If the programmers at Yahoo do any work on the Babelfish site that results in a change in the output format, our regular expression may stop matching, and we will no longer find our translation in the HTML.

Typically, when screen scraping, the search should be as general as possible given the circumstances. For example, in our recipe, we only search for the div with id="result" rather than search for that and the following style div. We do this on the assumption that the styling div is more likely to change than the result wrapping div.

Still, no matter how good our assumptions, we don't have much resilience to changes in this approach. This points out the advantage of using well-defined public interfaces for doing web service operations. Additionally, it's worth noting that the screen scraping approach might violate the remote site's terms of use. If the provider finds you are violating those terms, they may block your requests or send you scary legal threats to induce you to cease and desist.

See also

- *Display a stock price from Yahoo with a User-Defined Tag* recipe

Getting the Most out of Tags and User-Defined Tags

Posting an article to the News Module when the Admin adds a new Group

One topic that is always of interest to CMS Made Simple site builders is the interaction of different components. The ability of User-Defined Tags to interact with core APIs and the APIs of installed modules is one of the powerful characteristics that really sets CMS Made Simple apart from other systems.

This recipe pulls together a number of interactions. It begins with a UDT that works with the core News module to create a new News article. This UDT is then connected to a system event that gets triggered when the administrator adds a new group to the CMS administration area.

To accomplish these tasks, the recipe shows how to access module methods from a User-Defined Tag and how to handle parameters from events.

Getting ready

For this recipe, you will need login access to your site's Administration area with permission to "Modify User-Defined Tags", "Add Groups", and "Modify Events". It requires that the News module is installed and active.

How to do it...

1. Log in to your CMS Administration area.
2. Using the top menu, go to "**Extensions**" and click on "**User Defined Tags**".
3. Click on the "**Add User Defined Tag**" icon.
4. In the "**Name**" field, type "**add_news**".
5. In the "**Code**" field, type the following:

```
$gCms = cmsms();
$news_module = $gCms->GetModuleInstance('News');
$new_group = $params['group']->name;
$summary = 'The Admin has added the new group "'.$new_group.'!"';
$article = 'The Admin has added the new group "'.$new_group.'."'.
  ' This new group has no members yet, but will doubtless end up '.
  'being a credit to the community.';
if ($news_module != null)
  {
  $res = $news_module->AddNewArticle( 'General',
    'Group Added', $summary, $article);
  }
```

6. Click on the "**Submit**" button.
7. Using the top menu, go to "**Extensions**" and click on "**Event Manager**".
8. Click on the name of the "**Add Group Post**" event in order to modify it.
9. Select "**add_news**" from the dropdown menu, and click on the "**Add**" button.
10. Using the top menu, go to "**Users & Groups**" and click on "**Groups**".
11. Click the "**Add New Group**" button.
12. In the "**Name**" field type "**Programmers**" and click the "**Submit**" button.
13. View your site from the user side. Click on your "**Home**" page or any page that contains News.

News

General
Sep 26, 2010
Group Added
Category: General
Posted by: admin
The Admin has added the new group "Programmers!"
[More]

Sep 26, 2010
News Module Installed
Category: General
Posted by: admin

The news module was installed. Exciting. This news article is not using the Summary field and therefore there is no link to read more. But you can click on the news heading to read only this article.

14. Click on the details for the new News story, to confirm that the article body is set correctly.

News

Sep 26, 2010
Group Added

The Admin has added the new group "Programmers!"

Category: General
Posted by: admin

The Admin has added the new group "Programmers." This new group has no members yet, but will doubtless end up being a credit to the community.

Print
Return

Previous page: Modules
Next page: Menu Manager

How it works...

The User-Defined Tag in this recipe starts using the `cmsms()` function to get a reference to the `CmsObject`. The `CmsObject` is a resource that has methods for retrieving references to many important objects. We use the `CmsObject` to call the `GetModuleInstance()` method, with which we request a reference to the News module.

The `GetModuleInstance()` method can return one of two things: a null, meaning that it was unsuccessful, or a reference to the installed module. For the latter, the module needs to be installed, active, and not pending an upgrade.

Anytime we have a reference to an active module, we can call any of the public methods that the module supports. It's not always obvious, however, what public methods a module has. The vast majority of modules don't document their methods as an API for the simple reason that most module authors don't think of their modules as being general resources. Often, looking at the module source is the only way to figure out what methods are supported.

Still, to find what methods modules support, it's worth thinking about what kind of function you see a module perform, and what function you're hoping it will provide for you. Once you have a concrete idea, such as "I'd like my tag to be able to post a News article," it gives you an idea of what method to look for in the News module.

It this case, it turns out we're in luck, and the News module has a method called `AddNewsArticle()`, which does exactly what we were hoping it would. It takes a few parameters:

- $category—the category for the article
- $title—the article's title
- $summary—summary text for the article
- $text—the main article content
- $start_time—an optional publication starting time
- $end_time—an optional publication ending time
- $status—an optional status, which defaults to 'published'
- $icon—an optional icon filespec for the article

Before we look at the values we set up for these parameters, we need to think a bit about how this UDT will be called. We connected the tag to the "Add Group Post" event using the Event Manager. The description of the event states that it is "sent after a new group is created," and if we click on the information link in the Event Manager, we can see that the parameter it passes is called "group" and is a reference to the "affected group object".

When an event passes parameters to a UDT, they are made available by name from an associative array called $params. So, when we find that the event passes a Group object to our UDT via a parameter named "group," this really means we can get at that parameter using the $params['group'] syntax. So we know we can get a Group object with that reference, but we still don't know exactly what that object is like.

To determine this requires a quick look at the source of the Group object, that can be found in the lib/classes directory in the file class.group.inc.php. There we can see that the Group class only has Delete(), Save(), and SetInitialValues() methods. It also has $id, $name, and $active attributes, however, and they are not protected or private, so we can use them in our UDT.

So back in our UDT, we create strings for the News article and summary, using the $name attribute from the group object we expect to be passed in by the "Add Group Post" event. With those strings, we call the AddNewsArticle() method to create the news article.

There's more...

The explanation of this tag may seem to have a lot of hand-waving in it. What methods can we call on a module? Look at the source code. What gets handed to our UDT by the event? Look at the source code.

One of the frequent frustrations for new developers on CMS Made Simple is exactly this lack of central documentation for this kind of extension. While the documentation has a long way to go, the Core team has been and continues to add more information on Event parameters. Individual module authors may or may not provide good documentation of module methods.

Even with these efforts, the documentation remains sparse. Reading through the Wiki and the CMS Made Simple forum may provide clues. Using `debug_display()` to find variable contents is valuable. Sometimes you can get more information by talking to other developers. As you write more Tags and gain more familiarity with the system it becomes easier to intuit what may be available. But it remains that the best reference that exists is the source code itself.

See also

- Chapter 9, *Attaching a User-Defined Tag to an Event* recipe
- Chapter 9, *Finding what parameters an event passes using a User-Defined Tag* recipe

Reversing a string in two ways using a Smarty Modifier

One of the few things that a Tag can do that a User-Defined Tag cannot, is to act as one of the more exotic Smarty tags; specifically filters and modifiers. A Smarty modifier is used, as the name suggests, to modify the output of a Smarty tag before it is substituted into the template.

Modifiers are typically used to do things like reformat text, convert data (dates, numeric formats, and so on). They can be used to escape certain characters to prevent cross-site scripting (XSS) attacks, or to obfuscate e-mail addresses to stymie spam harvesting programs.

This recipe shows you how to write a Smarty modifier, which can reverse strings in two different ways: order of characters and case of characters.

Getting ready

For this recipe, you will need access to your site's Administration area with permission to "Manage All Content". You will also need privileges to create a file on the server.

How to do it...

1. Open your favorite text editing program, and create a new file.
2. Type the following code:

```
<?php
function smarty_cms_modifier_reverse($string, $invert_case=false)
  {
  if ($invert_case)
    {
    $retstr = '';
    $chars = str_split($string);
```

```
      foreach ($chars as $char)
        {
        if (strtolower($char) != $char)
          {
          $retstr .= strtolower($char);
          }
        else
          {
          $retstr .= strtoupper($char);
          }
        }
      }
    else
      {
      $retstr = $string;
      }
    return strrev($retstr);
    }
?>
```

3. Save this file as "`modifier.reverse.php`" in your CMS Made Simple base install's "`plugins`" directory.
4. Log in to your CMS Administration area.
5. Using the top menu, go to "**Content**" and select "**Pages**".
6. Click on the "**Add New Content**" button.
7. Enter "**Smarty Modifier Example**" into the "**Title**" and "**Menu Text**" fields.
8. In the "**Content**" text area, enter the following tags:

   {title|reverse}

   {title|reverse:true}
9. Click on the "**Submit**" button.
10. View your site from the user side. Click on the new "**Smarty Modifier Example**" page.

Smarty Modifier Example

elpmaxE reifidoM ytramS
ELPMAXe REIFIDOm YTRAMs

Previous page: User Defined Tags

Getting the Most out of Tags and User-Defined Tags

How it works...

This recipe, while slightly silly, shows how a Smarty modifier can be used to modify any string that Smarty displays. Since any content can be captured into a Smarty variable and displayed, this really represents the ability to process any content on an entire site.

Following the naming convention for Tags, we start by declaring our function with the name "`smarty_cms_modifier_reverse`". Decoding that function name, the first two pieces tell CMS Made Simple that this will be used by Smarty. The "`modifier`" tells Smarty that this function will act as a data modifier, and the last portion is the name of the modifier.

All Smarty modifiers receive at least one parameter, which is the data that they modify. In the case of this modifier, we're expecting a string of characters, so we name the parameter `$string`. While the modifier could be applied to any kind of data that Smarty outputs, the results will not necessarily be what we expect if we use it on an array or other data type.

Smarty modifiers can receive additional parameters, which will be separated by colon characters in the tag itself. In this case, we pass an optional Boolean parameter, which we'll use to decide whether or not to invert the case of every character.

The first portion of the Tag does just that: if the `$invert_case` parameter is set to true, we invert the case. This is accomplished by splitting the string into an array of characters, and testing to see if converting to lowercase changes anything—if it does, we can assume the character was uppercase, so we convert it to lowercase, otherwise we convert the character to uppercase. There are doubtless more efficient ways of converting a string's case, but this approach works well enough for our purposes.

Next, we pass our string through the PHP `strrev()` function to reverse the order of the characters, and return the converted string.

As demonstrated, we use our new modifier, and successfully reverse the title of a sample page in two different ways.

There's more...

You might discover an interesting problem with this modifier in the case where it performs only an order-reverse of the source string. Certain strings apparently cause it to simply shift spaces around. To demonstrate this problem, try using the modifier on one of the following cases:

- are we not drawn onward, we few, drawn onward to new era
- ma is as selfless as I am
- yawn a more roman way

The solution to this problem is left as an exercise for the reader.

See also

> *Adding Registered Trademark symbols to a name automatically* recipe

Adding registered trademark symbols to a name automatically

As mentioned, one of the few things that a Tag can do that a User-Defined Tag cannot is to act as a Smarty filter. A Smarty filter is called during the process of rendering a template; depending on the type of filter, it can be called before values are substituted into the template (referred to as a "pre-compile filter"), or it can be called after the substitutions are complete (referred to as a "post-compile filter").

Both kinds of filters are extremely powerful for doing global manipulation of the content on your site.

This recipe shows you how to use a Smarty post-compile filter tag to append a symbol after every instance of a given string. Specifically, this filter searches for the string "CMS Made Simple" and guarantees that this phrase is always tagged with a registered trademark symbol.

Such a filter prevents site users from having to remember to be careful with the use of trademarks while still protecting the rights associated with those trademarks. It's the kind of feature that makes corporate legal departments happy, and can make the person implementing the site, a hero with minimal effort.

Getting ready

For this recipe, you will need access to your site's Administration area with permission to "Manage All Content". You will also need privileges to create a file on the server.

How to do it...

1. Open your favorite text editing program, and create a new file.
2. Type the following code:

```php
<?php
function smarty_cms_postfilter_registeredtrademarker($tpl_output, &$smarty)
{
  $result = explode(':', $smarty->_current_file);
  if (count($result) > 0)
  {
    if ($result[0] == 'content')
```

Getting the Most out of Tags and User-Defined Tags

```
      {
      $tpl_output = str_replace('CMS Made Simple',
        'CMS Made Simple®', $tpl_output);
      }
    }
    return $tpl_output;
  }
?>
```

3. Save this file as "`postfilter.registeredtrademarker.php`" in your CMS Made Simple base install's "`plugins`" directory.
4. Log in to your CMS Administration area.
5. Using the top menu, go to "**Site Admin**" and select "**Global Settings**".
6. Click on the "**Advanced Setup**" tab.
7. Click on the "**Clear Cache**" button.
8. View your site from the user side.

Home

Congratulations! The installation worked. You now have a fully functional installation of CMS Made Simple® and you are *almost* ready to start building your site.

If you chose to install the default content, you will see numerous pages available to read. You should read them thoroughly as these default pages are devoted to showing you the basics of how to begin working with CMS Made Simple®. On these example pages, templates, and stylesheets many of the features of the default installation of CMS Made Simple® are described and demonstrated. You can learn much about the power of CMS Made Simple® by absorbing this information.

To get to the Administration Console you have to login as the administrator (with the username/password you mentioned during the installation process) on your site at http://yourwebsite.com/cmsmspath/admin. If this is your site click here to login.

Read about how to use CMS Made Simple® in the documentation. In case you need any help the community is always at your service, in the forum or the IRC.

License

CMS Made Simple® is released under the GPL license and as such you don't have to leave a link back to us in these templates or on your site as much as we would like it.

Some third party add-on modules may include additional license restrictions.

Next page: How CMSMS Works

^ Top

1.9

How it works...

When CMS Made Simple outputs a page, it follows a process of getting content from the database, calling all of the modules in the given page, and then compiling all of the module output and page content into the page template to provide the final output. There are hooks at various points in this process where the code can make changes; notable among these are the Smarty pre-compile and post-compile hooks. These are called before and after Smarty combines variables into templates, respectively.

This recipe uses the powerful post-compile filter to modify Smarty's output after it has been compiled.

Following the naming convention for Tags, we start by declaring our function with the name "smarty_cms_postfilter_registeredtrademarker". Decoding that function name, the first two pieces tell CMS Made Simple that this will be used by Smarty, the "postfilter" tells Smarty to call this function after compiling each template, and the last portion is the name of this specific postfilter.

The function receives two parameters from Smarty: the string which is the template output, and a reference to the Smarty object. Our tag function starts by determining something about the template that it's being passed. For each template that Smarty compiles in CMS Made Simple, it sets an internal variable named $_current_file, which describes that template. We could do our search and replacement on all templates, but for the sake of this recipe we're really only concerned about the page content.

This is where Smarty terminology can be a little confusing, since we're looking for content, but Smarty only processes templates. The key to clarifying this is to remember that CMS Made Simple passes even page content through Smarty as a template—this is how Smarty tags that are embedded in page content can be used.

So when our page content is being processed by Smarty, the $smarty->_current_file contains a string to identify it. For an English-language website, the default content block's string happens to be "content:content_en" while a second content block (set in the template with the tag {content block='second' label='Second Content Area'} or something similar) would have the identifier string "content:second".

Since we want to process all content blocks with our filter, we break the identifier string on the colon character, and if there is more than one piece, we check that the first is the string "content". If it is, we make the substitution within the template output of our target string with our target string followed by the registered trademark symbol.

Regardless of whether we modified the template output, we return it to the calling function.

If we were to be deploying this recipe in a production site, we may want to take another look at our str_replace() call. Consider the case where a user has entered content which includes both the search phrase and the registered trademark symbol: the implementation provided here would duplicate the symbol.

Getting the Most out of Tags and User-Defined Tags

There's more...

This recipe shows some of the power of a post-compile filter. Any kind of change that you can imagine to do to your page content can be performed here. The possibilities range from practical and utilitarian to whimsical:

- automatically remove obscenities from your site
- substitute old-style markup with CSS classes (for example, convert `<font ...>` tags into `<spans>`)
- replace instances of your company name with an image tag of your logo
- celebrate International Talk Like A Pirate Day by translating to "pirate-talk"

Handling more than just content blocks

In this recipe, we processed only content blocks, presumably to save some overhead. You may, however, want to process everything in your site, or everything but stylesheets, or maybe only module output.

For this kind of fine-grained processing control, take a look at the `$smarty->_current_page` variable. Some of the more common values it may contain include:

- `filespec`—when Smarty is compiling a static page template for the site admin area.
- `tpl_top:X`—when Smarty processes page_data variables
- `tpl_body:X`—when Smarty processes the `<body></body>` section of a page template
- `tpl_head:X`—when Smarty processes the `<head></head>` section of a page template
- `module_db_tpl:module_name;template_name`—when a module is compiling a template that is stored in the database
- `module_file_tpl:module_name;template_filename`—when a module is compiling a template that is on the filesystem
- evaluated template—when a dynamically created string is being processed as a template (likely from a module calling the ProcessTemplateFromData() method)
- `content:block_name`—site content
- `globalcontent:block_name`—a global content block
- temporary stylesheet—when Smarty processes a stylesheet

Pre-compile filters

The pre-compile filter is as powerful as the post-compile filter. Typically, you will want to process the page after the template substitutions have occurred. But if you are looking to filter or modify Smarty tags themselves, this is where you would do that.

When using a pre-compile filter, it's important to keep in mind that the filter will only be called when content is processed by Smarty. You may think this should happen on every page view—but it turns out that this is not how it works. If the asset has been cached, processing will only happen if the cache has expired or the asset has been changed.

See also

- *Reversing a string in two ways using a Smarty Modifier* recipe

4
Getting Started with Modules

In this chapter, we will cover:

- Creating the file structure for a module
- Creating a new module stub using the Skeleton module
- Creating a new module stub using the ModuleMaker module
- Breaking a module into multiple files
- Making a module localizable
- Using Smarty variables and templates with a module
- Calling methods on other Modules and specifying module dependencies

Introduction

The power of CMS Made Simple comes from a relatively lightweight core, coupled with great extensibility. If you're looking for a flexible, localizable content management system with fairly modest resource requirements, the basic distribution of CMS Made Simple will satisfy you. If, however, you want a complex website with interactive forms, user registration, e-commerce, image galleries, newsletters, guest books, polls, and so forth, these additional capabilities can be yours after just a few module installations.

The CMS Made Simple Module API is really the key to extending the CMS. It provides you with the means of integrating your code seamlessly into the operation of your website, as well as a rich API that will save you coding time. Once you understand modules, you can enhance CMS Made Simple in virtually any way you can imagine.

Getting Started with Modules

So what exactly is a module? In CMS Made Simple, a module is a class that extends the base CMS module class. The base class has a set of methods that are called by the CMS to do things like manage actions, respond to or generate events, or act as a tag within a page. When you create a module, you override methods, and use them to accomplish whatever it is your module is designed to do.

The CMS Made Simple Module API also contains a collection of methods that may be called to do typical tasks that are typical for a CMS add-in. There is a database abstraction layer with powerful tools for creating and modifying tables, querying and interacting with the database, and protecting against SQL-injection attacks. There is an interface to Smarty, the template subsystem used by CMS Made Simple, that allows for setting variables, and rendering several kinds of templates. There are tools for creating HTML forms, for managing input, for integrating interfaces into a site's admin panel, and more.

> You can read the technical documentation on the CMS Made Simple Module API at `http://www.cmsmadesimple.org/apidoc/`

This chapter will help you get started with creating modules. It starts with a recipe to help you understand the way that CMS Made Simple organizes module files. Next, there are recipes for getting a quick start with module development by using available tools. There are recipes to show you how to enable localization of your modules, so they can be translated into many languages. Lastly, there is a recipe that shows how you can make modules work together in concert for even more powerful results—and with even less work!

Creating the file structure for a module

CMS Made Simple has a straight-forward standard for the directory structure that is used by modules. For your module to work correctly, you will need to follow the conventions set out by the standard; fortunately, it is not complicated and will help keep your module files organized in a logical fashion.

This recipe shows you how to create the standard module directory structure.

Getting ready

For this recipe, you will need to have CMS Made Simple installed and working. You will need write access to the filesystem of the server where your CMS is installed. This recipe assumes you are using SSH to access the server, but other approaches such as FTP will work as well.

How to do it...

1. Use SSH to connect to your server.
2. Change your working directory to the modules directory of your CMS Made Simple installation directory, for example:

   `cd /var/www/mysite-root/modules`

3. Create your top level module directory:

   `mkdir MyModule`

4. Create the directory for the module's language files:

   `mkdir MyModule/lang`

5. Create the directory for the localized versions of the module's language files:

   `mkdir MyModule/lang/ext`

6. Create the directory for the module's template files:

   `mkdir MyModule/templates`

7. Create the directory for the module's icon (and other image files):

   `mkdir MyModule/images`

8. Set permissions for the Module directories:

   `chmod -R 755 MyModule`

Getting Started with Modules

How it works...

The following diagram graphically shows the directory structure you just created, and adds in some details about which files will go in which directory:

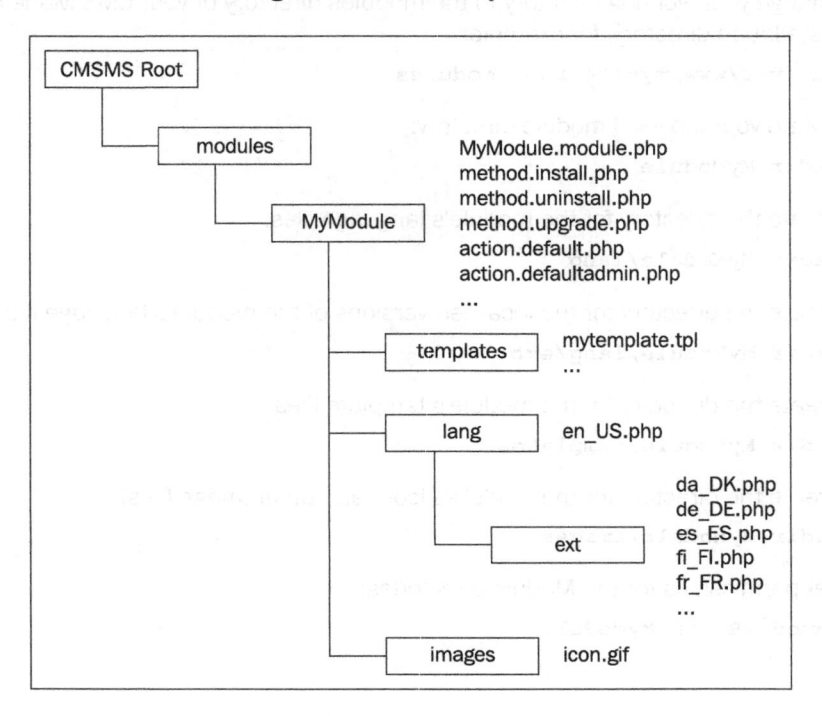

```
CMSMS Root
│
└── modules
    │
    └── MyModule        MyModule.module.php
        │               method.install.php
        │               method.uninstall.php
        │               method.upgrade.php
        │               action.default.php
        │               action.defaultadmin.php
        │               ...
        │
        ├── templates   mytemplate.tpl
        │               ...
        │
        ├── lang        en_US.php
        │   │
        │   └── ext     da_DK.php
        │               de_DE.php
        │               es_ES.php
        │               fi_FI.php
        │               fr_FR.php
        │               ...
        │
        └── images      icon.gif
```

The top-level `MyModule` directory is where you place your primary module file. The naming convention is simple: the module directory must be the module name (which is the string returned by the module's `GetName()` method), and the primary module file will be that same name followed by the extensions `".module.php"`.

> A number of other files may also be in the top-level directory. If you are following recommended practices and breaking your module into multiple files, all of the module action files will be kept here, as will the install, upgrade, and uninstall methods.

The template's subdirectory is, not surprisingly, where the file-based templates for your module are stored. In general, modules use file-based templates for their administration interfaces, and store their user-facing templates in the database. This enables site administrators to more easily customize the user-facing templates to match their site's look and feel. Many module authors will store the default versions of these user-facing templates as static files in the template's directory as well.

> The `lang` directory is where you store your file containing localization strings. If you are following recommended practices, you don't hardcode strings in your module; instead you refer to language keys, that are mapped via the localization file to the display strings.

By default, the top-level language file is the English localization, and is called `en_US.php`. Within the `lang` directory, however, is an `ext` directory containing other localizations. The name of this directory originates in the fact that the translations have been managed using Subversion externals.

> Individual localization files are named for their language and country codes, with the convention being the two-letter ISO 639-1 language code (in lowercase) followed by an underscore followed by the two-letter ISO 3166-1 country code followed by the `.php` extension. This allows for localizations even within a language, like separating Castilian and Mexican Spanish.

The last standard directory is the images directory. The only conventional use for this directory is a place to keep an "`icon.gif`" image, that will be used as the custom icon for the module in the CMS admin area. Of course, if your module requires any special image files, this is the ideal place to put those as well.

There's more...

When naming your module directory and your module file, it's important that the names match exactly the string that's returned by the module's `GetName()` method. Keep in mind that these names are case-sensitive. While you may be able to get away with mismatches on some case-insensitive filesystems, you will run into problems on any Unix-like platform.

Similarly, the names of the action files should agree in case with the names of the actions themselves, even though you may be able to use different case on case-insensitive filesystems. It's always best to err on the side of standardization, rather than be in the position of debugging under pressure the day you upload your development site to a production server.

Other files in your module directory

In many modules, including some core modules, you'll also see one or more other directories within the top-level directory for that module. Typical directories are classes, doc, includes, and/or lib. As a module author, you are free to create any structure that helps you organize your files. Using names that will make sense to others is desirable.

Getting Started with Modules

Sometimes, modules will include third-party PHP code as a library or use it to interface with other products. Keeping this code in a subdirectory of a module is perfectly acceptable—but don't forget that these directories are still accessible to the web server. Unless you set up restrictions in your web server configuration (or, say, through an Apache .htaccess file), a well-crafted URL can go directly to any file. So if you include a third-party product or library, be careful about any installation procedures or configuration scripts that come with them. You don't want to provide anything that an attacker could use to compromise your system.

Directly accessed scripts

You will occasionally see non-module files included in the module directories. These are PHP scripts that are not related to the module API, and which are not being used as libraries by a module. These are files that have entirely non-CMS entry-points, and which are called independently without any direct involvement of CMS Made Simple. Typically, they are support files that handle asynchronous uploads or return scaled images.

Normally, this practice is not recommended, although, the reasons are more philosophical than practical. Like third-party libraries, it's difficult to be sure that the non-module files are following good security procedures, and they lack the ability to use the built-in security features of the module API. Still, there are times when they are the only way to solve a problem. The conclusion is to avoid non-module scripts unless you can explain to yourself exactly why the same functionality can't be implemented within the module framework (or as a separate Tag).

See also

- *Chapter 1, Create a "Hello World" Module* recipe
- *Breaking a module into multiple files* recipe
- *Making a module localizable* recipe

Creating a new module stub using the Skeleton module

One quick way of getting started with writing a module is to install a stub module, and then customize it to do what you want. Doing so saves you from having to create numerous directories, figure out which files go where, or remembering which methods you need to implement to get started.

This recipe shows you how you can get started quickly using the Skeleton module.

Getting ready

For this recipe, you will need to have login access to the site's Administration area with permission to "Modify Modules" and "Manage All Content".

You will also need write access to the filesystem of the server where your CMS is installed. This recipe assumes you are using SSH to access the server, but other approaches such as FTP will work as well.

For the sake of this recipe, we will assume that the module you want to create is the `ProblemSolver` module.

How to do it...

1. Log in to your CMS Administration area.
2. Using the top menu, go to "**Extensions**" and click on "**Module Manager**".
3. If it is not the current tab, click on the "**Available Modules**" tab.
4. In the following alphabetical index list, click on "**S**".
5. Scroll down the page until you see "**Skeleton**" and click on the "**Download & Install**" link.
6. Once the installation has been completed, SSH to the server where you have CMS Made Simple installed.
7. Change your working directory to the module directory of your CMS Made Simple installation directory, for example:

   `cd /var/www/mysite-root/modules`

8. Rename the Skeleton directory to your module's name:

   `mv Skeleton ProblemSolver`

9. Change the active directory to be the `ProblemSolver` directory:

   `cd ProblemSolver`

10. Rename the `Skeleton.module.php` to `ProblemSolver.module.php`:

    `mv Skeleton.module ProblemSolver.module.php`

11. Using your favorite editor, edit `ProblemSolver.module.php`. Find the class declaration and change it from:

    `class Skeleton extends CMSModule`

    To

    `class ProblemSolver extends CMSModule`

Getting Started with Modules

12. Find the `GetName()` method, and change the return line from:

    `return 'Skeleton';`

    To

    `return 'ProblemSolver';`

13. Find the `GetVersion()` method and choose what version number you want to use for your first release. Change the return string to reflect that number.
14. Find the `GetAuthor()` method and replace "SjG" with your name.
15. Find the `GetAuthorEmail()` method and replace "sjg@cmsmodules.com" with your e-mail address.
16. Save the modified file.
17. Change the working directory to `lang`:

    `cd lang`

18. Using your favorite editor, edit `en_US.php`.
19. Change the friendly name string:

    `$lang['friendlyname'] = 'Pedantic Skeleton Module';`

    To

    `$lang['friendlyname'] = 'Problem Solver Module';`

20. Save the file.
21. Using the top menu, go to "**Extensions**" and click on "**Modules**".
22. See that your new Problem Solver module is available to install.

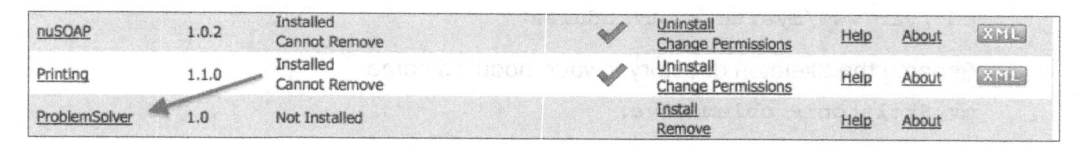

nuSOAP	1.0.2	Installed Cannot Remove	✓	Uninstall Change Permissions	Help	About	XML
Printing	1.1.0	Installed Cannot Remove	✓	Uninstall Change Permissions	Help	About	XML
ProblemSolver	1.0	Not Installed		Install Remove	Help	About	

23. At this point, and before you install the module, you probably want to go in and modify at least the `method.install.php` to be more appropriate for your purposes.
24. Customize away!

How it works...

Software re-use is a popular topic in computer science; shared libraries and object-oriented code are both ways to avoid rewriting code. Cut and paste, as this recipe demonstrates, is another way to save time and reuse code.

Chapter 4

> The Skeleton module was originally designed as an educational tool, but also serves as a shortcut for building modules. Not only is it an example application, but it is richly commented, and contains a wealth of information on the module API.

By copying a working module, and adapting it for your own uses, you save yourself the effort of creating all of the files and directories and can instead focus on implementing your specific project. If you follow the steps outlined earlier, you will be at the point where your module is recognized by CMS Made Simple as a valid module, and you could install it.

To completely convert the Skeleton module into your own module, however, you will want to get rid of all of the functionality that is not specific to the Skeleton example. This includes deleting the content of the action files, rewriting the install and uninstall method files, updating the language file and clearing extraneous strings, updating the `SetParameters()` method, and updating or removing the `GetNotificationOutput()` and `GetDashboardOutput()` methods.

One convenient way of working is to comment out all of the methods in the main module file, then going through them one-by-one to either update or remove them.

See also

- *Chapter 1, Create a "Hello World" module recipe*
- *Creating a new module stub using the ModuleMaker module recipe*

Creating a new module stub using the ModuleMaker module

The ModuleMaker module is a convenient tool for rapidly creating the basic framework for a new module. It uses a question-and-answer approach to determine what your requirements are, and outputs stub files that you can then populate to create your module.

This recipe walks you through a sample session with ModuleMaker, and shows you how to build a customized module stub in less than ten minutes.

Getting Started with Modules

Getting ready

For this recipe, you will need to have CMS Made Simple installed and working. Your installation will need to have the filesystem permissions set to enable the web server to create files in the modules directory. You will need login access to the site's Administration area as a member of the "admin" group, or as a member of a group with permission to "Modify Modules".

Once you have created the stub using Module Maker, you will need write access to the filesystem of the server where your CMS is installed in order to populate the stub files with your module code.

For this example, we'll create a module stub for our "Playlist" module, that will allow users to create and share musical playlists.

How to do it...

1. Log in to your CMS Administration area.
2. Using the top menu, go to "**Extensions**" and click on "**Module Manager**".
3. If it is not the current tab, click on the "**Available Modules**" tab.
4. In the alphabetical index list below, click on "**M**".
5. Scroll down until you find the listing for ModuleMaker.
6. Click on the "**Download & Install**" link.
7. Once the installation has completed, click on the link "**Return to Module Manager**" and confirm that Module Maker is listed as installed.
8. Using the top menu, go to "**Extensions**" and click on "**Module Maker**".
9. From here, there will be a series of question screens, that will allow you to configure your module. Starting on the first page, enter "playlist" for the "Module Name" field, and "Play List Module" for the "Friendly Name" field. For the "Module Description" field, enter:

    This module lets your users submit playlists to share with one another, and has an admin interface for you to manage playlists.

10. Click on the "**Next...**" button.
11. Enter your name for the "**Author Name**" and your e-mail for the "**Author Email**" and click on the "**Next...**" button.
12. Enter "**1.0**" for the "**Initial Version Number**" field, "**1.0**" for the "**CMS minimum version**" field, and "**1.999**" for the "**CMS Maximum version**" field, and click on the "**Next...**" button.
13. Since the module won't have any dependencies, simply click "**Next...**" on the module dependency page.

14. Check the checkbox to indicate that the module is a plugin module, and click on the "**Next...**" button.
15. Now we will enter some of the user-side actions that we think we'll need. The "default" action is already defined. So enter "**add_playlist**" into the "**Add a User-Side Method**" field and hit "**Add Another...**"
16. Enter "`view_playlist`" into the "**Add a User-Side Method**" field and the click on the "**Next...**" button.
17. Check the checkbox to indicate that the module will have an admin interface, and click on the "**Next...**" button.
18. Select "**the Content Menu**" from the "**Admin Section**" dropdown. Enter "**Administer user-submitted playlists**" into the "**Admin Description**" text area, and click on the "**Next...**" button.
19. Since our module will only have one specific admin permission, type "**Administer Playlists**" into the "**Module-specific Permission**" field and click on the "**Next...**" button. Select the "**Administer Playlists**" permission from the "**Default Admin-side Permission**" dropdown, and click on the "**Next...**" button.
20. Now, we create admin actions. The "defaultadmin" is already set up using the default permission we just defined; we'll use that for listing playlists. So type "`edit_playlist`" into the "**Add an Admin Method**" field, select "**Administer Playlist**" from the permission dropdown, and click on the "**Add Another...**" button.
21. Type "`delete_playlist`" into the "**Add an Admin Method**" field, select "**Administer Playlist**" from the permission dropdown, and click on the "**Add Another...**" button.
22. Type "`admin_settings`" into the "**Add an Admin Method**" field, select "**Administer Playlist**" from the permission dropdown, and click on the "**Next..**" button.
23. We will have two tabs in our Admin panel, so check the checkbox and click the "**Next...**" button.
24. Type "**Playlists**" into the "**Tab Name**" field, and click on the "**Add Another...**" button.
25. Type "**Configuration**" into the "**Tab Name**" field, and click on the "**Next...**" button.
26. Lastly, click on the "**Finished. Generate Module Stub**" button, and watch the Module Maker generate your stub.
27. Using the top menu, go to "**Extensions**" and click on "**Modules**" to view your new module.

News	2.11	Installed Cannot Remove	✓	Uninstall Change Permissions	Help	About	XML
nuSOAP	1.0.2	Installed Cannot Remove	✓	Uninstall Change Permissions	Help	About	XML
playlist	1.0	Not Installed		Install Remove	Help	About	
Printing	1.1.0	Installed Cannot Remove	✓	Uninstall Change Permissions	Help	About	XML

Getting Started with Modules

28. At this point, you would normally modify the "`method.install.php`" to set up any database tables your module will use. Once you have done this, click on the "**Install**" link next to your module.

29. Check the "**Content**" menu to confirm your module is showing in the correct menu.

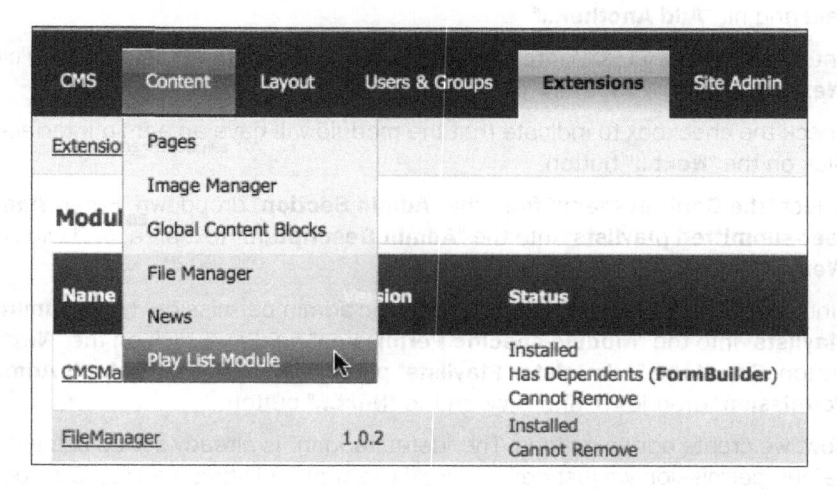

30. Click on the "**Play List Module**" link to see the default admin.

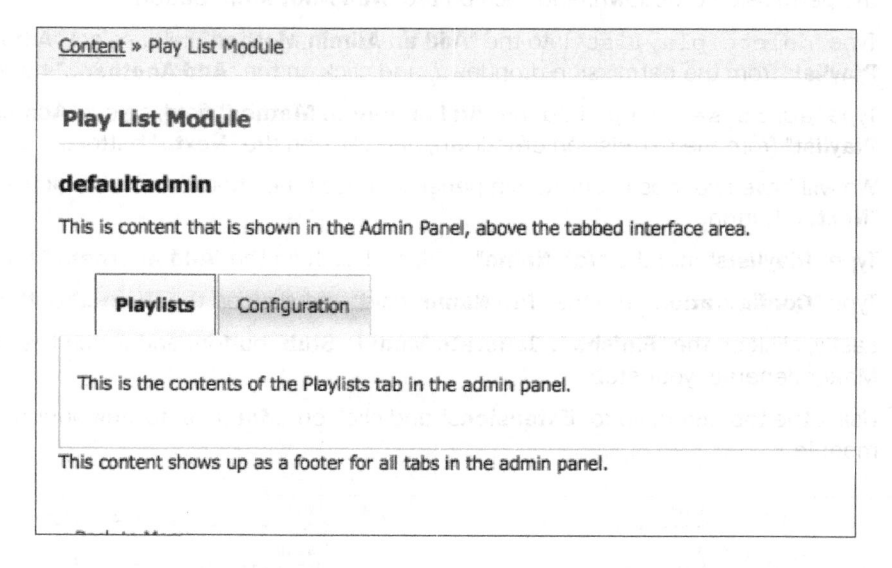

31. Now you can start editing the stub files, and implementing your module.

How it works...

This recipe walks you through the Module Maker's process for creating a stub module. Unlike customizing the Skeleton module, the code stub that this module outputs will not need any effort to remove extraneous code. Instead, you will be able to focus on the creation of your module functionality.

The Module Maker module includes a collection of standard methods that a typical module needs. By directing you through a set of questions, it uses your answers to create stubs of the files that you will need. Those stubs files are enough to allow you to install the new module, so you can see the basic layout and how the module will function. At that point, you can start editing the individual file stubs and make your module do what it is that it will do.

Module Maker will not implement your whole module for you, of course. What it does do is:

- Create the base module file and directories.
- Create the `method.install.php`, `method.uninstall.php`, and `method.upgrade.php` files.
- Create a basic language file.
- Create `action.default.php` and `action.defaultadmin.php` stubs.
- Create an `action.YOUR_ACTION.php` stub for each module action you tell it you want.
- Create any Admin-side permissions you tell it you want.
- Create a tabbed admin panel to your specification.
- Create an admin-side `action.YOUR_ADMIN_ACTION.php` stub with permission enforcement for each module admin action you tell it you want.

See also

- *Chapter 1, Create a "Hello World" Module* recipe
- *Creating a new module stub using the Skeleton module* recipe
- *Breaking a module into multiple files* recipe

Breaking a module into multiple files

A module in CMS Made Simple may be implemented in a single file. All that is required is that the file contains a subclass of CMSModule and overrides a few key methods.

Getting Started with Modules

Most modules, however, will typically evolve to contain some complicated functionality. As the amount of code in a module increases, keeping it all in a single file begins to make management difficult. Similarly, loading and parsing all of the module code on every request can lead to performance issues.

This recipe shows you how you can split a module into multiple files to improve its organization and reduce its footprint with respect to per-request resource requirements.

Getting ready

For this recipe, you will need write access to the filesystem of the server where your CMS is installed.

This recipe assumes you have a full module written monolithically with a single file, or a single file with an external language file.

How to do it...

1. Open your module file in your favorite editor.
2. Find your `Install()` method, and copy the contents of the method into a new file. When copying the method, copy everything after the initial opening curly brace and before the final closing curly brace.
3. Save this file in your module's root directory as "`method.install.php`".
4. Remove the `Install()` method from your original module.
5. Repeat this process for the `Uninstall()` method, saving the new file as "`method.uninstall.php`".
6. Repeat this process for the `Upgrade()` method, saving the new file as "`method.upgrade.php`".
7. Your `DoAction()` method will likely comprise a switch statement containing different cases to execute based upon the value of the action $name variable. Copy the content of each "case" statement into a new file, and save it in your module's root directory using the naming convention "`action.action_name.php`" where `action_name` is the string of that particular case's conditional.
8. Repeat this process for every case in the `DoAction()` switch statement.
9. Remove the `DoAction()` method from your module.

How it works...

For performance and organizational improvements, CMS Made Simple allows you to break a module into multiple files. This recipe shows you how to split out various methods, and to make your module more efficient.

For each method that can be separated from the main Module file, CMS Made Simple sets some variables. At a minimum, these include the variables that are passed to the analogous method as parameters, but also include a set of other useful variables. These other variables are:

- $gCms—a reference to the CmsObject
- $smarty—a reference to the global Smarty instance
- $db—a reference to the database connection object
- $config—a reference to the CMS Config object
- $filename—the fully qualified path of the file

Each split out file gets variables defined for the parameters it would have received as a method in a monolithic module file. So we have:

The Install() method and Uninstall() methods don't take any parameters, so their split-out file versions only have the variables described earlier.

The Upgrade() method takes two parameters: $oldversion and $newversion. These variables represent the pre-upgrade version number of the module and the post-upgrade version number of the module respectively. The method.upgrade.php file has these variables available as well.

The DoAction() method takes several parameters, that are also set as variables in a split out action.action_name.php file. These are:

- $name—the name of the action being called
- $id—a unique identifier of the module instance (used to differentiate multiple tag modules when embedded in a single page)
- $params—an associative array of parameters
- $returnid—the content_id of the page containing the module (if it's a tag module)

There's more...

One thing to be careful about, whether writing modules or any other code, is what happens when the web server requests a given file directly. For example, if someone enters the URL http://www.yoursite.com/modules/ModuleName.module.php into their browser's address bar, there won't be any harmful side effects, since the main module file is simply a class definition. The PHP will be executed, but it will simply be defining a class. It's the methods within the module that perform any actions. So this kind of access cannot cause any harm.

When you split out your actions into action.action_name.php files, this is no longer true! The content of one of those methods is right out there in the open. So if you have a "delete" action, it might be possible for someone to abuse it simply by typing the URL http://www.yoursite.com/modules/action.delete.php into their browser's address bar.

Getting Started with Modules

> To make sure that the only way an action is called is properly via the CMS, it's strongly advised to put the following code at the top of each split-out file:
>
> `if (!isset($gCms)) exit;`
>
> Since the CMS sets up the `$gCms` reference before calling any of the method or action files, this simple test will succeed when they are called correctly, and will fail if someone is trying to illicitly access them.

See also

- Chapter 1, Create a "Hello World" module recipe

Making a module localizable

CMS Made Simple has built-in support for making modules multilingual for both the administrators and the end users. If you are writing a module for your own personal use, you may be tempted to save some time and hardcode all of the strings and output to be only in your own native language. It turns out, however, that if a module is useful to you, there will be other people for whom it would be useful. If you share a module with others, it's worth the extra work to make it localizable. People from all over the world will thank you.

This recipe shows you the basic steps to making your CMS Made Simple module localizable.

Getting ready

This recipe assumes you're working with a module that was not written in a localized fashion to begin with. It also assumes that your project is in the CMS Made Simple Developer's Forge Subversion repository.

How to do it...

1. If you have not already done so, create a "lang" directory in your module's top-level directory.
2. Inside the "lang" directory, create a file named "en_US.php".
3. For each file of your module, locate any instance where a string is an output using an echo statement.
4. Take the text that is displayed, and add a line to your en_US.php file where you assign that text to a descriptive key.

   `$lang['descriptive_key'] = 'Text that is displayed';`

5. In your module file, replace the text with a call to `$this->Lang('descriptive_key')`

6. If your module uses templates that contain strings, edit the templates. Replace each string with a Smarty variable like `"{$descriptive_key}"`.

7. In the code that calls the template, assign the smarty variable

    `$smarty->assign('descriptive_key',$this->Lang('descriptive_key'));`

8. Add a line to your `en_US.php` file where you assign the original template text to the descriptive key.

    `$lang['descriptive_key'] = 'Text that was originally in the template';`

9. Once you have completely converted your module for localization, you will add it to the translation center. From the command line in the CMS base install directory, set up the Subversion externals (replacing "ModuleName" with your module's name):

    `svn propedit svn:externals modules/ModuleName/lang`

10. In the editor window that pops up, enter the following (replacing "ModuleName" with your module's name):

    `ext http://svn.cmsmadesimple.org/svn/translatecenter/modules/ModuleName/lang/ext`

11. Save the file and exit your editor.

12. Change the working directory to your module's base directory:

    `cd modules/ModuleName/`

13. Work some Subversion magic:

    ```
    svn cleanup lang
    svn update
    svn commit lang
    svn up lang
    ```

How it works...

There are two parts to localizing a module. The first part is making sure that all of the strings that are output are keyed to some kind of descriptive name that retrieves values from your language file. The process of converting a module from hardcoded strings to using a language file is time consuming, which is a good reason to implement your modules with language files in the first place. It slows down development by a small percentage of time, but it is a lot less painful than converting afterward.

Getting Started with Modules

Once a module has all of its strings in an external file, the process of translating is relatively straightforward from the module author's perspective. By using Subversion externals and adding the module to the Translation Center, your module becomes available to everyone on the translation team. All over the world, translation team members who use your module will be able to translate the strings to their own language.

Translated language files become automatically available to you via the Subversion externals. When you do a Subversion checkout or update of your module, those files will appear in the `lang/ext` directory. Then, when people change their language settings for the admin area or specify a front-end language for a page containing your module, the CMS system will select the appropriate language file. Instead of looking up the descriptive key in the English language file, it will look up the key in the appropriate file, and your strings will be shown in translation.

There's more...

This recipe described the process of adding a module to the translation center via the command line. If you are not using Subversion from the command line, the approach may be a bit different:

If you are a Windows user using TortoiseSVN, right-click on the icon of your module's working directory and select "**Properties**".

Chapter 4

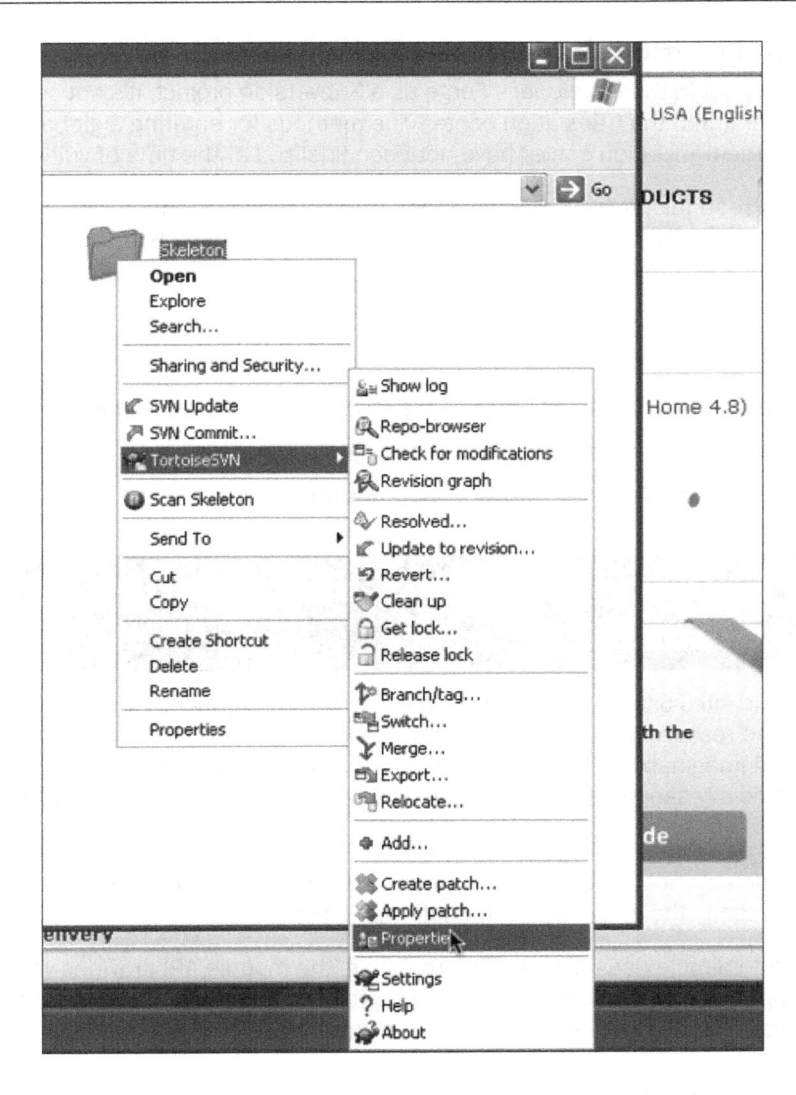

In the properties dialog box, click on "**New...**" and select "**svn:externals**" from the drop-down menu. In the edit box, enter the same external command as described in the command-line instructions.

If you are a Macintosh user and are using a graphical Subversion tool like svnX, you may need to open up the terminal and issue a few command-line files. As of version 0.9.13, there was no way to set SVN properties via the tool.

Localization of modules without Subversion

If your module is not in the Developer's Forge as a Subversion project, it's not currently possible to enter it into the translation center. The methods for entering a git-based repository into the translation center have not been finalized at the time of writing.

By the time you read this, however, an approach may have been standardized. Please check the CMS Made Simple wiki, or enquire in the CMS Made Simple IRC channel (#cms on `freenode.net`).

See also

- *Chapter 7, Creating an account on the CMS Made Simple Developer's Forge* recipe
- *Chapter 7, Adding your module to the Forge* recipe
- *Chapter 7, Creating your Subversion Repository* recipe

Using Smarty variables and templates with a module

People who build sites using CMS Made Simple choose the product for many different reasons, but one reason that comes up time and again is the ability to make it work with any layout or design imaginable. Unlike some systems, you're not trapped into a "block" model or one of a few officially sanctioned layouts. You can do pretty much anything you want.

When you write a module, it's important to remember that your module output should also uphold that philosophy of flexibility. It's less work to simply have your module output in a fixed format, but it lessens the value of your module significantly.

Since CMS Made Simple uses Smarty for templating, the module API provides you with access to Smarty templates and variables. This recipe explores the tools from the API, that you can use to make your module output just as flexible as the rest of the CMS system.

Getting ready

For this recipe, you will need access to your site's Administration area with permission to "Modify Modules".

You will also need write access to the filesystem of the server where your CMS is installed. This recipe assumes you are using SSH, but you could just as easily create the files on a local computer and transfer them via FTP.

How to do it...

1. Use SSH to connect to your server.
2. Change your working directory to the modules directory of your CMS Made Simple installation directory, for example:
   ```
   cd /var/www/mysite-root/modules
   ```
3. Create a top level module directory:
   ```
   mkdir SmartyDemo
   ```
4. Create the directory for the module's template files:
   ```
   mkdir SmartyDemo/templates
   ```
5. Open your favorite text editing program, and create a new file.
6. Type the following code:
   ```
   {foreach from=$text item=sentence}
     <p>{$sentence}</p>
   {/foreach}
   ```
7. Save this file as "text_template.tpl" in the `SmartyDemo/templates` directory.
8. Open your favorite text editing program, and create a new file.
9. Type the following code:
   ```php
   <?php
   class SmartyDemo extends CMSModule
      {
      function GetName()
         {
         return 'SmartyDemo';
         }

      function HasAdmin()
         {
         return true;
         }
      function GetVersion()
         {
         return '0.1';
         }
      function Install()
         {
         $this->SetTemplate('title_template','<h1>{$title}</h1>');
         }
   ```

```
function DoAction($action, $id, $params, $returnid)
  {
  $this->smarty->assign('title','The Rubaiyat');
  echo $this->ProcessTemplateFromDatabase('title_template');

  $subtitle_template = '<h2>{$subtitle}</h2>';
  $this->smarty->assign('subtitle','by Omar Khayyam');
  echo $this->ProcessTemplateFromData($subtitle_template);

  $text = array("Wake! For the Sun, who scatter'd into flight",
    "The Stars before him from the Field of Night,",
    "Drives Night along with them from Heav'n, and strikes",
    "The Sultan's Turret with a Shaft of Light.");
  $this->smarty->assign('text',$text);
  echo $this->ProcessTemplate('text_template.tpl');
  }
}
?>
```

10. Save this file in the SmartyDemo directory as "SmartyDemo.module.php".
11. Log in to your CMS Administration area.
12. Using the top menu, go to "**Extensions**" and click on "**Modules**".
13. Scroll down the list until you find "**SmartyDemo**" and click the "**Install**" link next to it.
14. Under the "**Extensions**" menu, select "**SmartyDemo**":

Extensions » SmartyDemo

SmartyDemo

The Rubaiyat
by Omar Khayyam
Wake! For the Sun, who scatter'd into flight

The Stars before him from the Field of Night,

Drives Night along with them from Heav'n, and strikes

The Sultan's Turret with a Shaft of Light.

« Back to Menu

How it works...

Within this tiny module, we demonstrate the three different ways of defining and rendering out Smarty templates from within a module. The first is a module database template, the second is a module data template, and the third is a file-based template.

When a module is rendering content on the user-side of a site, it will typically use templates, which are stored in the database. Storing the template in the database enables the module to create an interface where the site administrator can update those templates. Administrators can then customize the module output to match whatever site design they want.

For a module to be able to use a database template, the module has to know about the template. In this case, we define the template in our module's Install() method with a call to SetTemplate(). This method takes a template name, in this case "title_template", and the template itself. This title template contains some basic markup and a Smarty variable $title. In the DoAction() method, you can see that we assign $title a value with a call to $this->smarty->assign(). Now that both the template and the relevant variables are set up, we render this template with the ProcessTemplateFromDatabase() method.

When a module has text that needs substitutions like placing variables into an e-mail subject or displaying some kind of status string to the user, it can use Smarty (rather than inventing its own algorithms). This kind of data template is convenient and easy to use.

The next template we render, a data template, is just a string containing some markup and a Smarty variable. Unlike our database template example, we don't need to register it with the module in any way. We create the template when we need it, use Smarty to assign() a value for the variable, then we render the combination with the ProcessTemplateFromData() method.

The last approach demonstrated – a file template – is one you'd typically use for a module to display content to the site admin. It's a template that doesn't typically need to change on a site-by-site basis, but it does provide flexibility to the module author to change the layout without too much pain. As with the other template types, the variables within the template must be exported to Smarty with an assign(), and then the template is rendered with the ProcessTemplate() method. For file templates, the ProcessTemplate() method takes the template filename as a parameter, with the path to that file being defined as the template's directory within the module's base directory.

There's more...

In a production module, you would probably not want to do some of the things demonstrated here. Specifically, you wouldn't want to use three templates to output a single page, when you could use a single template!

Getting Started with Modules

Additionally, in a production module, you would want to localize your strings rather than hard-coding them. This way, when you release the module to the wider community, it can be used by people who speak different languages than you do.

Similarly, some of the shortcuts taken by this example (particularly the inflexible, monolithic implementation of the `DoAction()` method) are to be avoided.

$this->smarty versus $smarty

If you look at the code in the action files of modules that have been split into multiple files, you might be confused by the calls to Smarty methods that look like:

```
$smarty->assign('key','value');
```

instead of the

```
$this->smarty->assign('key','value');
```

shown here. There is no deep magic here, though. The base `DoAction()` method sets a number of variables in scope when calling an action file that is not passed as a parameter to the method that overrides the base `DoAction()` call. Not only is the module's Smarty handle directly in scope as `$smarty`, but a reference to the `CmsObject` is in scope as `$gCms`.

This turns out to make the module action files a little cleaner, although, you can still use the `$this->smarty` reference if you really wish to.

See also

- *Chapter 3, Making a variable available to Smarty from a User-Defined Tag* recipe
- *Breaking a module into multiple files* recipe
- *Making a module localizable* recipe

Calling methods on other modules and specifying module dependencies

In CMS Made Simple, modules are subclasses of the `CMSModule` object. Like other PHP objects, they comprise a set of methods which they use to accomplish their purpose. With the hundreds of modules in the CMS Forge, there is a lot of functionality available.

You can sometimes save yourself a great deal of work by using another module as a library or API rather than re-implementing the functions yourself. Some modules, in fact, exist for that very reason. They serve as standard APIs for important functionality that was not used in so many circumstances to merit being part of the CMS Core, but deemed useful nevertheless.

This recipe will demonstrate using one such module, the CMS Mailer, to generate an e-mail. It will also show how to formalize the dependencies between modules to make it easier for the administrator to manage module installations.

Getting ready

For this recipe, you will need access to your site's Administration area with permission to "Modify Modules."

You will also need write access to the filesystem of the server where your CMS is installed.

For demonstration purposes, this recipe assumes that you do not have the CMS Mailer modules installed, while – in all likelihood – you actually do. If you want to step through exactly along with the recipe, you can uninstall CMS Mailer; otherwise, you can skip the steps that make the assumption it's not installed.

How to do it...

1. Use SSH to connect to your server.
2. Change your working directory to the modules directory of your CMS Made Simple installation directory, for example:

    ```
    cd /var/www/mysite-root/modules
    ```

3. Create a top level module directory:

    ```
    mkdir MailDemo
    ```

4. Open your favorite text editing program, and create a new file.
5. Type the following code:

    ```php
    <?php
    class MailDemo extends CMSModule
      {
      function GetName()
        {
        return 'MailDemo';
        }

      function HasAdmin()
        {
        return true;
        }
      function GetVersion()
        {
        return '0.1';
    ```

```
        }
      function Dependencies()
        {
        return array('CMSMailer'=>'1.73');
        }
      function DoAction($action, $id, $params, $returnid)
        {
        $mail = $this->GetModuleInstance('CMSMailer');
        if ($mail !== FALSE)
          {
          $mail->reset();
          $mail->SetSubject('Spammers');
          $mail->SetBody("To whom it may concern;\nIf you are seeking
    the spammers who stopped by ".
              "last week, they have been fed to the cat.\nSincerely,\n_
    SjG_");
          $mail->AddAddress('you@yourdomain.com','Your Name');
          $res = $mail->Send();
          }
        }
      }
    ?>
```

6. Save this file as "MailDemo.module.php" in the MailDemo directory.
7. Log in to your CMS Administration area.
8. Using the top menu, go to "**Extensions**" and click on "**Modules**".
9. Scroll down the list until you find "**MailDemo**" and click on the "**Missing Dependency**" link.

CMSMailer	2.0	Not Installed		Install
FileManager	1.0.2	Installed Cannot Remove	✓	Uninstall Change Permissions
MailDemo	0.1	Not Installed	→	Missing Dependency Remove

10. The next page will show you what unsatisfied dependency or dependencies exist:

Chapter 4

Dependencies for MailDemo Module

Name	Minimum Version	Installed
CMSMailer	1.73	False

« Back to Menu

11. Click on the "**Back to Menu**" link.
12. Click on the "**Install**" link next to the CMS Mailer module.
13. Now the `MailDemo` module should have an "**Install**" link next to it. Click that link.

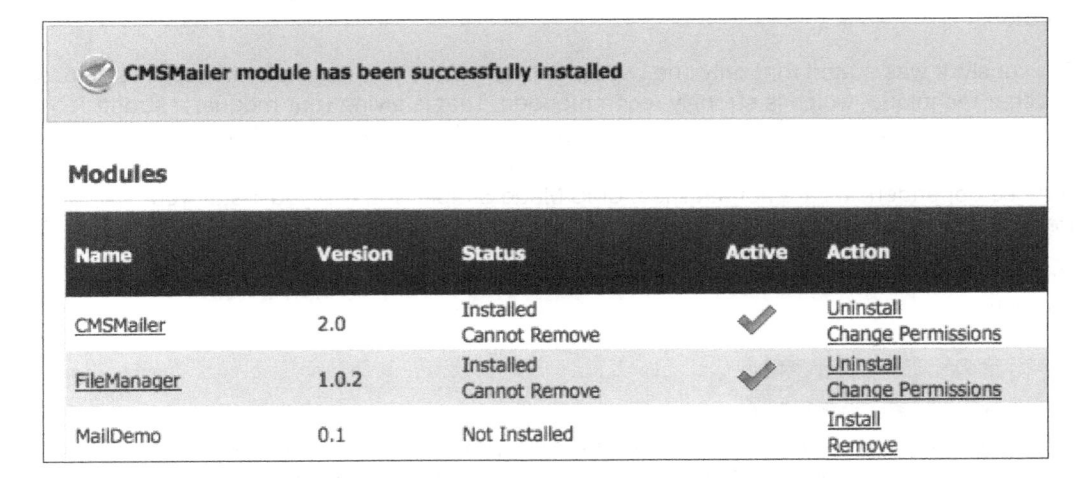

CMSMailer module has been successfully installed

Modules

Name	Version	Status	Active	Action
CMSMailer	2.0	Installed Cannot Remove	✓	Uninstall Change Permissions
FileManager	1.0.2	Installed Cannot Remove	✓	Uninstall Change Permissions
MailDemo	0.1	Not Installed		Install Remove

14. Under the "**Extensions**" menu, select "**MailDemo**." The page will be blank, but you should receive the e-mail.

			hide details 8:51 PM
from	CMS Administrator		
to	Samuel <cranky.old.module.author@gmail.com>		
date	Tue, Oct 5, 2010 at 8:51 PM		
subject	Spammers		

To whom it may concern;
If you are seeking the spammers who stopped by last week, they have been fed to the cat.
Sincerely,
SjG

Getting Started with Modules

How it works...

It is surprising how many modules end up sending e-mail in one way or another, which is only one reason why this recipe should be useful. The techniques outlined, of course, can be used for any module to integrate with any other module. Once your module has a reference to another module, it can use any public methods from that module. The CMS Mailer Module is designed to be used as an API for other modules to utilize; many other modules had no such thing in mind when they were designed, but turned out to be quite useful to other modules regardless.

To call methods on another module, there is only one critical call, which is part of the module API. That method call is `GetModuleInstance()`. It is passed a module name, and optionally a version requirement, and returns a reference to the module object, or a FALSE if it is unsuccessful. Once you have a reference to the module object, you can call its public methods.

Previously, it was stated that only one critical call is needed to integrate modules, but there's another technique, which is strongly recommended. That is giving your module a strong dependency upon the other module. As demonstrated in this recipe, modules support a `GetDependencies()` method, which returns an associative array of modules and versions. If those dependencies are not satisfied, CMS Made Simple won't let you install your dependent module.

Building solid dependencies is a good way to help ensure that your module will function correctly.

There's more...

Normally, when calling methods of another module, you will want to call methods that are intended for external use. While most module authors are not thinking of their modules as an API, they may well think about some of the methods as being more general—these are often identified by being specifically called out in the module help, or by more extensive comments in the module code.

By calling methods that are intended for outside use, your integration will less likely break when the author of the other module makes changes. Contrariwise, it's something you will want to think about when writing your modules! By documenting your methods, other modules can take advantage of your hard work. Similarly, your module can be a "good citizen" by buffering external modules from changes you make internally—one of the promises of Object-Oriented programming. This means that if you were to change a method to take an array instead of a StdClass, for example, you might choose to implement the change as a new method, and use the old method to reformat the incoming parameters and call the new one.

Dependencies and ModuleManager

Module dependencies are not only used to prevent installation of modules that don't meet requirements—they are also used by the Module Manager to automatically install an entire dependency tree. If your dependencies are well-defined, the administrator will be able to install your module in a single operation, rather than hunt around for why a module is breaking.

This feature of the Module Manager has an underutilized side-effect—it is possible to create "meta-modules", which are simply collections of dependencies. If every site you build uses the same five modules, you could create a meta-module that has dependencies for those five modules. Then, using the Module Manager, you could install all five of the modules in a new CMS Made Simple installation with a single click.

Error checking

In a production module, you would probably not want to do some of the things demonstrated here.

When getting a reference to the CMS Mailer module instance, you would probably want to do something to indicate a problem to the user or site admin if you get a FALSE response. Typically, this would only happen if the other module was inactivated, uninstalled, or in the midst of an upgrade, although, it can also happen in low-memory conditions. Regardless, it's important to know when it's failing. Likewise, checking the return value from the `$mail->send()` method and handling any error conditions would probably be wise.

Additionally, in a production module, you would want to localize your strings rather than hard-coding them. This way, when you release the module to the wider community, it can be used by people who speak different languages than you do.

Similarly, some of the shortcuts taken by this example (particularly the inflexible, monolithic implementation of the `DoAction()` method) are to be avoided.

See also

- Chapter 3, *Posting an article to the News Module using a User-Defned Tag* recipe

5
Using the Database API

In this chapter, we will cover:

- Creating a database table when a module gets installed
- Creating a database index when creating a table
- Making a database query from a module
- Creating and using a database sequence
- Altering a database table when a module gets upgraded
- Cleaning up when a module is uninstalled

Introduction

Content Management Systems are often divided into two philosophical camps based upon how they approach the task of managing content: with structure or without structure. Simplistically, a structured system has one or more rigid, record-oriented formats for all pages, while an unstructured system is more free-form, allowing the users to organize the content of pages as they see fit.

In reality, most CMSes are hybrids, and CMS Made Simple is no exception. Page content in CMS Made Simple is generally unstructured content, where the site administrator uses the WYSIWYG editor or HTML directly to format the content. Some structure can be imposed by putting one or more content blocks in a page template, but, by and large, pages are free-form.

Using the Database API

Where CMS Made Simple really reveals its hybrid nature is through modules. Core modules like News, for example, are a combination of fixed record formats and free-form areas. Many modules create purely record-oriented interfaces for entering, listing, and displaying data.

Any module that manages data (whether rigidly structured, free-form, or a combination of both) will need a way to initialize its data storage in the database. A module will need a way to access the data in the database. And, since requirements change over time, a module will need a way to update or remove its data storage structures.

This chapter gives an introduction to the database API. It focuses on the basics of creating database tables and sequences, simple population of data, upgrading database tables and data, and removing data when the module is uninstalled. The chapter also gives an example of querying records. While other chapters will give more depth on specific database operations, and will cover important topics like data sanitizing, this chapter should be enough to give you a good basic understanding of the API's capabilities.

The recipes in this chapter all require that you have access to your site's Administration area with permission to "Modify Modules," and write access to the filesystem of the server where your CMS is installed.

Creating a database table when a module gets installed

Although a few modules interact only with the core CMS Made Simple database tables, most of the modules you will create will have a need for their own data storage. Fortunately, the module API provides you with methods for creating database tables in a database-independent fashion.

The module installation method is the ideal place to create any database tables your module will need. This recipe shows you how, using the example of a module for organizing music collections.

How to do it...

1. Using any of the methods described in *Chapter 4, Getting Started with Modules*, create a new module stub for your Music Collection module.
2. Using your favorite editor, edit your module's `method.install.php`.
3. Type in the following code:

   ```php
   <?php
   if (!isset($gCms)) exit;

   $taboptarray = array('mysql' => 'TYPE=MyISAM');
   $dict = NewDataDictionary($db);
   $fields = "
   ```

```
            track_id I KEY,
            name C(255) NOTNULL,
            play_count I DEFAULT 0,
            average_rating N,
            description X";
    $sqlarray = $dict->CreateTableSQL(cms_db_prefix().'module_music_
    collection',
        $fields, $taboptarray);
    $dict->ExecuteSQLArray($sqlarray);
    ?>
```

4. Log in to your CMS Administration area.
5. Using the top menu, go to "**Extensions**" and select "**Modules**".
6. Find your new Music Collection module in the list, and click the "**Install**" link.
7. Using the program of your choice, view your database, and look at the table that was created.

Field	Type	Length	Unsigned	Zerofill	Binary	Allow Null	Key	Default
track_id	int	11	☐	☐	☐	☐	PRI	
name	varc...	255	☐	☐	☐	☐		
play_count	int	11	☐	☐	☐	☑		0
average_rating	deci...	10,0	☐	☐	☐	☑		NULL
description	text		☐	☐	☐	☑		NULL

INDEXES

Non_unique	Key_name	Seq_in_index	Column_name	Collation	Cardinality	Sub_part	Packed	Comm
0	PRIMARY	1	track_id	A	0	NULL	NULL	

How it works...

Microsoft developed ActiveX Database Objects (ADO) in the 1990s as a way of making it easier to write database code that would work across multiple products, including non-SQL-based products. The idea is that rather than writing code for the peculiarities of any particular datastore, you can write code for a library that implements the common capabilities of a large set of datastores. The abstraction provided by the library removes the requirement for knowing finicky details of your data storage system.

Using the Database API

ADOdb takes the concepts that Microsoft popularized, and brings them to the PHP world, although ADOdb is less about abstracting across datastores than it is about abstracting across multiple SQL- based databases. Most relational database systems use the Structured Query Language (SQL) as their primary query interface—which may lead you to wonder why an abstraction layer is required for different databases. As William Abikoff famously observed, "in the computer world, a standard is a rule followed except most of the time". Different implementations of SQL make different interpretations of datatypes and even some query syntax. Furthermore, the way code connects to a database isn't part of the standard, and varies by database system.

CMS Made Simple uses ADOdb not only for abstracting the database connection, but also its resources for database-independent table creation. What this means is that you can describe a database table using a simple meta-language, and you don't have to worry exactly what datatype your underlying database creates.

CMS Made Simple also provides a mechanism for creating database tables (or other initialization) when a module is installed. The `method.install.php` is a special piece of code that is only run when the site administrator first installs a module. It can be used for any kind of setups that are required, whether creating files, or, as in this case, creating database tables.

The CMS passes a `$db` variable to the install method, that is a reference to the ADOdb database object. This will be used for all of our interactions with the database.

We create an array called `$taboptarray`. This contains a set of optional, database-specific flags that will be passed into the system when we create the actual SQL—in other words, this is where we can override the abstraction layer and be platform-specific. Fortunately, it's completely optional (in this case, we're stating that if the database is MySQL, we'll tell it to create tables using MySQL's specific ISAM table implementation).

The next step is creating an abstract data dictionary by instantiating a class called `NewDataDictionary`. This is ADOdb's object for describing data tables.

Next, we describe our data table. The format for this is a simple comma-delimited string, where each item represents a column in the table, and has a name, a datatype, and other possible options. We describe a table with five fields:

- `track_id`—an integer, which is the key for the record
- `name`—a string up to 255 characters long and which cannot be null
- `play_count`—an integer, which defaults to being 0
- `average_rating`—a numeric field
- `description`—a long text field

This string is passed to the Data Dictionary's `CreateTableSQL()` method, along with the name of the table we want to create, and our database-specific option list. What is returned from `CreateTableSQL()` is an array of SQL commands that are specific to the database system used by your CMS Made Simple install. You don't have to know anything about this array, however; you can pass it directly to the Data Dictionary's `ExecuteSQLArray()` method, that will execute the SQL commands and create your database table.

There's more...

The different versions of the SQL Standard specify somewhere between a dozen and twenty datatypes. Some database management systems implement thirty or more datatypes. Here's a table of the high-level datatypes supported by ADOdb, and which should be safe to use with the databases that are supported by CMS Made Simple.

Type	Definition
C	Character string, using varchar or varchar2 type. Length from 1-255 characters.
X	Long character string, using Varchar or Text type. Length from 1-4000 characters.
XL	Very long character string, using Text or CLOB type. Length is maximum supported by underlying database.
C2	Multibyte character string. Improves unicode compatibility with some databases. Length from 1-255 characters
X2	Long multibyte character string. Improves unicode compatibility with some databases. Length is maximum supported by underlying database.
D	Date
T	Timestamp
TS	High resolution (sub-second) timestamp. Some databases implement this as a standard Timestamp.
L	Boolean
I or I4	4-byte integer
I1	1-byte integer
I2	2-byte integer
I8	8-byte integer
F	Floating point number
N	Numeric or decimal type

For more details, visit the documentation for ADOdb's datadict class at http://phplens.com/lens/adodb/docs-datadict.htm

Using the Database API

ADOdb or ADOdb-lite?

CMS Made Simple actually ships with two different versions of the ADOdb database abstraction layer—ADOdb and ADOdb-lite. By default, CMS Made Simple uses the "lite" version, although you can override this in your `config.php`.

The differences between ADOdb and ADOdb-lite are:

- The "lite" version supports a subset of the functions provided by ADOdb.
- The "lite" version supports fewer database systems. This may not matter to you, as only MySQL and PostgreSQL support is provided in the CMS Made Simple distribution, regardless of ADOdb version.
- The "lite" version implements a DBDate method to work with date and time types, while the full version has a SQLDate method, which may require edits to the drivers for your specific database.

Normally, you'll want to use ADOdb-lite. However, if you want to use CMS Made Simple with a database system other than MySQL, PostgreSQL, SQLite, or Sybase, you should use the full ADOdb. In any case, if you want to use a database system other than MySQL or PostgreSQL, you will need to track down drivers for your specific database and install them into CMS Made Simple installation (check `http://adodblite.sourceforge.net/` or `http://adodb.sourceforge.net/` to find those drivers).

See also

- *Creating a database index when creating a table* recipe
- *Altering a database table when a module gets upgraded* recipe
- *Cleaning up when a module is uninstalled* recipe

Creating a database index when creating a table

When your module accesses the database, it is usually either to store or to retrieve data. You have defined a schema for your data, and stored it using relational algebra in one or more tables. For most CMS-related applications, you do a lot more querying from the database than you do inserting or changing data; for example, you may add a News article once, but it is displayed every time someone hits the front page of your website.

Relational database management systems have been refined over decades to manage tabular data with very high performance. In the simplest case, each row in a database table is referenced by its key (for example, "`employe_id`"), and the database automatically creates an index to aid looking up rows by primary key. But frequently, you will want to search a table by some other column: first name or last name. Because the table is not organized according to these fields, the database has to perform a full table scan—that is, it has to look at every row in the database to find the records that match your criteria. If you have a dozen records, this will still be fast. But when your table has thousands, tens of thousands, or millions of records, a full table scan will destroy your site's performance.

By creating an index, you are telling the database to keep an internal map of the values for a given column in the table. This internal map is organized to facilitate searching, and often takes the form of a binary tree, hash, or B+ tree. Using an index means that every time you save a record into that table, the database has to do extra work to keep that index up-to-date, but the trade-off is that when it comes to reading records, the database has far less work to do. Adding an index can speed some queries by orders of magnitude.

This recipe shows you how to create additional indexes for your tables, using the example of a module that maintains a roster of Knights for our Round Table.

How to do it...

1. Using any of the methods described in *Chapter 4, Getting Started with Modules* create a new module stub for your Knight Roster module.
2. Using your favorite editor, edit your module's `method.install.php`.
3. Type in the following code:

   ```php
   <?php
   if (!isset($gCms)) exit;

   $taboptarray = array('mysql' => 'TYPE=MyISAM');
   $dict = NewDataDictionary($db);

   $fields = "
     knight_id I KEY,
     first_name C(80) NOTNULL,
     last_name C(80) NOTNULL,
     victories I DEFAULT 0,
     defeats I DEFAULT 0";
   $sqlarray = $dict->CreateTableSQL(cms_db_prefix().'module_knight_roster',
     $fields, $taboptarray);
   $dict->ExecuteSQLArray($sqlarray);

   $sqlarray = $dict->CreateIndexSQL(cms_db_prefix().'mod_kr_nameidx',
   ```

Using the Database API

```
        cms_db_prefix().'module_knight_roster', 'last_name,first_name');
    $dict->ExecuteSQLArray($sqlarray);
    $sqlarray = $dict->CreateIndexSQL(cms_db_prefix().'mod_kr_vicidx',
        cms_db_prefix().'module_knight_roster', 'victories');
    $dict->ExecuteSQLArray($sqlarray);
    ?>
```

4. Log in to your CMS Administration area.
5. Using the top menu, go to "**Extensions**" and select "**Modules**".
6. Find your new Knight Roster module in the list, and click the "**Install**" link.
7. Using the program of your choice, view your database, and look at the table and indexes that were created.

Field	Type	Length	Unsigned	Zerofill	Binary	Allow Null	Key	Default
knight_id	int	11	☐	☐	☐	☐	PRI	
first_name	varchar	80	☐	☐	☐	☐		
last_name	varchar	80	☐	☐	☐	☐	MUL	
victories	int	11	☐	☐	☐	☑	MUL	0
defeats	int	11	☐	☐	☐	☑		0

INDEXES

Non_unique	Key_name	Seq_in_index	Column_name	Collation	Cardinality	Sub_part	Packed	Com
0	PRIMARY	1	knight_id	A	0	NULL	NULL	
1	cms_mod_...	1	last_name	A	NULL	NULL	NULL	
1	cms_mod_...	2	first_name	A	NULL	NULL	NULL	
1	cms_mod_...	1	victories	A	NULL	NULL	NULL	

How it works...

The syntax of the table creation code used by ADOdb is explained in the previous recipe, "Creating a database table when a module gets installed." Essentially, we are using the ADOdb `NewDataDictionary()` class to generate database-specific SQL from a field description.

We define our table as having the following fields:

- `knight_id`—a unique identifier for the knight, this will be an integer and the primary key for the table.
- `first_name`—the knight's first name, a string of up to 80 characters, which must be populated when a record is saved.
- `last_name`—the knight's last name, another string of up to 80 characters, which must be populated when a record is saved.

- `victories`—an integer count of the number of times the knight has won when tilting, which defaults to zero.
- `defeats`—an integer count of the number of times the knight has lost when tilting at the tournament, defaulting to zero.

With the record defined, we create the database-specific SQL using the `CreateTableSQL()` method and then create the table itself with the `ExecuteSQLArray()` method. If we were to stop here, we'd have a perfectly serviceable database table, optimized for retrieval by the unique `knight_id`. But what if we want to retrieve knights from our database by name, or select knights with fewer than a set number of victories? Those queries would require full table scans at this point. So we will create indexes.

The `NewDataDictionary` class has a `CreateIndexSQL()` method, which takes as parameters the table name, the name of the index to create, and the fields of the table to index. For most database management systems, index names need to be unique, even if they are rarely used directly. Typically, the database's query optimizer will identify which indexes to use; you only need to specify the index name in complex queries when you want to override the query optimizer's best guess.

In our first case, we create an index on the knight's `last_name`, `first_name` combination. In some database systems, this will create a single aggregate index, while in other systems it will actually create two separate indexes. In either case, it will give a big performance boost for searching by `last_name` or by the `last_name`, `first_name` combination. In some database systems, it will give a performance boost when searching by `first_name` as well.

We generate the SQL via the `CreateIndexSQL()` method, and execute the SQL using the `ExecuteSQLArray()` method.

In our second case, we create an index on the knight's victories.

There's more...

To demonstrate the advantage of these indexes, we load up a database with 100,000 sample knights. For this example, we'll use MySQL to see the performance advantage. First, we turn on database profiling, and then run a few queries without any indexes:

```
mysql> set profiling=1;
Query OK, 0 rows affected (0.00 sec)


mysql> select * from cms_module_knight_roster where first_name='Robin'
and last_name like 'Not%';
+------------+------------+----------------------------------+------------+-
--------+
| knight_id  | first_name | last_name                        | victories  |
defeats    |
```

Using the Database API

```
+----------+-------------+----------------------------------+-----------+---------+
|     1800 | Robin       | Not-Quite-as-Brave-as-Launcelot  |        18 |     253 |
+----------+-------------+----------------------------------+-----------+---------+
1 row in set (0.05 sec)

mysql> select count(*) from cms_module_knight_roster where victories > 350;
+----------+
| count(*) |
+----------+
|    29803 |
+----------+
1 row in set (0.05 sec)
```

And now we repeat the process with the same table, but this time with the indexes described earlier. Then we display profiling information:

```
mysql> show profiles;
+----------+------------+------------------------------------------------------------------------------------+
| Query_ID | Duration   | Query                                                                              |
+----------+------------+------------------------------------------------------------------------------------+
|        1 | 0.05230500 | select * from cms_module_knight_roster where first_name='Robin' and last_name like 'Not%' |
|        2 | 0.04476100 | select count(*) from cms_module_knight_roster where victories > 350                |
|        3 | 0.00072600 | select * from cms_module_knight_roster where first_name='Robin' and last_name like 'Not%' |
|        4 | 0.02537000 | select count(*) from cms_module_knight_roster where victories > 350                |
+----------+------------+------------------------------------------------------------------------------------+
4 rows in set (0.00 sec)
```

The first two queries listed are without the indexes, and the second two queries are those same queries with our indexes in place. As you can see, the numeric query was almost twice as fast, and the more complicated query involving the knight's name was more than seventy-two times faster!

When considering times in milliseconds, it's initially hard to care about speedups, even of orders of magnitude. Where this will become important is where your queries involve multi-table joins. As the relational algebra gets complicated, the time for operations can become exponential of the number of tables involved. In these cases, indexes will make the difference between unacceptable query times and reasonable performance.

See also

- *Creating a database table when a module gets installed* recipe
- *Creating and using a Database Sequence* recipe
- *Altering a database table when a module gets upgraded* recipe

Making a database query from a module

A significant percentage of CMS Made Simple modules exist to process data: they manage lists of things, they allow users to create, track, and manage records, and they store relationships between disparate collections of information, and so on. The mechanism behind much of this data processing is the backend database. Rather than implementing its own data storage system, CMS Made Simple works with a number of Relational Database Management Systems (RDBMs) including popular Free/Open Source databases like MySQL and PostgreSQL.

As discussed throughout this chapter, CMS Made Simple provides a database API, which allows modules to access the database. This recipe shows how to use the database API to query a list of all site Admin users and the groups that they belong to.

How to do it...

1. Use SSH to connect to your server.
2. Change your working directory to the modules directory of your CMS Made Simple installation directory, for example:
   `cd /var/www/mysite-root/modules`
3. Create a top level module directory:
   `mkdir Personnel`
4. Create the directory for the module's template files:
   `mkdir Personnel/templates`

Using the Database API

5. Open your favorite text editing program, and create a new file.
6. Type the following code:
   ```php
   <?php
   class Personnel extends CMSModule
       {
         function GetName()
            {
            return 'Personnel';
            }
         function GetVersion()
            {
            return '0.1';
            }

         function IsPluginModule()
            {
            return true;
            }

         function SetParameters()
            {
            $this->RegisterModulePlugin();
            }
       }
   ?>
   ```
7. Save this file as "Personnel.module.php" in the Personnel directory.
8. Open your favorite text editing program, and create a new file.
9. Type the following code:
   ```php
   <?php
   if (!isset($gCms)) exit;
   $db=$gCms->GetDb();
   $personnel=array();
   $results = $db->Execute('select u.first_name, u.last_name, g.group_name from '.
      cms_db_prefix().'users u, '.cms_db_prefix().'groups g, '.cms_db_prefix().
      'user_groups ug where u.user_id=ug.user_id and g.group_id=ug.group_id;');
   while ($results && $row=$results->FetchRow())
      {
      $personnel[]=$row;
      }
   $smarty->assign('personnel',$personnel);
   $count = $db->GetOne('select count(*) from '.cms_db_prefix().'users');
   $smarty->assign('usercount',$count);
   ```

```
echo $this->ProcessTemplate('list.tpl');
?>
```

10. Save this file in the Personnel directory as "`action.default.php`".
11. Open your favorite text editing program, and create a new file.
12. Type the following code:

```
<h2>{$usercount} Users</h2>
<ul>
{foreach from=$personnel item=entry}
  <li>{$entry.first_name} {$entry.last_name}, {$entry.group_name}</li>
{/foreach}
</ul>
```

13. Save this file in the Personnel/templates directory as "`list.tpl`".
14. Log in to your CMS Administration area.
15. Using the top menu, go to "**Extensions**" and click on "**Modules**".
16. Scroll down the list until you find "**Personnel**" and click the "**Install**" link next to it.
17. Using the top menu, go to "**Content**" and select "**Pages**".
18. Click on the "**Add New Content**" button.
19. In the "**Title**" and "**Menu Text**" fields, enter "**Site Management**".
20. In the "**Content**" text area, enter "**{Personnel}**" and click on the "**Submit**" button.
21. View your site from the user side, and go to the new "**Site Management**" page.

Site Management

6 Users

- Ada Lovelace, Admin
- E.B. White, Editor
- Horace Greeley, Editor
- Coco Chanel, Designer
- Frank Lloyd Wright, Designer
- Tom Every, Designer

Previous page: User Defined Tags

Using the Database API

How it works...

We start this recipe by going through the creation of a very simple module structure, as described in *Chapter 4, Getting Started with Modules*. We create our module's main file, `Personnel.module.php`. In this file, we override the `GetName()` and `GetVersion()` methods to return the module name and a reasonable version number, respectively.

When we override the `IsPluginModule()` method to return a "true" value, we're telling the CMS core that this module can be embedded in a content page as a Smarty tag. We also override the `SetParameters()` method, where we call the `RegisterModulePlugin()` method. This call sets up our module tag as the module name, so that the module can be included in a page using the `{Personnel}` syntax rather than the more cumbersome `{CMSModule module='Personnel'}` tag.

Once we have our module's base file created, we create a file for the default action, which is where all the real activity will take place. As usual, we start by confirming that the `$gCms` variable is in scope. This reference to the CmsObject will be defined if this PHP file is called via the CMS, but not if someone used their browser to go directly to the `action.default.php`. This safety measure helps guarantee that the code will be called only in the context we expect it to be.

Next, we get a reference to the database object, which we will use for all of our database interactions. The first of these interactions is direct execution of a SQL query that joins the core User table with the core Group table using the `User_Groups` table for the many-to-many relationship. The `Execute()` method takes a SQL string as its first parameter, and an optional array of parameterized values for the second. In this case, we are not passing parameters to the query. We do, however, take care to refer to the core tables using the `cms_db_prefix()` function. This function returns the database prefix that is used by this particular CMS installation.

The `Execute()` method returns either a Boolean `false`, or an `ADORecordSet`. So we create a loop that continues while that result is not false, and while it is able to return rows from the query. The `FetchRow()` method, as set up by default in CMS Made Simple, takes a row and stores it into an associative array with the database column name as the key and the column's value as the value. In our loop, we simply push this associative array onto the end of an empty array; in other words, we create a data structure, that is a list of associative arrays, each representing one row that's returned from the database.

Once we have this data structure, we assign it to a Smarty variable for later processing.

The next query is designed to get us the number of users in the CMS core User table. We can't simply count the records we got with the last query, since, a given user may belong to multiple groups. Our previous query returns one record for each membership in a group, and won't return any record for a user who does not belong to any group.

So, this query uses an SQL `count(*)` command, which – in the absence of other relational algebra – will return a single value. Because we are guaranteed a single result, we can use the shortcut `GetOne()` method, which returns the single value returned by the query. If you use the `GetOne()` method on a query that returns multiple fields and/or multiple rows, it will discard all but the first field of the first row returned, and give you that value back.

As mentioned earlier, we bind the `$count` variable to a Smarty variable, and then process the "`list.tpl`" template through Smarty. This template displays the user count (using the quick and dirty non-localized string "`Users`" in the template), and then iterates through the `$personnel` data structure, reformatting it as an unordered list. The output of the processed template is then substituted in for the module's tag in the page.

See also

- Chapter 3, *Using URL parameters in a User-Defined Tag* recipe
- Chapter 4, *Using Smarty variables and templates with a module* recipe

Creating and using a database sequence

In relational databases, tables almost always have a unique identifier for each row, known as the primary key. While there are occasional reasons to do otherwise, it's common practice to use an otherwise meaningless integer for this key. This unique identifier can be used for joining the table or for identifying a row when you perform an update.

When adding data to a database table, it is expected that you will provide a value for this key. So where do you get an integer value that you can rely on to be unique?

This recipe shows you how to use the ADOdb facility for creating unique integer sequences, and for getting values from the sequence.

How to do it...

1. Create a module stub by any of the methods described in *Chapter 4, Getting Started with Modules*. Call your new module "`Planets`".
2. Using your favorite editor, create a new file and type the following code:
   ```php
   <?php
   if (!isset($gCms)) exit;
   
   $taboptarray = array('mysql' => 'TYPE=MyISAM');
   $dict = NewDataDictionary($db);
   
   $fields = "
     planet_id I KEY,
     name C(255)";
   ```

Using the Database API

```
    $sqlarray = $dict->CreateTableSQL(cms_db_prefix().'module_
planets',
      $fields, $taboptarray);
    $dict->ExecuteSQLArray($sqlarray);
    $db->CreateSequence(cms_db_prefix().'module_planet_seq');
    $insert_sql = 'insert into '.cms_db_prefix().
      'module_planets (planet_id,name) values (?,?)';
    $planet_id = $db->GenID(cms_db_prefix(). 'module_planet_seq');
    $res = $db->Execute($insert_sql,array($planet_id,'Mercury'));
    $planet_id = $db->GenID(cms_db_prefix(). 'module_planet_seq');
    $res = $db->Execute($insert_sql,array($planet_id,'Venus'));
    $planet_id = $db->GenID(cms_db_prefix(). 'module_planet_seq');
    $res = $db->Execute($insert_sql,array($planet_id,'Earth'));
    $planet_id = $db->GenID(cms_db_prefix(). 'module_planet_seq');
    $res = $db->Execute($insert_sql,array($planet_id,'Mars'));
    $planet_id = $db->GenID(cms_db_prefix(). 'module_planet_seq');
    $res = $db->Execute($insert_sql,array($planet_id,'Jupiter'));
    $planet_id = $db->GenID(cms_db_prefix(). 'module_planet_seq');
    $res = $db->Execute($insert_sql,array($planet_id,'Saturn'));
    $planet_id = $db->GenID(cms_db_prefix(). 'module_planet_seq');
    $res = $db->Execute($insert_sql,array($planet_id,'Uranus'));
    $planet_id = $db->GenID(cms_db_prefix(). 'module_planet_seq');
    $res = $db->Execute($insert_sql,array($planet_id,'Neptune'));
    $planet_id = $db->GenID(cms_db_prefix(). 'module_planet_seq');
    $res = $db->Execute($insert_sql,array($planet_id,'Pluto?'));
    ?>
```

3. Save this file in the `modules/Planets` directory as "`method.install.php`".
4. Log in to your CMS Administration area.
5. Using the top menu, go to "**Extensions**" and click on "**Modules**".
6. Scroll down the list until you find "**Planets**" and click the "**Install**" link next to it.
7. Using the MySQL command line or your favorite graphical database tool, take a look at your CMS install database:

planet_id	name
1	Mercury
2	Venus
3	Earth
4	Mars
5	Jupiter
6	Saturn
7	Uranus
8	Neptune
9	Pluto?

How it works...

In this recipe, we create a very simple table for collecting planets; it contains only a unique identifier and a name field. We also create a sequence for generating the unique identifiers. A database sequence can be thought of as a way of tracking the IDs that have been used for IDs in a database table, and which is guaranteed to give us an as-yet unused ID when we ask. Depending on the database system, they are implemented in a variety of ways, but thanks to ADOdb, we don't have to worry about those details. We just can be confident that every time we ask, we'll be getting back a unique integer.

The syntax of the table creation code used by ADOdb is explained in detail in a previous recipe, "*Creating a database table when a module gets installed*". Essentially, we are using the ADOdb `NewDataDictionary()` class to generate database-specific SQL from a field description. We define our table structure in the `$fields` variable, create the database-specific SQL using the `CreateTableSQL()` method and then create the table itself with the `ExecuteSQLArray()` method.

Next, we create the sequence. The syntax of the `CreateSequence()` method is extremely simple—it takes the name of the sequence as its parameter. It optionally takes a starting ID as well, but in this case we'll let it start with the default value.

Once we have our sequence established, we can get values from it by using the `GenID()` method. This method takes the sequence name as its parameter.

The rest of this method simply generates an ID for each planet, and inserts a record using that ID for the value of `planet_id`.

Using the Database API

There's more...

For the databases which support it, there's an even easier way to handle unique identifiers—auto-increment. For some databases, you could replace the `method.install.php` mentioned earlier with this one:

```php
<?php
if (!isset($gCms)) exit;

$taboptarray = array('mysql' => 'TYPE=MyISAM');
$dict = NewDataDictionary($db);

$fields = "
  planet_id I KEY AUTOINCREMENT,
  name C(255)";

$sqlarray = $dict->CreateTableSQL(cms_db_prefix().'module_planets',
  $fields, $taboptarray);
$dict->ExecuteSQLArray($sqlarray);

$insert_sql = 'insert into '.cms_db_prefix().
  'module_planets (name) values (?)';
$res = $db->Execute($insert_sql,array('Mercury'));
$res = $db->Execute($insert_sql,array('Venus'));
$res = $db->Execute($insert_sql,array('Earth'));
$res = $db->Execute($insert_sql,array('Mars'));
$res = $db->Execute($insert_sql,array('Jupiter'));
$res = $db->Execute($insert_sql,array('Saturn'));
$res = $db->Execute($insert_sql,array('Uranus'));
$res = $db->Execute($insert_sql,array('Neptune'));
$res = $db->Execute($insert_sql,array('Pluto?'));
$last_id = $db->Insert_ID();

?>
```

As you can see, when we create our field description, we pass the "AUTOINCREMENT" flag along with our `planet_id` definition. Later, when we're inserting rows into our table, we omit mentioning the `planet_id` at all—the database will take care of that for us.

Often, however, you need to know the unique identifier of a row that was just inserted into the database. For example, if you had a dependent table of moons, you would need to know which `planet_id` to associate with each moon. If you use sequences, that value is available to you in a variable you retrieved from the sequence. In the case of auto-incrementing fields, ADOdb has a method `Insert_ID()`, which will make the value available, as shown after we create Pluto in the previous code.

Deciding between Sequences and Auto-increment

It sure seems like auto-increment is much easier to use, or at a minimum more compact. Why would you use sequences when you could use auto-increment? The answer to this question really depends on whether you want to guarantee your code is portable across multiple databases. Auto-increment is supported by MySQL, PostgreSQL, and MS SQL Server. Some versions of PostgreSQL return internal IDs, which aren't guaranteed to be consistent if you dump and restore databases, although this shouldn't cause any trouble unless your program logic has some expectation about the order of record IDs.

One philosophy espoused by this book is to write code to be as flexible and portable as possible, even if it means a little more work. This principle arises from painful experience, and the observation that many requirements that are ostensibly carved in stone have a tendency to change unexpectedly. By putting in a small effort up front, you can save yourself from significant headaches in the future. Still, you may not share that philosophy, or may be working for a specific proprietary need; either case may affect your approach when it comes to sequences.

See also

- *Creating a database table when a module gets installed* recipe
- *Altering a database table when a module gets upgraded* recipe

Altering a database table when a module gets upgraded

One thing to which you should accustom yourself as a module author is the continuous need for change. As your module gets used, in addition to the vast volumes of fan mail you will undoubtedly receive, you will also be deluged by feature requests, suggested changes, bug reports, and various other complaints. Some of this communication will motivate you to make changes, and possibly even new releases of your module.

In the course of your new development, you may find yourself needing to make changes to your database structures in addition to your code. The CMS Made Simple module API anticipates this need, and provides a method for performing such changes. This recipe will demonstrate how it works.

How to do it...

1. Use SSH to connect to your server.
2. Change your working directory to the modules directory of your CMS Made Simple installation directory, for example:

   ```
   cd /var/www/mysite-root/modules
   ```

Using the Database API

3. Create a top level module directory:

   mkdir Monsters

4. Using your favorite editor, create a new file and type the following code:

   ```php
   <?php
   class Monsters extends CMSModule
     {
     function GetName()
       {
       return 'Monsters';
       }

     function GetVersion()
       {
       return '0.1';
       }
     }
   ?>
   ```

5. Save this file in your new directory as "Monsters.module.php".

6. Create a new file, and type in the following code:

   ```php
   <?php
   if (!isset($gCms)) exit;

   $taboptarray = array('mysql' => 'TYPE=MyISAM');
   $dict = NewDataDictionary($db);

   $fields = "
     monster_id I KEY AUTOINCREMENT,
     name C(255),
     habitat C(80)";

   $sqlarray = $dict->CreateTableSQL(cms_db_prefix().'module_monster',
     $fields, $taboptarray);
   $dict->ExecuteSQLArray($sqlarray);

   $insert_sql = 'insert into '.cms_db_prefix().
     'module_monster (name,habitat) values (?,?)';

   $res = $db->Execute($insert_sql,array('Ghoul','Graveyard'));
   $res = $db->Execute($insert_sql,array('Will o\' the Wisp','Swamps and Marshes'));
   $res = $db->Execute($insert_sql,array('Devil','The Crossroads at Midnight'));
   $res = $db->Execute($insert_sql,array('Guiron','Planet Terra'));
   ?>
   ```

7. Save this file as "`method.install.php`".
8. Install your module, and check the database using your favorite tool.

monster_id	name	habitat
1	Ghoul	Graveyard
2	Will o' the Wisp	Swamps and Marshes
3	Devil	The Crossroads at Midnight
4	Guiron	Planet Terra

9. After having your module used for a while, you decide that you need to track the weakness of each monster too. So, using your favorite editor, update "`method.install.php`" to be:

```php
<?php
if (!isset($gCms)) exit;

$taboptarray = array('mysql' => 'TYPE=MyISAM');
$dict = NewDataDictionary($db);

$fields = "
  monster_id I KEY AUTOINCREMENT,
  name C(255),
  habitat C(80),
  weakness C(80)";
$sqlarray = $dict->CreateTableSQL(cms_db_prefix().'module_monster',
    $fields, $taboptarray);
$dict->ExecuteSQLArray($sqlarray);

$insert_sql = 'insert into '.cms_db_prefix().
   'module_monster (name,habitat,weakness) values (?,?,?)';
$res = $db->Execute($insert_sql,array('Ghoul','Graveyard','Fire'));
$res = $db->Execute($insert_sql,array('Will o\' the Wisp','Swamps and Marshes','Magic Missile'));
$res = $db->Execute($insert_sql,array('Devil','The Crossroads at Midnight','Fiddle-playing Contests'));
$res = $db->Execute($insert_sql,array('Guiron','Planet Terra','Battle with Gamera'));

?>
```

10. Using your favorite editor, create a new file and type in the following code:

```php
<?php
if (!isset($gCms)) exit;
```

Using the Database API

```php
    $dict = NewDataDictionary( $db );
    switch($oldversion)
    {
     case "0.1":
      $sqlarray = $dict->AddColumnSQL(cms_db_prefix()."module_monster", "weakness C(80)");
      $dict->ExecuteSQLArray($sqlarray);
      $update_sql = 'update '.cms_db_prefix().
        'module_monster set weakness=? where name=?';
      $res = $db->Execute($update_sql,array('Fire','Ghoul'));
      $res = $db->Execute($update_sql,array('Magic Missile','Will o\' the Wisp'));
      $res = $db->Execute($update_sql,array('Fiddle-playing Contests','Devil'));
      $res = $db->Execute($update_sql,array('Battle with Gamera','Guiron'));
    }
    ?>
```

11. Edit "`Monsters.module.php`" and change the `GetVersion()` method to return "`0.2`"

12. Log in to your CMS Administration area, and go to the Modules panel. Note the "**Upgrade Needed**" message next to your Monsters module. Click on the "**upgrade...**" link.

13. Confirm that the upgrade has made the desired changes to the database.

monster_id	name	habitat	weakness
1	Ghoul	Graveyard	Fire
2	Will o' the Wisp	Swamps and Marshes	Magic Missile
3	Devil	The Crossroads at Midnight	Fiddle-playing Contests
4	Guiron	Planet Terra	Battle with Gamera

How it works...

When a module gets new features, it often needs to make changes to its database tables. This recipe demonstrates the facility provided by the CMS Made Simple module API to enable these changes.

The first part of this recipe involves the creation of a sample module for keeping track of various monsters and where they are found. This sample module comprises the "`Monsters.module.php`" file and the related "`method.install.php`". The workings of the base module file and the install method file are described in other recipes, so we won't discuss them here.

When we decide to create version 0.2 of the Monsters module, we have to do a few things. The new version of the module needs to work for someone who is installing the module for the first time, so we simply rewrite our "method.install.php" to create and populate the database tables the way we want them. Next, we update the version number string returned by GetVersion(). Now, someone can install the module, and immediately be working with version 0.2.

But we still have to do something for the people who had installed version 0.1 and who are upgrading to version 0.2. There is a special method that gets called when the site administrator clicks on the "**Upgrade**" link for a module, named "method.upgrade.php". This method receives a few useful parameters. Like the install method, there is the $gCms reference to the CmsObject, and the $db reference to the ADOdb database abstraction object. There are also two other variables, $oldversion and $newversion, which contain the version number of the installed version and the version to which we are upgrading, respectively.

Typically, in the method.upgrade.php, there will be a PHP switch statement using the $oldversion as the test expression. Each block of the switch statement will contain the operations required to perform the upgrade from $oldversion to the next version. In this switch statement, there will be no "break" command at the end of each block. If done this way, a user may successfully upgrade from any historical version to the latest version, as execution will begin with the first match, and drop through all subsequent blocks as well.

In this recipe, we're adding a column to our database table. The NewDataDictionary object has the AddColumnSQL() method for that, which generates an SQL array that we can execute with the ExecuteSQLArray() method.

Modifying the table structure, however, may not be sufficient to make an upgraded database match a fresh installation. You may need to update the extant data to make sure it works with the new version. This recipe demonstrates simplistic updating of existing records; however, in a complex module upgrade you may need more complex logic to copy data from one table to another, to reformat data, or do other transformations.

There's more...

Sometimes, your upgrade may require more complex changes than simply adding columns to tables. The NewDataDictionary class has a number of useful methods for transforming database tables, including:

- ChangeTableSQL($table_name, $fields)—uses the same field definition syntax as CreateTableSQL(), and creates each column that's not already defined, or alters the type of any column that does exist. This method has $options as an optional parameter, and an optional flag to drop the existing table data before making changes.

Using the Database API

- `RenameTableSQL($table_old_name, $table_new_name)`—renames the table.
- `RenameColumnSQL($table_name, $old_column_name, $new_column_name)`—renames columns.

Of course, you can always create new tables using the `CreateTableSQL()` method, or drop unused tables using `DropTableSQL()`. For full details on these and other `NewDataDictionary` methods, consult http://phplens.com/lens/adodb/docs-datadict.htm.

See also

- *Creating a database table when a module gets installed* recipe
- *Cleaning up when a module is uninstalled* recipe

Cleaning up when a module is uninstalled

When a site administrator uninstalls a module, they are telling the system that they no longer want or need the functionality that the module provides. A good module doesn't waste resources or create unnecessary clutter, and therefore, when uninstalled, should remove all traces of itself.

This recipe shows you how to create a method that gets called when your module is uninstalled, and how to clean up database tables and sequences that it has created.

How to do it...

1. Create a module stub by any of the methods described in *Chapter 4, Getting Started with Modules*. Call your new module "Enemies."

2. Using your favorite editor, create a new file and type the following code:
   ```php
   <?php
   if (!isset($gCms)) exit;
   
   $taboptarray = array('mysql' => 'TYPE=MyISAM');
   $dict = NewDataDictionary($db);
   
   $fields = "
     enemy_id I KEY,
     name C(255),
     planned_fate X";
   
   $sqlarray = $dict->CreateTableSQL(cms_db_prefix().'module_enemies',
     $fields, $taboptarray);
   $dict->ExecuteSQLArray($sqlarray);
   ```

```
$db->CreateSequence(cms_db_prefix().'module_enemies_seq');
?>
```

3. Save this file as "method.install.php".
4. Create a new file, and type in the following code:

```
<?php
if (!isset($gCms)) exit;
$dict = NewDataDictionary($db);
$sqlarray = $dict->DropTableSQL( cms_db_prefix().'module_enemies');
$dict->ExecuteSQLArray($sqlarray);
$db->DropSequence( cms_db_prefix().'module_enemies_seq');
?>
```

5. Save this file as "method.uninstall.php".
6. Install your module, and check the database structure.

    ```
    mysql> describe cms_module_enemies;
    ```

Field	Type	Null	Key	Default	Extra
enemy_id	int(11)	NO	PRI		
name	varchar(255)	YES		NULL	
planned_fate	text	YES		NULL	

    3 rows in set (0.00 sec)

    ```
    mysql> describe cms_module_enemies_seq;
    ```

Field	Type	Null	Key	Default	Extra
id	int(11)	NO			

    1 row in set (0.00 sec)

7. Populate the database with your enemy list. If you wish to create a form to help do this, consult *Chapter 6, Using the Module Form API.*

Using the Database API

8. View the data in your database using your favorite database GUI tool.

enemy_id	name	planned_fate
1	Vizzini	Iocane Poisoning
2	Count Rugan	Heart cut out
3	Rodent of Unusual Size	Kill with fire

9. Decide that it's a bad idea to keep a list of enemies. Log in to your CMS Administration area.
10. Using the top menu, go to "**Extensions**" and click on "**Modules**".
11. Scroll down the list until you find "**Enemies**" and click the "**Uninstall**" link next to it.
12. Check the database to verify that your table has been removed:

    ```
    mysql> describe cms_module_enemies;
    ```

    ```
    ERROR 1146 (42S02): Table 'cmsmadesimple.cms_module_enemies' doesn't exist
    ```

    ```
    mysql> describe cms_module_enemies_seq;
    ```

    ```
    ERROR 1146 (42S02): Table 'cmsmadesimple.cms_module_enemies_seq' doesn't exist
    ```

How it works...

This recipe demonstrates that there is an inverse of the commands that are used to create tables and sequences in the database.

As described elsewhere in this chapter, the "`method.install.php`" is called when the admin installs a module. We create an ADOdb `NewDataDictionary()`, and use its methods to create SQL for table and index creation, and then call the `ExecuteSQLArray()` method to pass that SQL to the database.

The "`method.uninstall.php`" is the counterpoint to the "`method.install.php`". It only gets called when the site administrator clicks on the "**uninstall**" link on the module page. Like the install method, the uninstall method gets called with a few variables already instantiated; specifically, the `$gCms` variable, which is a reference to the CmsObject, and the `$db` variable, which is a reference to the ADOdb object.

In our uninstall method, we create a `NewDataDictionary` object, just as we did in the install method. This time, however, instead of calling the `CreateTableSQL()` method, we call the `DropTableSQL()` method, passing it the name of the table we wish to drop. We then pass the resulting SQL array to the database with the `ExecuteSQLArray()` method.

Similarly, the sequence that was created with the `CreateSequence()` method gets dropped with the `DropSequence()` method, which also takes the name of the sequence as a parameter.

There's more...

It's always a question for the module author whether or not actually deleting the database tables is the right thing to do when uninstalling a module. After all, deleted data is not reversible—unless the user has kept backups, once you drop that data, it's gone.

Some users get into the bad habit of uninstalling and re-installing modules to remedy issues when they upgrade their CMS to a new version. If the uninstall method of the module drops their data, they will get an unpleasant surprise. On the other hand, if the module does not drop the data, users may complain that their database is bloated with obsolete records.

In the end, you will need to decide for yourself whether or not to keep data around when a module is uninstalled.

See also

- *Creating a database table when a module gets installed* recipe
- *Altering a database table when a module gets upgraded* recipe

Using the Module Form API

In this chapter, we will cover:

- Creating a basic form in a module
- Restricting and sanitizing parameters to a module
- Using `debug_display` to see what parameters your module is receiving
- Embedding your module output in a different page after a form submission
- Making your module display its output without disrupting the rest of the page
- Creating checkboxes that always submit a value

Introduction

The primary purpose of any computer program is to accept input, do something with it, and output something meaningful based upon the processed input. Websites are no different; they format and display dynamic or static content depending on the user's requests. As early as the HTML 2.0 standard, there has been the concept of interactive forms for websites, that provides additional means of supplying data to the web server. Content management is one of the many tools that use this form capability to optimize the process of accepting and displaying data via websites.

Less abstractly, it's clear that the majority of the modules have interfaces where either the site administrator or the site's end-users can enter form data. Whether it's the admin creating a News article, an end-user submitting a contact form, or a more complex system, these interactions use HTML forms. For a content management system to be useful, it has to make the input of information easy, and HTML forms are a great way to make that input simpler.

Using the Module Form API

The CMS Made Simple module API has a large collection of methods that make the creation of forms and form elements consistent and standards-compliant. It also contains utilities for handling form submissions and making the submitted data available to modules. These methods not only make creation of forms that are valid HTML, but they help solve some common problems that crop up when more than one independent module is included in a single site page.

This chapter includes recipes to demonstrate using the form API to create forms, give some insight into understanding the parameters returned by form submissions, and show some options regarding where form output is displayed.

Most of the recipes in this chapter will require access to your site's Administration area with permission to "Modify Modules" and "Manage All Content", as well as write access to the filesystem of the server where your CMS is installed.

Creating a basic form in a module

This recipe encapsulates the primary purpose of many modules: it creates a form that an end-user can fill out, and stores the provided data into a database table. Not only does it demonstrate the basics of creating different form inputs, processing the form submission, and storing the data in a database table, but provides a typical install method that initializes the database table for use. It does all of this in a localizable fashion, so the module can be easily translated to work in other languages. In just a few pages of code, it provides much of a working application: all it lacks is some means of displaying and/or administering the submitted data (and possibly some data validation).

How to do it...

1. Using any of the methods described in *Chapter 4, Getting Started with Modules*, create a new plug-in type module stub for your UFO Sighting Report module, and call it "`UFOTracker`".

2. Using your favorite editor, edit your module's `method.install.php`, and type in the following code:

```
<?php
if (!isset($gCms)) exit;

$db = $this->GetDb();
$dict = NewDataDictionary( $db );

$fields="
  sighting_id I KEY AUTOINCREMENT,
  name C(40),
  shape C(10),
  had_lights I,
```

```
        description X ";
    $sqlarray = $dict->CreateTableSQL(
        cms_db_prefix()."module_ufotracker",$fields);
    $dict->ExecuteSQLArray($sqlarray);

    ?>
```

3. Using your favorite editor, edit your module's `action.default.php` and type in the following code:

```
<?php
if (!isset($gCms)) exit;

$message = '';

if (isset($params['submit']))
  {
  // process the form
    $db->Execute('insert into '.cms_db_prefix().
      'module_ufotracker (name,shape,had_lights,description)
        values (?,?,?,?)',
      array($params['reporter_name'],$params['type'],
        isset($params['lights'])?'1':'0',$params['description']));
    $message = $this->Lang('sighting_saved');
  }

$smarty->assign('form_start',
  $this->CreateFieldsetStart($id, 'fieldset',
    $this->Lang('title')).
  $this->CreateFormStart($id, 'default', $returnid));

$smarty->assign('input_name',
  $this->CreateInputTextWithLabel($id, 'reporter_name',
    isset($params['reporter_name'])?$params['reporter_name']:'',
    40, 80, '', $this->Lang('name')));

$ufo_types = array($this->Lang('cigar')=>'cigar',
  $this->Lang('saucer')=>'saucer',
  $this->Lang('sphere')=>'sphere');
$smarty->assign('input_type',
  $this->CreateInputRadioGroup($id, 'type', $ufo_types,
    isset($params['type'])?$params['type']:''));

$smarty->assign('input_lights',
  $this->CreateInputCheckbox($id, 'lights', 'lights',
    isset($params['lights'])?$params['lights']:''));
$smarty->assign('label_lights',
```

Using the Module Form API

```php
        $this->CreateLabelForInput($id, 'lights',
          $this->Lang('lights')));
    $smarty->assign('title_description',
      $this->Lang('title_description'));
    $smarty->assign('input_description',
        $this->CreateTextArea(false, $id,
          isset($params['description'])?$params['description']:'',
          'description'));

    $smarty->assign('submit',
        $this->CreateInputSubmit($id, 'submit', $this->Lang('submit')));
    $smarty->assign('form_end',
        $this->CreateFormEnd().
        $this->CreateFieldsetEnd());

    $smarty->assign('message',$message);

    echo $this->ProcessTemplate('report_form.tpl');
    ?>
```

4. Using your favorite editor, edit your module's `lang/en_US.php`, and make sure it contains (in addition to any other strings you need):

    ```php
    <?php
    $lang['title']='Sighting Report';
    $lang['cigar']='Cigar-Shaped';
    $lang['saucer']='Saucer-Shaped';
    $lang['sphere']='Spherical';
    $lang['lights']='UFO was accompanied by blinky lights';
    $lang['name']='Your Name';
    $lang['title_description']='Please describe what you saw:';
    $lang['submit']='Register your sighting';
    ?>
    ```

5. Next, create a new file, containing the following markup:

    ```
    {if $message!=''}<h2>{$message}</h2>{/if}
    {$form_start}
    <p>{$input_name}</p>
    <p>{$input_type}</p>
    <p>{$input_lights}{$label_lights}</p>
    <p>{$title_description}<br />{$input_description}</p>
    <p>{$submit}</p>
    {$form_end}
    ```

6. Save this file in your module's templates directory as `"report_form.tpl"`
7. Edit your `UFOTracker.module.php` file, and make sure you have a `SetParameters()` method that contains at least the line:

   `$this->RegisterModulePlugin();`
8. Log in to your CMS Administration area. Using the top menu, go to "**Extensions**" and select "**Modules**".
9. Find "**UFOTracker**" in the module list, and click on the "**install**" link.
10. Using the top menu, go to "**Content**" and select "**Pages**".
11. Click on the "**Add New Content**" button.
12. Enter "**UFO Report**" into the "**Title**" and "**Menu Text**" fields.
13. In the "**Content**" text area, put the tag for your module: `{UFOTracker}`.
14. Click the "**Submit**" button.
15. View your site from the user side, and go to the "**UFO Report**" page:

UFO Report

Sighting Report

Your Name

○ Cigar-Shaped ○ Saucer-Shaped ○ Spherical

☐ UFO was accompanied by blinky lights

Please describe what you saw:

(Register your sighting)

Using the Module Form API

How it works...

This recipe introduces the basics of using the CMS Made Simple Form API by building a simple system to report UFO sightings. We start by creating a basic module structure; this process is detailed in other recipes, so won't be described here. In our `method.install.php`, we create a database table for storing the details of the UFO sightings: the name of the person reporting, the shape of the UFO, whether or not it had blinky lights, and a description of the experience. The table will be populated with data from a form that the site's users fill out.

To simplify, we will use the default action of the module to both display the form and to process the form submission. When building modules, you may choose to make separate actions for displaying forms and handling their responses, especially if the code is complex—this way, you can keep the files smaller and better organized.

Our `action.default.php` starts with the standard safety check, to make sure that `$gCms` is defined. Next, we define a `$message` variable, that will be used to present status messages to the user. For now, we'll skip the next conditional section, and talk about the creation of the form itself.

To make our module flexible, we create a Smarty variable for each element in the form. As you'll see, each form element is created by making an API call. These methods have one parameter in common: they all require an `$id`. The `$id` variable is defined for us by the CMS, and is automatically in scope. It is used to alter the field names generated in the HTML, and serves to cleanly isolate the fields of one module's forms from any other module's forms. This allows multiple modules to display forms on a single page without having to worry about whether field names are already are already being used by another.

We begin by defining the "`form_start`", that combines the beginning of a `fieldset` and the opening tag of the form. The `fieldset` is created using the `CreateFieldsetStart()` method. This method takes the `$id` mentioned earlier, a name for the `fieldset`, and a legend string. Throughout this recipe, we use the API's `Lang()` method whenever passing strings, so that the module can be easily localized. The other part of the "`form_start`" Smarty variable is the form opening tag. This is generated with the `CreateFormStart()` method. This method takes the `$id`, the destination action, and a `$returnid` variable. The `$returnid` variable is also provided for us by the CMS, and is used to determine which CMS page will be used to display the results of the form submission. We set our action to be default, which means that the form submission will call this same file: `action.default.php`.

Next, we define some more form fields. We create the `reporter_name` field using the `CreateInputTextWithLabel()` method. It uses the ubiquitous `$id` variable, a field name (in this case, "reporter_name"), an initial value for the text input, the display width of the field in characters, the maximum number of characters, and a string to use for the label for the field.

> The field name determines how the value is passed back to the module. In this case, we name our field "reporter_name", which means that the data that the user enters into the field will be sent to the module as $params['reporter_name']. Another notable thing in this method call is how we set the initial value of the field. That funny clause uses the isset() function to see if the module had been submitted with a value for the reporter_name parameter. If so, that value is used as the initial value, otherwise the field is set to be blank. This little trick is especially useful if there is validation of form values going on—the user's data will not vanish if they get one field wrong.

Next, we assign create an array to use for selecting UFO types. The array contains name/value pairs, that are used in the next API method, CreateInputRadioGroup(). The names are what will be displayed in the form, and the values are what will be passed if that radio button is selected. The method takes the $id variable, a field name ("type"), the array of name/value pairs, and the value of any pre-selected radio buttons. We use the same trick as in the reporter_name field, of checking if a value was submitted for this input.

After the radio button group, we create a checkbox for blinky lights. This uses the CreateInputCheckbox() method, which takes the $id, the field name ("lights"), the value that will be submitted if the box is checked ("lights"), and the current selected value (our isset trick). Since the checkbox field doesn't automatically have a label, we create a label for it using the CreateLabelForInput() method, which takes the $id, the name of the field that the label will attach to, and the text of the label.

We create a title for the description field, using a simple Smarty assignment. This could also have been done using the CreateLabelForInput() method used earlier.

We also generate a text area for the description, using the CreateTextArea() method. This method's first parameter is whether or not to supply a WYSIWYG editor, that will typically only apply on the admin side. It also takes the $id variable, the default content of the text area, and the name to use ("description").

We create a submit button for the form using the CreateInputSubmit() method, that takes the $id, a field name, and the text for the button.

Finally, we create a form_end variable, that uses the CreateFormEnd() and CreateFieldsetEnd() methods to cleanly close the form and fieldset tags, respectively. We then render out the form using the ProcessTemplate() method, specifying our layout in the file report_form.tpl.

Using the Module Form API

When the user fills out the form, and hits submit, the execution will call this same `action.default.php`, as specified in the `form_start` tag. Let's revisit that conditional near the top of the file—if the `$params['submit']` is defined, we are handling a form submission. So we insert a record into the database using the values of the fields, which we get from the `$params` array. Our name, shape, and description fields are all very straightforward, but you'll see that the lights field requires an extra trick. This is because a checkbox field only returns a value if checked, and doesn't submit anything to the server otherwise.

When the record is inserted, we place a message into the `$message` variable. If you look at the `report_form.tpl` template, you'll see that we use a Smarty conditional to only display the message if it's not empty. We use this to tell the user that their submission has been received.

There's more...

The module Form API supports a number of form element creation methods in addition to those used in this recipe:

- `CreateTooltip`—for creating an icon or word that will pop up a tooltip when the user's mouse is positioned over it
- `CreateTooltipLink`—for creating a link that will pop up a tooltip when the user's mouse is positioned over it
- `CreateFrontendFormStart`—for starting forms that will not appear in any admin interface (essentially a more specific version of `CreateFormStart`)
- `CreateInputText`—for creating simple text input fields
- `CreateInputFile` and `CreateFileUploadInput`—for creating a file upload input field (the difference being `CreateInputFile` has an "accepts" parameter to restrict file types)
- `CreateInputPassword`—for creating an obscured password input field
- `CreateInputHidden`—for creating hidden fields
- `CreateInputReset`—for creating a form "reset" button (often found dangerously close to form "submit" buttons for some strange reason)
- `CreateInputDropdown`—for creating a drop-down input field
- `CreateInputSelectList`—for creating a selection list or multi-selection list input

> For details on the API, refer to the documentation of the CMS Module class at http://www.cmsmadesimple.org/apidoc/CMS/CMSModule.html.

See also

- Chapter 4, *Breaking a module into multiple files* recipe
- Chapter 4, *Making a module localizable* recipe
- Chapter 4, *Using Smarty variables and templates with a module* recipe
- Chapter 5, *Creating a database table when a module gets installed* recipe

Restricting and sanitizing parameters to a module

The internet can be a wretched hive of scum and villainy, and any well-written module takes some measures to protect itself from attack. One element in a good, layered defense involves validating the type of data being submitted to a module.

The CMS Made Simple module API has a formal process for declaring which parameters a module expects, and some limited control over their type. Using these methods can be a good first-line of defense against both SQL-injection and Cross-Site Scripting type attacks.

How to do it...

1. Use SSH to connect to your server.
2. Change your working directory to the modules directory of your CMS Made Simple installation directory, for example:

   `cd /var/www/mysite-root/modules`

3. Create a top level module directory:

   `mkdir Armor`

4. Open your favorite text editing program, and create a new file.
5. Type the following code:

```
<?php
class Armor extends CMSModule
  {
  function GetName()
    {
    return 'Armor';
    }
```

Using the Module Form API

```php
function GetVersion()
  {
  return '0.1';
  }

function IsPluginModule()
  {
  return true;
  }

function GetHelp()
  {
  return 'Armor Test';
  }

function SetParameters()
  {
  $this->RegisterModulePlugin();
  $this->RestrictUnknownParams();

  $this->CreateParameter('int_param', -1, 'An Integer');
  $this->SetParameterType('int_param',CLEAN_INT);

  $this->CreateParameter('string_param', '', 'A String');
  $this->SetParameterType('string_param',CLEAN_STRING);

  $this->CreateParameter('none_param', '', 'Anything goes!');
  $this->SetParameterType('none_param',CLEAN_NONE);

  $this->SetParameterType(
    CLEAN_REGEXP.'/anyfloat.*/',CLEAN_FLOAT);
  }
function DoAction($action, $id, $params, $returnid)
  {
  echo '<h1>'.$id.'</h1>';
  debug_display($params);
  }
}
?>
```

6. Save this file as "Armor.module.php" in the directory you just created.
7. Log in to your CMS Administration area.
8. Using the top menu, go to "**Extensions**" and click on "**Modules**".

9. Scroll down the list until you find "**Armor**" and click the "**Install**" link next to it.
10. Using the top menu, go to "**Content**" and select "**Pages**".
11. Click on the "**Add New Content**" button.
12. In the "**Title**" and "**Menu Text**" fields, enter "**Armor Test**".
13. In the "**Content**" text area, enter "`{Armor}`" and click on the "**Submit**" button.
14. View your site from the user side, and go to the new "**Armor**" page.

```
Armor Test
                    id
m56ef6
Debug: (1.120117) - (8200)
Number of elements: 2
Array
(
    [module] => Armor
    [action] => default
)
```

15. Using the value for the `$id` variable displayed, try passing various parameters by adding them to the URL, for example:

    ```
    http://www.yoursite.com/index.php?page=armor-test&m56ef6int_param=1
    ```

    ```
    http://www.yoursite.com/index.php?page=armor-test&m56ef6int_param=test
    ```

    ```
    http://www.yoursite.com/index.php?page=armor-test&m56ef6int_param=1&m56ef6string_param=<script>alert('hi')</script>
    ```

    ```
    http://www.yoursite.com/index.php?page=armor-test&m56ef6anyfloat1=1.5&m56ef6none_param=<script>alert('hi')</script>
    ```

How it works...

This recipe shows one of the mechanisms built into the module API to help prevent unexpected or unwanted parameter values being passed to your module. Essentially, you provide your module with some rules that dictate what parameters it should expect, and some details about the types of values that they may contain.

Using the Module Form API

We start with our `SetParameters()` method, where we specify that we don't want to allow parameters other than the ones that we formally register. We do this by making a call to `RestrictUnknownParams()`. In and of itself, this restriction is not a real security measure—stray parameters that don't get used can't really cause us any trouble. But by restricting to declared parameters, we will see warnings if we use a parameter that we didn't declare. In other words, this is useful for us as module authors to remind us to declare the incoming parameters.

Sanitizing parameters has two separate parts. The first, where we call the `CreateParameter()` method, declares the parameter to the API. It takes three arguments, the first being the parameter name, the next the default value, and the third a help string, that is displayed at the end of the module's "help" text. This description is optional, but will make it much easier for the people who use your module.

Once a parameter is declared, we can tell the API what type it is. We do this with the `SetParameterType()` method, by passing in the parameter name and the type. The type system is fairly limited; you have a choice of a few predefined types:

Type Code	Definition
CLEAN_INT	guarantees the parameter has an integer value
CLEAN_FLOAT	guarantees that the parameter has a numeric or floating point value
CLEAN_STRING	guarantees that the parameter is a string that has been passed through an html entity encoding (in other words, it's safe to display directly without risk of cross-site scripting attacks)
CLEAN_FILE	allows an uploaded file
CLEAN_NONE	allows value to be passed through without modification

There's also a special type of declaration that can be passed to `SetParameterType()` by prefixing your parameter name with the string "CLEAN_REGEX" followed by the regular expression for your parameter name to match. In our recipe, we set up a filter that will match any parameter, that has a name beginning with "anyfloat" and maps those parameter values to floating point numbers.

There's more...

The `SetParameterType()` method may be useful for guaranteeing that parameters that should, say, be integer IDs are in fact integers, but it should not be mistaken for doing deep cleaning of parameters. This filtering should be good enough to clean up parameter values for inclusion in HTML pages that are displayed to the user or admin. It will prevent cross-site scripting (XSS) attacks, but it really is a rudimentary filter, and is designed to be used in conjunction with other security measures. In particular, you should not count on using this method to make parameters safe for inclusion directly in SQL calls, passing to `exec()`, or writing to files.

CLEAN_STRING and entity encoding

There's one unexpected result that the CLEAN_STRING filter can cause, which is double-encoding of form field values. This happens in the case where you sanitize the incoming parameter with a `SetParameterType` of CLEAN_STRING, and then use that parameter for the default value of a form field. The reason double encoding takes place is that the CLEAN_STRING filter performs an HTML entity encode, and most of the form API methods also perform an HTML entity encode on the default values they receive.

This is typically a problem when a form fails validation, and displays the original values to the user for correction. The form values get returned to the module as parameters, and those parameters are passed directly to the form field creation methods.

Thus, if you see user-supplied values in forms with odd strings like "&amp;" in them, be sure to call `html_entity_decode()` on your parameter before passing it to the form field creation method.

See also

- *Chapter 3, Using URL parameters safely in a User Defined Tag recipe*
- *Using debug_display or error_log to see what parameters your module is receiving recipe*

Using debug_display or error_log to see what parameters your module is receiving

Sometimes when developing a module, particularly when dealing with forms, it is useful to dump out the incoming parameters to see exactly what input your module is receiving. This recipe shows a pair of methods for displaying that information: one directly to your web browser, the other to your PHP error log.

Using the Module Form API

How to do it...

1. Use SSH to connect to your server.
2. Change your working directory to the News module's directory of your CMS Made Simple installation directory, for example:

   `cd /var/www/mysite-root/modules/News`

3. Using your favorite editor, edit `action.editarticle.php`, and immediately after the `$gCms` test, add a debug statement. The first three lines will look like:

   ```
   <?php
   if (!isset($gCms)) exit;
   debug_display($params,'Parameters');
   ```

4. Log in to your CMS Administration area.
5. Using the top menu, go to "**Content**" and click on "**News**".
6. Click on the title of any News article to edit it. Observe the debug output:

News

Debug display of 'Parameters':(0.000172) - (8200)
Number of elements: 2
Array
(
    [articleid] => 1
    [action] => editarticle
)

*Author:
admin

*Title:

News Module Installed

---

7. In your SSH session, edit "`action.addcategory.php`" adding the same debug statement in the third line.
8. Back in the CMS Administration area, use the top menu to select "**Content**" and click on "**News**".
9. Click on the "**Categories**" tab, and then click on the "**Add Category**" button.
10. Observe the debug information.
11. Enter "**Example**" into the "**Name**" field and select "**General**" in the "**Parent**" drop-down.

12. Click on the "**Submit**" button. Notice that you didn't get a chance to see your debug information before the page redirected to the main News page.

13. In your SSH session, edit "`action.addcategory.php`" again, making it so that the top three lines are:

    ```
    <?php
    if (!isset($gCms)) exit;
    error_log(debug_display($params,'Parameters',false, false));
    ```

14. Repeat steps 8 to 12, but using "**Example 2**" in the "**Name**" field.

15. Look at your PHP error logs, and look for your debug information:

    ```
    [04-Nov-2010 23:55:54] Array
    (
        [name] => Example 2
        [parent] => 1
        [submit] => Submit
        [action] => addcategory
    )
    ```

How it works...

There are several methods of getting debug information when developing a PHP program. There's the `echo()` function, for outputting any kind of information whatsoever. There's the `print_r()` function, which formats variables for easy human comprehension, and `var_dump()`, that does the same with added variable type information. Then there are extensions, which allow you to use a true debugger with PHP.

The CMS Made Simple API provides a general purpose function for outputting debug information. It's essentially a nice wrapper for PHP's `print_r()` function, but provides some nice options. If you simply pass it a variable, it will display that variable along with timing information since the first call to `debug_display()`.

The other parameters `debug_display()` supports are an optional title, the ability to suppress display to the browser, and whether or not to format the output using HTML. By default, `debug_display()` will output to the browser and use HTML.

In our first use in this recipe, we used just the basic `debug_display()` output along with a title. We passed in the `$params` array, and were able to see what parameters were being received by the `editarticle` action.

Using the Module Form API

We weren't able to see any output in our next usage, however, since the `addcategory` action redirects to the main News module page after performing an update. In this second case, we set the parameters for `debug_display()` to suppress both HTML formatting and display in the browser, and send its output to the PHP `error_log()` function. This way, regardless of whether the browser redirects elsewhere, we can view the debug information by looking in the PHP error log.

See also

- Chapter 1, *How to use CMS debug mode* recipe
- Chapter 2, *Seeing what Smarty variables are available to your template* recipe
- Chapter 10, *Setting special diagnostic messages for debug mode* recipe

Making your module display its output without disrupting the rest of the page

When a plug-in type module displays a form, it's typically either embedded in the content or in the page template. When the module processes the form input, and displays some kind of response to it, the results generally replace the content area of the page template. This recipe shows how you can place a form within the content area that will leave the surrounding content even after the form is submitted.

How to do it...

1. Create a plug-in type module stub using any of the approaches described in Chapter 4, *Getting Started with Modules*. Call your module "Absurdists" and make sure to have it call `$this->RegisterModulePlugin()` from the `SetParameters()` method.

2. Using your favorite text editing program, change your module's `action.default.php` to the following:

   ```
   <?php
   if (!isset($gCms)) exit;

   $playwrights = array('Samuel Beckett'=>'beckett',
     'Eugène Ionesco'=>'ionesco',
     'Jean Genet'=>'genet',
     'Tom Stoppard'=>'stoppard');

   $message = '';
   if (isset($params['submit']))
     {
   ```

```php
      // process the form
      if ($params['playwright'] == 'beckett')
          echo '"Go on failing. Go on. Only next time, try to fail
              better."';
      if ($params['playwright'] == 'ionesco')
          echo '"Ideologies separate us. Dreams and anguish bring us
              together."';
      if ($params['playwright'] == 'genet')
          echo '"Anyone who knows a strange fact shares in its
              singularity."';
      if ($params['playwright'] == 'stoppard')
          echo '"Life is a gamble, at terrible odds - if it was a bet
              you wouldn\'t take it. "';
      echo '<br />--'.array_search(
        $params['playwright'],$playwrights);
      }
$smarty->assign('form_start',$this->CreateFormStart($id,
  'default', $returnid));
$smarty->assign('input_playwright',
  $this->CreateInputRadioGroup($id, 'playwright', $playwrights,
    isset($params['playwright'])?$params['playwright']:''));
$smarty->assign('submit',
  $this->CreateInputSubmit($id, 'submit', 'Display a Quotation'));
$smarty->assign('form_end', $this->CreateFormEnd());
echo $this->ProcessTemplate('form.tpl');
?>
```

3. In your module's templates directory, create a file named "form.tpl" containing the following:

```
{$form_start}
  <p>{$input_playwright}</p>
  <p>{$submit}</p>
{$form_end}
```

4. Log in to your CMS Administration area.
5. Using the top menu, go to "**Extensions**" and click on "**Modules**".
6. Scroll down the list until you find "**Absurdists**" and click the "**Install**" link next to it.
7. Using the top menu, go to "**Content**" and select "**Pages**".
8. Click on the "**Add New Content**" button.

Using the Module Form API

9. In the "**Title**" and "**Menu Text**" fields, enter "**Absurdists**".

10. In the "**Content**" text area, turn off the WYSIWYG editor (if it's enabled), and type in the following:

    ```
    <p>Theatre of the Absurd is predicated on the idea that there is
    no fundamental purpose. Some notable playwrights in the movement
    include:</p>
    {Absurdists}
    ```

11. Go to your new "**Absurdists**" page on the user side:

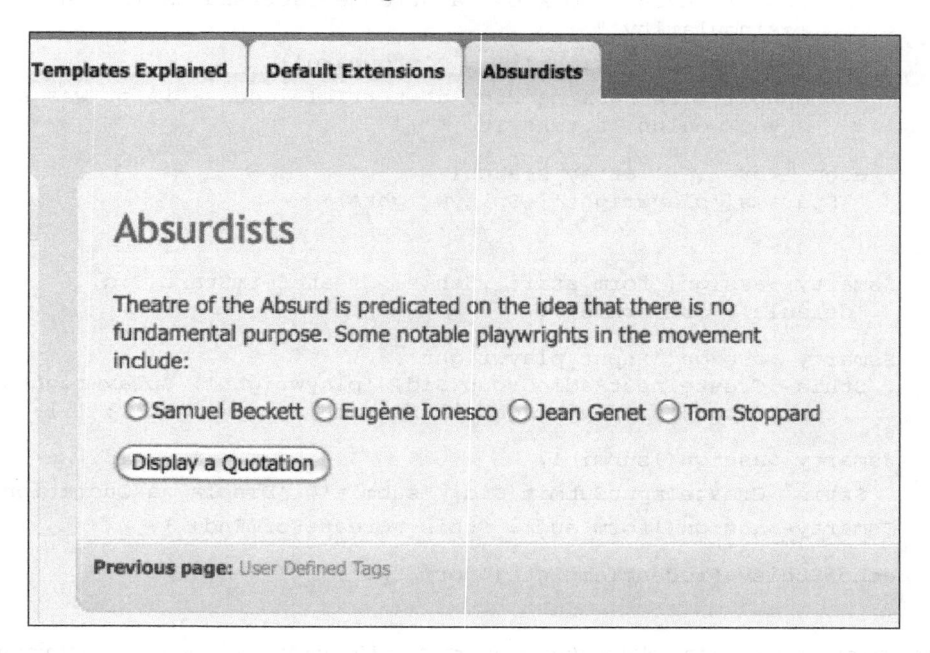

    | Templates Explained | Default Extensions | Absurdists |

    Absurdists

    Theatre of the Absurd is predicated on the idea that there is no fundamental purpose. Some notable playwrights in the movement include:

    ○ Samuel Beckett ○ Eugène Ionesco ○ Jean Genet ○ Tom Stoppard

    (Display a Quotation)

    Previous page: User Defined Tags

12. Click on a radio button and then the "**Display a Quotation**" button.

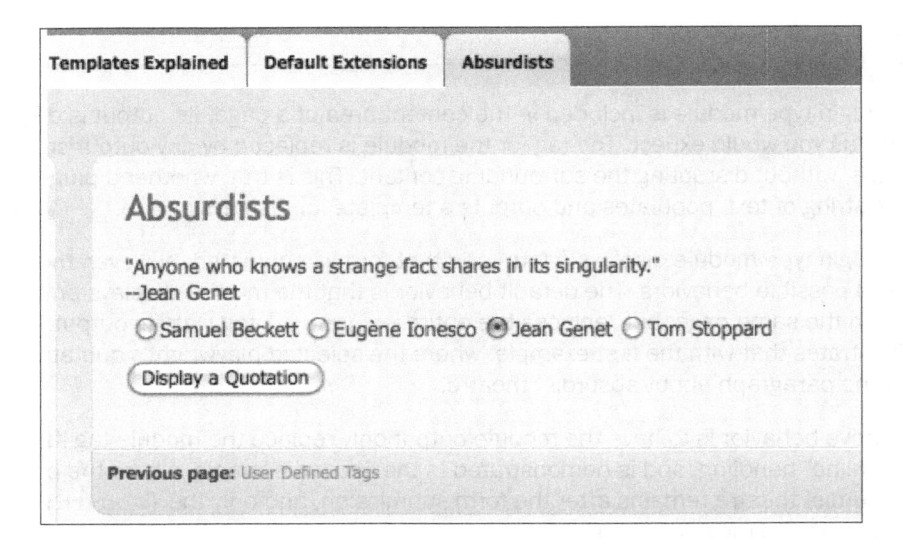

13. Edit your `action.default.php`, and change the line where the `form_start` variable is set to:

    ```
    $smarty->assign('form_start',
      $this->CreateFormStart($id, 'default',
      $returnid,'post','',true));
    ```

14. Once again, go to your "**Absurdists**" page on the user side, select a radio button, and click on the "**Display a Quotation**" button:

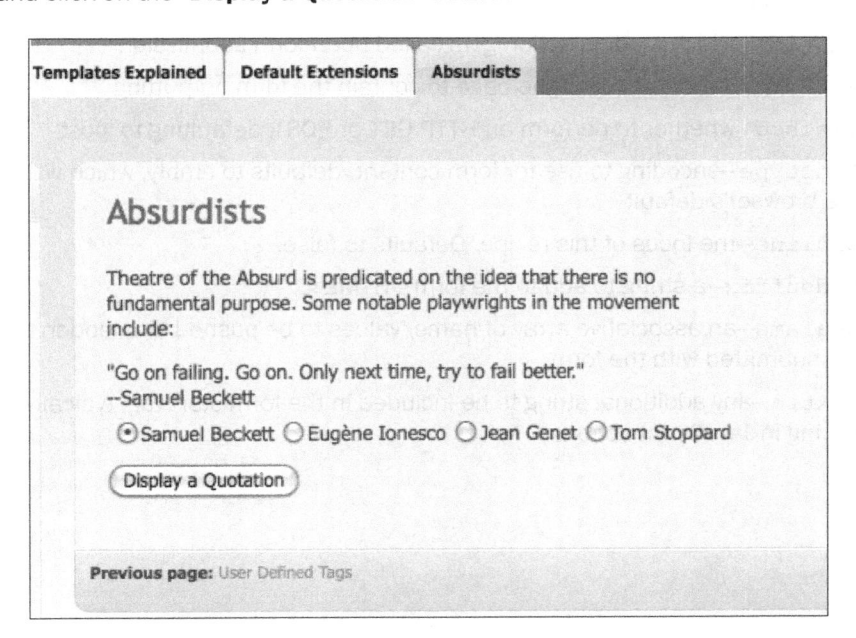

Using the Module Form API

How it works...

When a plugin type module is included in the content area of a page, its output is displayed very much as you would expect. The tag for the module is replaced by any output created by the module, without disrupting the surrounding content. This is true whether a plug-in module outputs a string of text, populates and outputs a template, or displays a form.

When a plugin type module displays a form and that form is submitted, however, there are several possible behaviors. The default behavior is that the module displays any form response in the same page, but replaces the entire {content} tag with its output. This recipe illustrates that with the first example, where the selected playwright's quotation replaces the paragraph about absurdist theatre.

An alternative behavior is to have the module output only replace the module tag itself. This is called "inline" handling, and is demonstrated in the second example, where the paragraph about absurdist theatre remains after the form submission, and only the {Absurdists} tag is replaced with the module output.

You can specify how you want your module form to behave when you declare your form start. The CreateFormStart() method has a Boolean parameter for inline behavior, which defaults to false. To change this, you'll need to make the call to CreateFormStart() with more than the typical three parameters, however, since this flag is the sixth parameter to the function. To review, the parameters to CreateFormStart() are:

- $id—the module identifier, to differentiate from other module forms on the same page
- $action—which module action gets called upon form submission
- $returnid—content ID of the page to contain the form outputting
- $method—whether to perform an HTTP GET or POST, defaulting to 'post'
- $enctype—encoding to use for form content, defaults to empty, which will use the browser's default
- $inline—the focus of this recipe. Defaults to false.
- $idsuffix—a string to add to the form's HTML ID
- $params—an associative array of name/values to be pushed into hidden fields that get submitted with the form
- $extra—any additional string to be included in the form start tag, typically used for linking in JavaScript actions

There's more...

In addition to the default and inline behaviors for form submission, there is yet another possible behavior, which is explored in a separate recipe in this chapter. This other approach causes any results of a form submission displayed in a different page than the one containing the form.

See also

- *Creating a basic form in a module* recipe
- *Chapter 4, Using Smarty variables and templates with a module* recipe
- *Embedding your module output in a different page after a form submission* recipe

Embedding your module output in a different page after a form submission

You may want to display a module's form submission response in a page other than the page containing the form. The form API has a provision for doing exactly that. This recipe will show you how.

How to do it...

1. Create a plugin type module stub using any of the approaches described in *Chapter 4, Getting Started with Modules*. Call your module "Flavors".
2. Using your favorite text editing program, change your module's action.default.php to the following:

```
<?php
if (!isset($gCms)) exit;

$flavors = array('Sour'=>'sour', 'Bitter'=>'bitter',
   'Sweet'=>'sweet', 'Salty'=>'salty', 'Umami'=>'umami');

if (isset($params['flavor']))
  {
  echo 'Yum ... '.array_search($params['flavor'],$flavors);
  return;
  }

$smarty->assign('form_start',
   $this->CreateFormStart($id, 'default', $params['target']));
```

Using the Module Form API

```
    $smarty->assign('input_flavor',
      $this->CreateInputRadioGroup($id, 'flavor', $flavors));

    $smarty->assign('submit',
      $this->CreateInputSubmit($id, 'submit', 'Submit'));
    $smarty->assign('form_end', $this->CreateFormEnd());

    echo $this->ProcessTemplate('form.tpl');
    ?>
```

3. In your module's templates directory, create a file named "`form.tpl`" containing the following:

```
{$form_start}
  <p>{$input_flavor}</p>
  <p>{$submit}</p>
{$form_end}
```

4. Log in to your CMS Administration area.
5. Using the top menu, go to "**Extensions**" and click on "**Modules**".
6. Scroll down the list until you find "**Flavors**" and click the "**Install**" link next to it.
7. Using the top menu, go to "**Content**" and select "**Pages**".
8. Click on the "**Add New Content**" button.
9. In the "**Title**" and "**Menu Text**" fields, enter "**You Say...**".
10. In the "**Content**" text area, type "**this will be replaced**" and click on the "**Submit**" button.
11. In the content list, click to edit your new "**You Say...**" page. Look at the URL in your browser's address bar for the part where it says `content_id=X`, where X is some number. Remember this number.
12. Click on the "**Cancel**" button.
13. Click on the "**Add New Content**" button.
14. In the "**Title**" and "**Menu Text**" fields, enter "**Flavors**".
15. In the "**Content**" text area, turn off the WYSIWYG editor (if it's enabled), and type in the following:

    ```
    <p>Pick your favorite:</p>
    ```

    ```
    {cms_module module='Flavor' target='79'}
    ```

16. Click on the "**Submit**" button.
17. Go to your new "Flavors" page on the user side.

Chapter 6

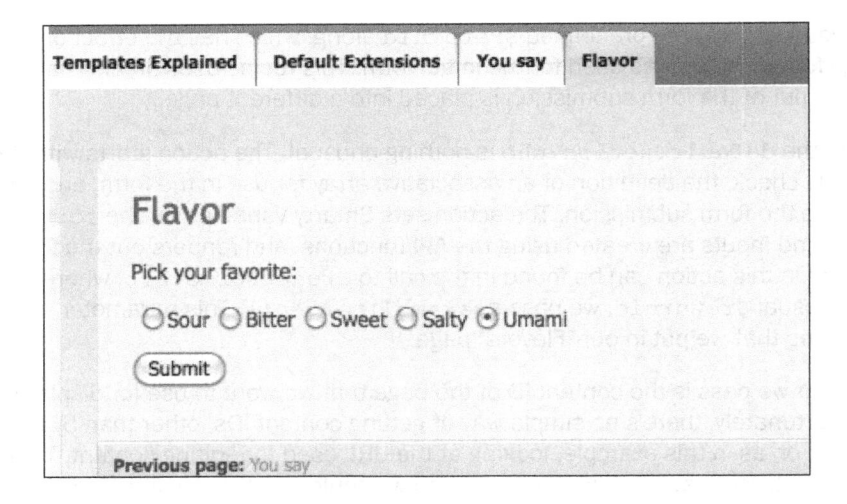

18. Select one of the radio buttons, and click on "**Submit**". View the result, and note that it's on the "**You say...**" page.

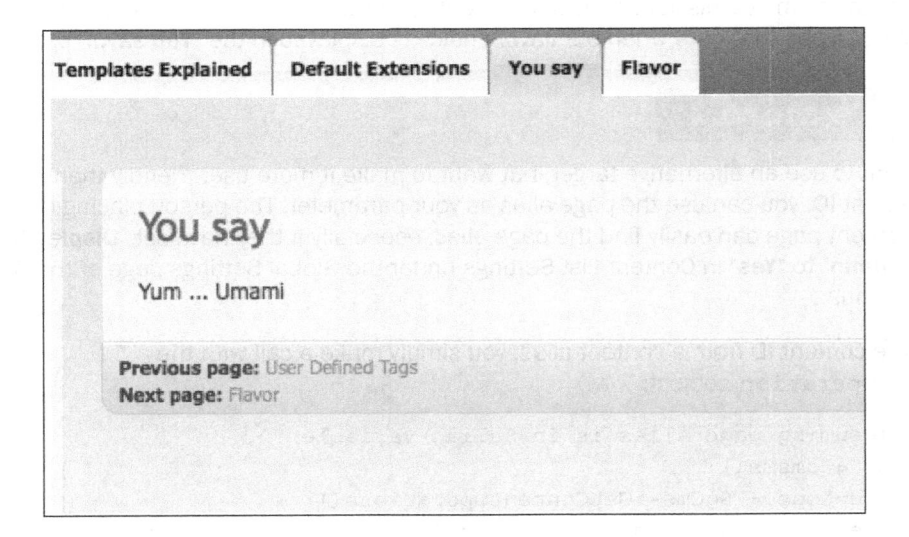

How it works...

When you create a form declaration with the module's Form API, you almost always pass at least three variables. The `$id` tells the CMS which module to pass the parameters, and the `$action` tells which module action to execute. The third variable, `$returnid`, tells the CMS which page to use to "contain" the output.

Using the Module Form API

Normally, you just pass the predefined `$returnid` along, which has the effect of using the same page for output as was used for the initial form. This recipe uses an alternative content id, so the output of the form submission is placed into a different page.

The code in the `default.action.php` is nothing unusual. The action starts with the `$gCms` safety check, the definition of an associative array for use in the form, and code for responding to the form submission. The action sets Smarty variables for the `form_start`, `form_end`, and inputs are created using the API functions, and renders out the form. The only atypical code in this action can be found in the call to `CreateFormStart`, where instead of passing the usual `$returnid`, we pass `$params['target']`. This parameter value is set in the module tag that we put in our "Flavors" page.

The value that we pass is the content ID of the page that we want to use for displaying the results. Unfortunately, there's no simple way of getting content IDs, other than by looking at the database or, as in this example, looking at the URL used for editing content. That's why we created our target page first in this recipe, so we could find that ID and place it into the module tag.

When a form is declared using a `$returnid`, it will use that content page to display the results of the form submission, replacing the entire `{content}` tag in that destination page. We can see that here when our flavor choice is displayed in the "**You say...**" page.

There's more...

If you want to use an alternative target, but want to make it more user-friendly than requiring your content ID, you can use the page alias as your parameter. The person placing the tag into a content page can easily find the page alias, especially if they have set "**Display the Alias Column**" to "**Yes**" in Content List Settings under the Global Settings page of the Site Admin menu.

To get the content ID from a content alias, you simply make a call with the `ContentOperations` object:

```
// assuming page alias is in $alias variable
$gCms = cmsms();
$contentops = $gCms->GetContentOperations();
$content_id = $contentops->GetPageIDFromAlias( $alias );
```

Modules and multi-page forms

It often comes up that module authors want to embed different steps of a multi-page form operation into separate content pages. They put their module tag into each of the pages, and use the `$returnid` to direct from one to the other. Yet it never seems to work—the parameters vanish!

The reason you can't do this daisy-chaining of module actions and pages is that the module's `$id` variable is set on a per-page basis, and it won't match up on subsequent requests.

For what it's worth, it's probably better to have your multi-form module keep all its actions within a single content page anyway, since you don't have to worry about users entering directly in the midpoint of the process by going to a later content page. Your module can handle the state, and your subtemplates can be used to visually separate the steps.

See also

- *Creating a basic form in a module* recipe
- *Chapter 4, Using Smarty variables and templates with a module* recipe
- *Making your module display its output without disrupting the rest of the page* recipe

Creating checkboxes that always submit a value

When working with HTML forms, many programmers are surprised to learn that a checkbox only submits a value if the box is checked. There are a number of ways to deal with this situation. This recipe shows one technique that helps make the processing of form data more compact and less error-prone.

How to do it...

- Create a plugin type module stub using any of the approaches described in *Chapter 4, Getting Started with Modules*. Call your module "Drinks". Make sure your `SetParameters()` method makes a call to `RegisterModulePlugin()`.
- Using your favorite text editing program, change your module's `action.default.php` to the following:

```
<?php
if (!isset($gCms)) exit;

if (isset($params['submit']))
  {
  if (isset($params['milk']))
    {
    $this->SetPreference('tea',$params['milk']);
    }
```

Using the Module Form API

```
        echo 'A proper cup of tea '.
           $this->GetPreference('tea','avoids').' milk.';
      }
    $smarty->assign('form_start',
        $this->CreateFormStart($id, 'default', $returnid));
    $smarty->assign('input_milk',
        $this->CreateInputCheckbox($id, 'milk', 'contains',
        $this->GetPreference('tea')).
        $this->CreateLabelForInput($id, 'milk', 'Tea requires milk'));
    $smarty->assign('submit',
        $this->CreateInputSubmit($id, 'submit', 'Submit'));
    $smarty->assign('form_end', $this->CreateFormEnd());
    echo $this->ProcessTemplate('form.tpl');
    ?>
```

- In your module's templates directory, create a file named "`form.tpl`" containing the following:
  ```
  {$form_start}
    <p>{$input_milk}</p>
    <p>{$submit}</p>
  {$form_end}
  ```
- Log in to your CMS Administration area.
- Using the top menu, go to "**Extensions**" and click on "**Modules**".
- Scroll down the list until you find "**Drinks**" and click the "**Install**" link next to it.
- Using the top menu, go to "**Content**" and select "**Pages**".
- Click on the "**Add New Content**" button.
- In the "**Title**" and "**Menu Text**" fields, enter "**Tea**".
- In the "**Content**" text area, type "**{Drinks}**" and click on the "**Submit**" button.
- On the user side, go to your new Tea page. Check the checkbox, and click on "**Submit**".

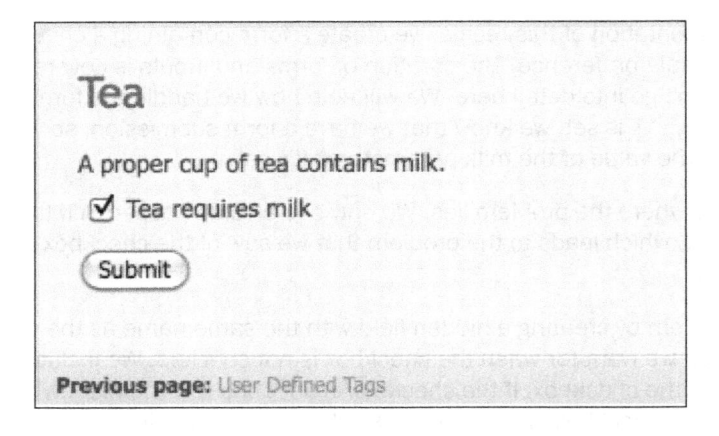

> [Screenshot: Tea page showing "A proper cup of tea contains milk." with checked "Tea requires milk" checkbox and Submit button.]

- Uncheck the checkbox, and click "**Submit**" again. Ponder why the tea is still requiring milk.
- Alter the checkbox creation code in `action.default.php` to the following:

  ```
  $smarty->assign('input_milk',
    $this->CreateInputHidden($id,'milk','avoids').
    $this->CreateInputCheckbox($id, 'milk', 'contains',
      $this->GetPreference('tea')).
    $this->CreateLabelForInput($id, 'milk', 'Tea requires milk'));
  ```

- On the user side, go to your new Tea page. Uncheck the checkbox, and click on "**Submit**".

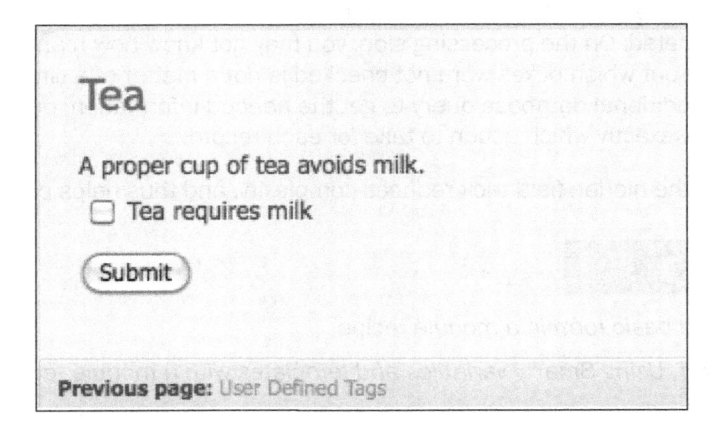

> [Screenshot: Tea page showing "A proper cup of tea avoids milk." with unchecked "Tea requires milk" checkbox and Submit button.]

How it works...

This recipe actually points out a peculiarity in the HTML standard, dating back to the HTML 2.0 standard (RFC 1866), where it is stated that an unchecked checkbox in a form should not submit anything back to the server.

Using the Module Form API

In our first implementation of this recipe, we create a form containing a checkbox, and use it to set a module preference. The creation of forms and inputs is covered in other recipes, so we won't go into detail here. We will note how we handle the form submission: if $params['submit'] is set, we know that we have a form submission, so we set the milk preference using the value of the milk parameter, if it's set.

This, of course, is where the problem lies. We only see a value passed in if the checkbox has been checked, which leads to the problem that we saw of the checkbox unintentionally being rechecked.

We solve the problem by creating a hidden field with the same name as the checkbox field, and with the value we want for when the checkbox is not checked. We include this hidden field in the form before the checkbox. If the checkbox is not checked, the hidden field value comes through, while if the checkbox is checked, PHP will use the last value seen in the form, which will be the checkbox's value.

This way, we can set our preference value with the parameter with impunity—we can even remove the isset() test and not have to worry about warnings that the parameter is not defined.

There's more...

In this example, it would be just as easy to add an "else" clause to the conditional clause where we test to see if $params['milk'] is set. In that "else" clause, we could set the preference to "avoid," and get the same effect as the hidden field trick.

Consider the case where your form's purpose is to choose which records in a list should be kept and which deleted. On the processing side, you may not know how many records are in the list, so figuring out which boxes were not checked is not a matter of a simple conditional. You could do an additional database query to get the needed information, or you could use this trick to specify exactly which action to take for each record.

In cases like this, the hidden field trick reduces complexity, and thus helps prevent errors.

See also

- *Creating a basic form in a module* recipe
- *Chapter 4, Using Smarty variables and templates with a module* recipe

7
Your Module and the Community

In this chapter, we will cover:

- Creating an account on the CMS Made Simple Developer's Forge
- Adding your module to the Forge
- Creating your Subversion Repository
- Using Subversion while developing your module
- Publishing a module release
- Creating your Git repository
- Using Git while developing your module
- Deciding on Git versus Subversion

Introduction

Open Source software derives its strength and vitality from the community of people who create and use it. By sharing code that you develop for an Open Source project, you not only increase the value of the project, but the value of your code. The more useful functionality that the overall project has, the more users it will attract. The more users, the more testing, feedback, and possibly more contracts the developers will receive. In the ideal case, it forms a positive feedback loop that benefits everyone.

There's more to the community than just sharing code, of course. There are discussions where people help one another solve problems. There are people who help publicize the project. There are get-togethers that build a sense of camaraderie. All of these are components of the community. However, the central part of an Open Source community is the sharing of source.

There are multiple levels to sharing code: there is not only distribution of the final product, but there is also collaboration during development. To support both of these ends, the CMS Made Simple project has a subsection of the main website, which is called the Developer's Forge. The Forge serves as a central point for hosting modules or other CMS-related projects. It provides a release management system that integrates with the built-in Module Manager, so you can distribute your modules. It provides tracking systems for Bugs and Feature Requests, so you can interact with your end users in an organized fashion. It also provides source-control repositories, so you can have all the benefits of a revision-control system and collaborate with multiple developers.

This chapter has recipes that give a quick overview of signing up for the Developer's Forge, registering your project on the Forge, using two of the supported revision control systems, and releasing new versions of your project to the world. You'll see how to take advantage of all that the Forge offers, and how to foster an active community around your project.

Creating an account on the CMS Made Simple Developer's Forge

If you're going to share your modules with the rest of the world, there are two ways you can do it. You can create your own website, where you post your modules for download, and find some means of posting updates, tracking bugs, and managing feature requests. Once you have your site up and functioning, you'll need to somehow get the word out to other CMSMS users.

The other approach, of course, is to use the extant facilities of the CMS Made Simple Developer's Forge. The Forge is designed to make it easy for you to post your modules, manage bug reports (BRs), and track feature requests (FRs). As we'll see elsewhere in this chapter, the Forge also integrates source revision control, translation tools, and more.

Getting ready

To create an account on the Developer's Forge, all you need is a web browser, a valid e-mail address, and a few minutes of your time.

How to do it...

1. With your web browser, go to `http://dev.cmsmadesimple.org`.
2. Click on the "**login**" icon on the right.

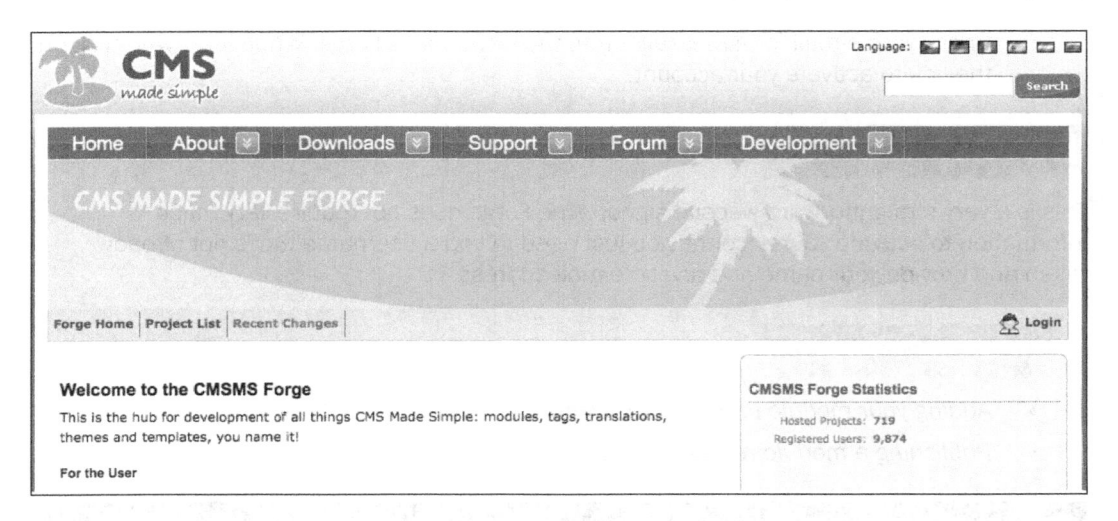

3. Under the login credentials form, click on the "**Sign Up**" link:

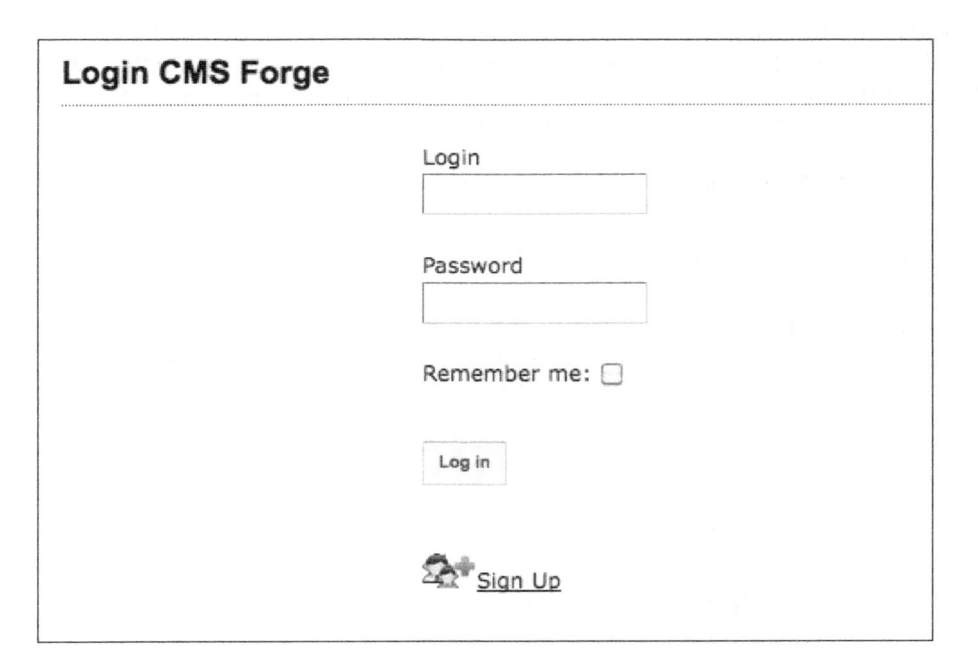

4. Fill in the form: place your desired username in the "**Login**" field, your full name, your e-mail, and your desired password in their respective fields. Click on the "**Signup**" button.

Your Module and the Community

5. Check your e-mail for a message from the Developer's Forge. When it arrives, click on the link to activate your account.

How it works...

This is a very straightforward website signup. The Forge does not require very much information to activate your account: you just need to find a username that's not already taken and provide your name and a valid e-mail address.

See also

- *Adding your module to the Forge* recipe
- *Publishing a module release* recipe

Adding your module to the Forge

Once you have an account on the Developer's Forge, you can share your module with the world. You don't need to have already written your module before adding it to the Forge. In fact, there are good reasons for adding it to the Forge before you begin writing it (so that you can have a source control repository, for example).

This recipe walks you through the process of adding your module to the Forge.

Getting ready

All you need at this point is a web browser, and an account on the CMS Made Simple Developer's Forge. This recipe assumes that the project you're publishing on the Forge is a module, but the basic steps are the same for all kinds of projects.

How to do it...

1. With your web browser, go to `http://dev.cmsmadesimple.org` and log in with your account.
2. Click on the "**Register New Project**" link.

Chapter 7

| Forge Home | Project List | My Page | Edit Profile | Recent Changes | | Logged in as: sjg - Logout |

Home Page for sjg

Personal Information
User Id: 110
Login Name: sjg

Participate
Register New Project

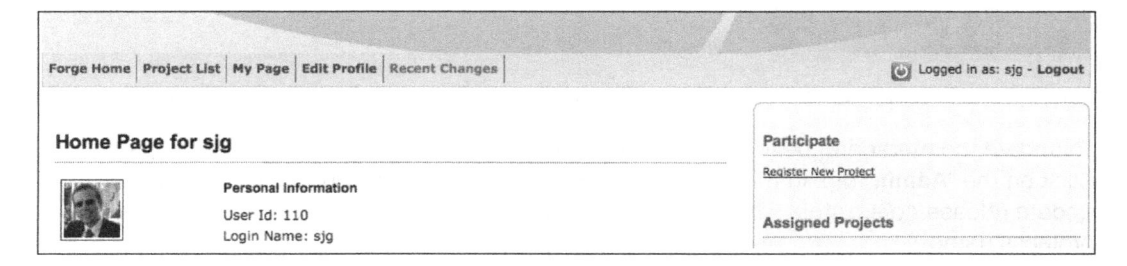

Assigned Projects

3. Start filling out the form by entering your module's name in the "**Full Name**" field.
4. In the "**Unix Name**" field, come up with a "machine-friendly" name for your module—it should be short and contain only alphanumeric characters. This will be used in the URL for your project.
5. In the "**Project Purpose**" field, give a brief explanation of the reason someone would use your module.
6. In the "**Description**" field, give a description of your module. This is what most people will see when they're reading about your module on the Developer's Forge.
7. In the "**Project Type**" drop-down, select "**Module**".
8. In the "**License**" drop-down, select the license you wish to use for your module.
9. For repository type, select your preferred revision control system (other recipes in this chapter can be used to help you choose). For this example, we'll use Subversion, so select "SVN".
10. Click on the "**Register**" button.
11. Await the e-mail telling you that your project has been approved.

How it works...

When you register your module on the Developer's Forge, the information is sent to the Forge administrators for approval. Once they approve your project, several things happen:

- First, the system adds your module's details to the database, which means people visiting the Forge can find your project when they search.
- Next, the system creates a Bug Tracker and a Feature Request system for your module, which means that you have a structured way of interacting with your user community.
- Last but not least, the system creates a revision control repository for you (unless you opted to use GitHub).

Once your project is approved, you can begin using these facilities immediately.

Your Module and the Community

There's more...

Forge projects can have more metadata than you enter when you first register them.

To update the metadata, begin by logging in to the Forge and going to your project's page. Click on the "**Admin**" tab. In this panel, you can update details on your project, add tags, update release notes, state when you think your next release will occur, or even change the project's name.

This Admin panel is also your interface for adding collaborators to your project. Checking the "**Show Request to Join**" checkbox will cause a link to show on the project's page, that lets other Forge users request to participate in your project (you can approve or deny on a per-request basis). Even without that checkbox checked, this panel allows you to add Forge users with permission to contribute to or administer the project.

See also

- *Creating an account on the CMS Made Simple Developer's Forge* recipe
- *Adding your module to the Forge* recipe
- *Creating your Subversion Repository* recipe
- *Chapter 4, Making a module localizable recipe (Apply necessary styles)*s
- *Publishing a module release* recipe

Creating your Subversion Repository

The value of a source-code revision control system cannot be overstated. It enables distributed development—multiple people can work on code simultaneously without worrying about clobbering one another's work. It takes the risk out of making changes, since you can always see what code changed, when it changed, and who changed it. There is a learning curve to using revision control, but once you get the hang of it, you'll never want to go back to keeping backup zip files or directories again.

> Subversion, also known as "SVN", is one of the most popular revision control systems in use today, and is one of the choices available for projects on the CMS Made Simple Developer's Forge.

This recipe shows how to import your project into SVN.

Getting ready

This recipe assumes that you have already created an account on the Developer's Forge, in this case with the username "`coder123`". We further assume that your project is a module that implements a "What You Get Is What You Actually Meant" editor called "WYGIWYAM" and that the UNIX name on the Developer's Forge is "wygiwyam". Last, we'll assume that you chose "SVN" as your repository type, and that you're using the command-line for interacting with Subversion.

How to do it...

1. In your terminal, go to your module's directory:

   `cd modules/wygiwyam`

2. Create a main branch in the SVN repository named "`trunk`":

   `svn mkdir http://svn.cmsmadesimple.org/svn/wygiwyam/trunk -m "Created Trunk" --username coder123`

3. Import your module into the repository:

   `svn import http://svn.cmsmadesimple.org/svn/wygiwyam/trunk -m "Initial import"`

4. Now, you will want your module directory to be a working set, so rename it and check it out as a working set:

   `cd ..`

   `mv wygiwyam wygiwyam.old`

   `svn checkout http://svn.cmsmadesimple.org/svn/wygiwyam/trunk wygiwyam`

How it works...

While there are many ways of using Subversion for revision control, a conventional organization involves a "`trunk`", that is the main line of development. From this trunk, developers can create "branches", which are copies of the trunk that can be changed, committed, rolled back, and/or worked on without fear of damaging the main stream of development. When and if the code in a branch becomes approved for the main development line, it can be merged into the trunk.

Therefore, when creating a Subversion repository for our project, the first thing we do is create the trunk. Because Subversion uses directories within the main repository for the trunk and branches, we create our trunk with the "`svn mkdir`" command. The `-m` flag allows us to provide a message that will be associated with the change.

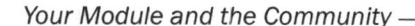

The `--username` flag, unsurprisingly, is how we authenticate ourselves to the server. It will challenge us for a password, that, in most cases, will be cached for subsequent operations.

Once we have the trunk established, we import our wygiwyam module.

The final thing we need to do before using the repository is make sure we're using a working set—the term for a local collection of code that's being managed by the repository. So we rename our original code directory, and check out a working copy. Within the checked out directory will be hidden `.svn` directories, that give Subversion the information it needs to know which repository the code belongs to and what the current state of the code is.

There's more...

You may choose to work with a GUI tool for Subversion rather than working from the command line. Under Windows, the TortoiseSVN (http://tortoisesvn.tigris.org/) client is very popular. On the Mac, there is SvnX (https://code.google.com/p/svnx/) and Linux boasts a variety of GUI clients, such as KDESvn (http://kdesvn.alwins-world.de/). There are also cross-platform tools like RapidSVN (http://rapidsvn.tigris.org/).

You will find that any of these GUI tools can do all of the steps outlined in this recipe, although they may require right-clicking or other mouse work.

Subversion Documentation

Even at its simplest, Subversion is a system with vast numbers of operations and commands. It is far more complex than can be documented here. Fortunately, there is an outstanding free guide to working with Subversion, which can be found online (http://svnbook.red-bean.com/).

See also

- *Creating an account on the CMS Made Simple Developer's Forge* recipe
- *Adding your module to the Forge* recipe
- *Using Subversion while developing your module* recipe

Using Subversion while developing your module

Subversion has dozens of commands, that, when coupled with their various options, result in hundreds or thousands of possible operations. Fortunately, for the purposes of developing small projects like CMS modules, only a small subset of these commands are used on a regular basis.

This recipe walks you through some typical use patterns.

Getting ready

You will need to have a project already committed into svn on the CMS Made Simple Developer's Forge. For the sake of this recipe, we'll say we're working on a database backup and restore module, that has the UNIX name "`dbrescue`". We also assume that you have a working set of the trunk checked out into a local directory.

How to do it...

1. Make sure you are in your module's directory:

    `cd modules/dbrescue`

2. Update your working set from the repository by typing the following command:

    `svn up`

3. Work on your module. Make changes, test, make more changes, until you feel like you've reached a point where your code is stable and is a state to which you might want to return. Check what's changed:

    `svn status`

4. Look at the output from the command:

    ```
    samuelg$ svn status
    M       dbrescue.module.php
    M       templates/error.tpl
    ?       templates/rescue.tpl
    ```

5. The question mark indicates that Subversion doesn't know about a file. If you're going to want to commit it, you need to tell Subversion with the "`add`" command:

    `svn add templates/rescue.tpl`

6. Now, if you repeat your "`status`" command, you'll see that Subversion knows it will be committing the new file:

    ```
    samuelg$ svn status
    M       dbrescue.module.php
    M       templates/error.tpl
    A       templates/rescue.tpl
    ```

7. If you don't recall what changes you have made, ask Subversion to tell you:

    `svn diff templates/error.tpl`

8. The output will show you all of the changes:

    `samuelg$ svn diff templates/error.tpl`

Your Module and the Community

```
Index: templates/error.tpl
===================================================================
--- templates/error.tpl      (revision 2)
+++ templates/error.tpl      (working copy)
@@ -1,2 +1,3 @@
 <h3>{$title_error}</h3>
-{if $message!=''}<p>{$message}</p>{/if}
+{if $message!=''}<p class="error">{$message}</p>{/if}
```

9. If you're satisfied that the changes make sense and that you want to preserve them, commit your changeset:

   `svn commit -m "Updated database handling, added CSS class to error messages."`

10. Repeat this process.

How it works...

Working with Subversion can be quite simple. As this recipe shows, you can check out the latest changes using the "`svn update`" command (that also accepts the convenient abbreviation "`svn up`"). After updating, your working copy will be up-to-date with the latest version in the repository.

As you work, your local copy of the code gets out of synch with the version in the repository. Subversion helps you identify the changes that you've made. The "`status`" and "`diff`" commands are very helpful for identifying which files you have made changes to, and what those changes are.

When you're ready to preserve your changes, you commit to the repository. If you omit the `-m` flag, Subversion will open up an editor for you to enter your commit message. It's important to give a good commit message: you'll refer to commit messages when you want to understand changes that you or other people made, when you release a module and are writing the changelog and release notes, or just to remind yourself of what you were thinking when you modified a particular file.

There's more...

If you're working with other people on your project, you may discover that someone else has also made changes while you've been doing your work. When you go to commit, you'll receive an error message:

`svn: Commit failed (details follow):`
`svn: File or directory 'dbrescue.module.php' is out of date; try updating`

```
svn: resource out of date; try updating
```

If this happens, normally you'll perform an update, and Subversion will take care of merging all of the changes:

```
svn up
```

Normally, you'll see a message "**At Revision X**" where X is the current committed revision number. Then you can check in your code.

But sometimes the changes are too complicated for Subversion to resolve without intervention: this is when you have made a change in the same line(s) as someone else, but they have committed their code first. This is called a conflict, and it's your responsibility as the second committer to resolve it. You'll know there's a conflict from the scary message that Subversion sends you:

```
samuelg$ svn up
Conflict discovered in 'dbrescue.module.php'.
Select: (p) postpone, (df) diff-full, (e) edit,
        (mc) mine-conflict, (tc) theirs-conflict,
        (s) show all options:
```

At this point, look at the conflicted file by responding "`dc`" for "display conflict". Usually, you'll quickly see what the problem is:

```
    function MinimumCMSVersion()
    {
<<<<<<< MINE (select with 'mc') (225)
       return "1.9.1";
||||||| ORIGINAL (225)
       return "1.8";
=======
       return "1.9";
>>>>>>> THEIRS (select with 'tc') (225)
```

In this case, both coders updated the minimum CMS Version from 1.8, but chose different values. In this case, we'll go with the more specific requirement, and key in "`mc`" to tell Subversion that my version is the correct one. Once the conflict is resolved, you can once again check in your changes normally with "`svn commit`".

More useful Subversion commands

As stated before, Subversion has many commands and operations, and this recipe just scratches the surface of what you can do with it. For in-depth documentation, refer to the free guide that can be found online (http://svnbook.red-bean.com/).

Here are a few other commands that you might find useful in day-to-day work:

- svn log—displays the commit messages for a given file
- svn mv—rename a file in the repository
- svn rm—remove a file from the repository
- svn revert—undo a change that you had not yet committed, like an add, rename, or delete
- svn copy—used to make copies of a repository, which is how Subversion handles branching
- svn merge—used to merge changes between different branches of a project

Viewing and reverting to earlier revisions

One of the powerful features of using Subversion, and indeed its primary purpose, is maintaining access to different revisions.

For example, you can check the log to see what's changed:

```
samuelg$ svn log dbrescue.module.tpl
------------------------------------------------------------------------
r77 | samuelg | 2010-11-22 21:10:11 -0800 (Mon, 22 Nov 2010) | 1 line

Fix for Forge bug report #3744, switched preg_replace with str_replace
------------------------------------------------------------------------
r75 | samuelg | 2010-11-20 14:05:32 -0800 (Sat, 20 Nov 2010) | 19 lines

Tried to optimize the admin display queries.
```

Once you know which version you want to compare, you can use a command you already know, "diff" to compare two versions:

```
samuelg$ svn diff -r r77 dbrescue.module.tpl


Index: dbrescue.module.tpl
===================================================================
--- dbrescue.module.tpl     (revision 77)
+++ dbrescue.module.tpl     (working copy)
```

```
- $result = preg_replace('/class="([^"]+)"/','class="$1_list"',$result);
+ $result = str_replace('class="admin"','class="admin_list"', $result);
```

The output format is a bit cryptic, but it's not too hard to see what the change was. Lines that were removed are prefixed with a minus sign, while lines that were added are prefixed with a plus sign. A changed line is the equivalent of a deletion and an addition, which is how this one-line change is shown.

The `-r` flag, designating version, can be used in a large number of Subversion commands. When used with some commands like "diff" it can take two revision numbers separated by a colon (for example, `svn diff -r r12:r22`).

When used with commands like "checkout", the `-r` flag allows you to check out previous revisions of your code, and can be used on a single file, a directory, or an entire working set.

See also

- *Creating an account on the CMS Made Simple Developer's Forge* recipe
- *Adding your module to the Forge* recipe
- *Creating your Subversion Repository* recipe

Publishing a module release

So you've been working on your module for some time now, and you've gotten it to a state where it's useful. You created a project for it on the Developer's Forge, and you've been committing it to Subversion.

As it is, people can already take advantage of your module. They can click over to the "**Code**" tab of the project page, and get the details so that they can check it out of Subversion. Still, the vast majority of CMS users don't have the knowledge or skills to use Subversion—wouldn't it be great if your module would just automatically show up for them in the Module Manager?

By formally creating a module release, that's exactly what will happen. This recipe shows you how.

Getting ready

This recipe assumes that you already have a module under development, and that you also have a Developer's Forge account.

Your Module and the Community

How to do it...

1. Log in to your CMS Administration area.
2. Using the top menu, go to "**Extensions**" and click on "**Modules**".
3. Click on the "**XML**" button next to your module, and save the exported file in some easily accessible directory.

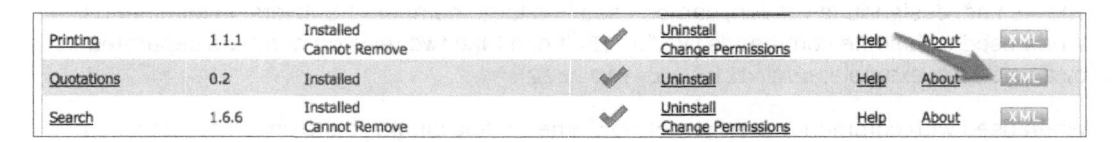

Printing	1.1.1	Installed Cannot Remove	✓	Uninstall Change Permissions	Help	About	XML
Quotations	0.2	Installed	✓	Uninstall	Help	About	XML
Search	1.6.6	Installed Cannot Remove	✓	Uninstall Change Permissions	Help	About	XML

4. With your browser, log in to your CMS Developer's Forge account. On the top navigation, click on "**My Page**".
5. In the right-hand pane, click on the name of your project under "**Assigned Projects**".
6. Click on the "**Admin**" tab for your project.
7. Scroll down to the "**File Packages**" pane. Since this is your first release, create a file package by typing "**Releases**" into the "**Add File Package**" text field, and click the "**Add Package**" button.

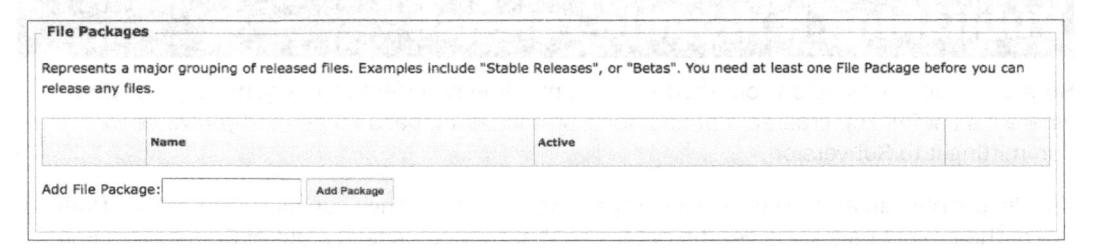

File Packages

Represents a major grouping of released files. Examples include "Stable Releases", or "Betas". You need at least one File Package before you can release any files.

| Name | Active |

Add File Package: [   ] [Add Package]

---

8. Scroll back down to the "**File Packages**" pane, and click on the "**Add Release**" button next to your new "**Releases**" file package.

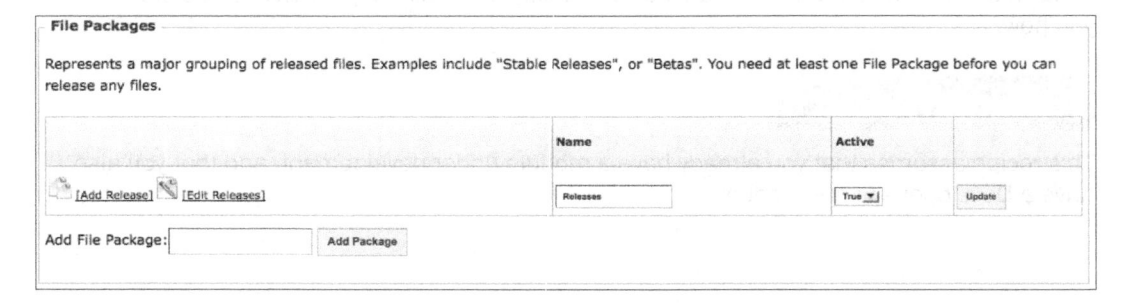

File Packages

Represents a major grouping of released files. Examples include "Stable Releases", or "Betas". You need at least one File Package before you can release any files.

| | Name | Active | |
| [Add Release] [Edit Releases] | Releases | True ▼ | Update |

Add File Package: [   ] [Add Package]

Chapter 7

9. We're releasing version 1.0 of our module, so enter "**1.0**" in the "**Release Name**" field.
10. Check the box to add this version to the bug tracker, and click "**Create New Release**".
11. You will see the "**Edit Release**" page. Start by entering your release notes and change log into the provided text areas, and click on the "**Update Release**" button.
12. The page will reload and report that the release has been updated. Scroll down to the "**Add Files to Release**" pane. Use the browse button to find your module's XML file on your local filesystem (from step 3).
13. Click the "**Upload**" button.

How it works...

When someone is using a CMS Made Simple installation, and clicks on the Module Manager in their admin area, they are looking at the published releases that are exported from the Developer's Forge. While the Developer's Forge knows about modules and other code that it manages in revision control, it only exports code to the Module Manager from formal releases that have been uploaded in XML format. So to publish your module, the first step is to obtain an XML file for it.

The CMS Made Simple admin area allows you to export any active module into an XML file. As long as your web server is configured correctly, clicking on the XML button will force the generation of the file, and your browser will ask you to save it.

The next few steps are creating a file package on the Developer's Forge. File packages are an organizational tool for code published on the Forge for cases where you need more than just version numbers. For example, if you want to formally release beta and release candidate packages for each version of your module, you could put those in separate file packages. Similarly, if you had different development trees for your module for use under different versions of PHP, you could have a file package for PHP 4.x, PHP 5.x, and so on. In our case, however, we did the minimum required and created a "**Releases**" file package for all of our releases.

Once we have a file package, we create a release within that package. When creating a release, it's common practice to name the release for the version of the module. By checking the box to add the release to the Bug Tracker, it allows people reporting bugs to tie the report to a specific version of the module.

Each release can have both release notes and a change log associated with it, that can be viewed by users on the Forge. These metadata describe the release to users, and are important reading for them.

Your Module and the Community

Although we uploaded a single XML file, a release may have more than one file associated with it. Files other than the XML file will not appear to users in the Module Manager, but will be visible to users who look at the "**Files**" tab for a project on the Developer's Forge. This is often used to provide the module in alternative formats, such as a `.zip` file or a `.tar` file. It can also be used to provide optional data or assets that can be used with a module release. Even if uploading additional files for a given release, do not upload multiple XML files, or it will confuse the Module Manager.

Once you have created a release and uploaded a valid XML file for it, you're done. Your module will now be available to everyone via the Module Manager! Post a message in the Forum to tell people about your fantastic new module, tweet the news, and, perhaps, have yourself a glass of your favorite beverage to celebrate.

There's more...

The first thing you did when you created your release was adding release notes and a change log. What exactly is the distinction between these two descriptors? The terms are often used interchangeably, or together as a single title. There is no hard and fast rule for what information you place where, but here are some loose guidelines:

Release notes are for information regarding how people will use the release. It's the advertising copy for this release that tells people why they should upgrade. It also offers any warnings that might make someone decide not to upgrade—if you're releasing a new version that won't cleanly import data from a previous version, for example, this is the place to warn users. This is also where you might thank the people who contributed to the release, either as sponsors, coders, or testers.

The change log is more of a list of specific changes. It enumerates new features and new functionality. Some programmers list which bugs were fixed by providing the bug ID number from the Forge. The change log is sometime simply a cleaned up version of the output from a "`svn log`" command, a fact that should serve as an incentive for writing good commit messages.

See also

- *Creating an account on the CMS Made Simple Developer's Forge* recipe
- *Adding your module to the Forge* recipe
- *Using Subversion while developing your module* recipe

Creating your Git repository

In an earlier recipe, we discussed the value of using a source control system. Revision control not only allows you to track the history of a project and roll back to previous versions, but modern revision control systems enable distributed simultaneous development.

Git is a relative newcomer in the revision control world, but as it was designed by the original author of Linux, it has had a large audience from its inception. It's increasingly popular for open source development, and is one of the choices available for projects on the CMS Made Simple Developer's Forge. This recipe shows how to create a local Git repository and import your project into a remote repository on the Developer's Forge.

Getting ready

This recipe assumes that you have already created an account on the Developer's Forge with the username "`coder123`". Like in the Subversion recipe, we assume that your project is a module that implements a "What You Get Is What You Actually Meant" editor called "WYGIWYAM" and that the UNIX name on the Developer's Forge is "wygiwyam". Last, we'll assume that you chose "git" as your repository type, and that you're using the command-line for interacting with Git.

How to do it...

1. With your browser, log in to your CMS Developer's Forge account. On the top navigation, click on "**Edit Profile**".
2. If you haven't already added an SSH key, do so. For instructions for this process, go to `http://help.github.com/key-setup-redirect`.
3. If you haven't already configured your identity in git, type the following two commands (using your own name and e-mail address, as appropriate):

    `git config --global user.name "Isaac Newton"`

    `git config --global user.email "sir_isaac@cambridge.edu"`

4. In your terminal, go to your module's directory:

    `cd modules/wygiwyam`

5. Initialize your local git repository:

    `git init`

6. Tell git that the master repository is on the Developer's Forge:

    `git remote add origin git@git.cmsmadesimple.org:wygiwyam.git`

7. Add your module files to the repository and commit them:

    `git commit -am "Initial Import" *`

8. Push your local repository to the Developer's Forge:

    `git push origin master`

Your Module and the Community

How it works...

Unlike Subversion where there is a single central repository and everyone using it creates dependent working sets, Git is decentralized. Every developer working on a project keeps a copy of the entire repository along with its history, and when local branches are merged in, they get copied to everyone as well.

We create a local repository using the "`git init`" command—that's all there is to it. We could start working with it immediately, and have most of the benefits of revision control. We have our own repository with all of its power sitting entirely on our local filesystem.

But one of the reasons for using revision control software is to collaborate with others, so we need to give other people a way to access our repository. Instead of setting up a service on our local machine, it's preferable to set up a public repository on a shared server, in this case, the CMS Made Simple Developer's Forge.

So we use Git's "`remote`" command to tell it to use the Developer's Forge as a public repository. We give the remote repository the alias "`origin`", that follows a common naming convention for repositories that will be cloned by multiple people. The "`git@git.cmsmadesimple.org:wygiwyam.git`" is just a fancy form of resource locator for git, which you can get from your project's "**Code**" tab on the Developer's Forge.

Now, we can work on our module locally. Our first step is to add and commit all of our working files. We used a shortcut to do this: we added using the `-a` flag as part of the commit instead of separately adding the files and then committing.

In Git, our main working version of the repository is called "`master`" by convention, and since we have not created or checked out any new branches, our commit goes to the "`master`" branch. Even though we have informed Git about our remote repository, our commits don't automatically propagate. When we want to make the remote repository current with our changes, we have to push them using the "`git push`" command. We provide it with the alias of the remote repository (origin) and which branch we wish to push (master).

There's more...

> You may feel more comfortable working with a GUI tool than using the command line. There are some GUI tools for Git that make this possible. Under Windows, the TortoiseGIT (`https://code.google.com/p/tortoisegit/`) client, based on TortoiseSVN, is popular. On the Mac, there is GitX (`http://gitx.frim.nl/`) and Katana (`http://dekorte.com/projects/shareware/Katana/`). Linux boasts a variety of GUI clients, such as GitG (`http://git.gnome.org/browse/gitg/`). Git is distributed with a cross-platform tool called git-gui.

You will find that any of these GUI tools can do all of the steps outlined in this recipe, although, they may require right-clicking or other mouse work.

> Git is a complex system with large number of operations and commands. It is far more involved than can be fully documented here. Fortunately, the team that created GitHub, (a commercial enterprise providing free and paid remote repositories) has a good reference website documenting the use of Git. This site is online at http://gitref.org.

See also

- *Creating an account on the CMS Made Simple Developer's Forge* recipe
- *Adding your module to the Forge* recipe
- *Using Git while developing your module* recipe

Using Git while developing your module

Git is a feature-rich system, and has entire books documenting its uses. Unless you're creating a project as large and complex as the Linux kernel, however, you probably won't need to understand everything that Git can do.

This recipe demonstrates some typical approaches to using Git for managing a small project.

Getting ready

You will need to have your Git repository set up, with your project already committed into it. You will need to have set up a remote repository on the CMS Made Simple Developer's Forge. For the sake of this recipe, we'll say we're working on a mapping module, that has the UNIX name "ajaxmaps", and we're just starting the development of version 1.1 of the module.

How to do it...

1. Make sure you are in your module's directory:

    ```
    cd modules/ajaxmaps
    ```

2. Merge in any changes from the remote repository to your local master branch by typing the following command:

    ```
    git pull origin
    ```

3. Create a working branch:

   `git branch version1.1`

4. Check out the new branch:

   `git checkout version1.1`

5. Work on your module. Make changes, test, make more changes, until you feel like you've reached a point where your code is stable and is a state to which you might want to return. Check what's changed:

   `git status`

6. Look at the output from the command:

   ```
   samuelg$ git status
   # On branch version1.1
   #
   # Changed but not updated:
   #   (use "git add <file>..." to update what will be committed)
   #
   #       modified:   action.generate_coords.php
   #       modified:   action.display_map.php
   #
   # Untracked files:
   #   (use "git add <file>..." to include in what will be committed)
   #
   #       action.update_map.php
   no changes added to commit (use "git add" and/or "git commit -a")
   ```

7. Git needs to be told which files it will be including in a commit, so we'll tell it to add the two modified files and the untracked file:

   `git add action.generate_coords.php action.display_map.php action.update_map.php`

8. Now we repeat our "`status`" command:

   ```
   samuelg$ git status
   # On branch version1.1
   # Changes to be committed:
   #   (use "git reset HEAD <file>..." to unstage)
   #
   #       modified:   action.generate_coords.php
   #       modified:   action.display_map.php
   ```

```
#   new file:      action.update_map.php
```

9. We're satisfied with our changes, so we commit them:

   ```
   git commit -m "Implemented feature to update maps, bug fixes."
   ```

10. Repeat this process as you develop the new version.

11. When we're ready to release this version, we will merge the branch into the master branch. We do this by checking out the master:

    ```
    git checkout master
    ```

12. And then merging in the branch:

    ```
    git merge version1.1
    ```

13. We might then want to push our code to the public remote repository. First, we merge in any changes on the remote:

    ```
    git pull origin
    ```

14. And then push our changes:

    ```
    git push origin master
    ```

How it works...

One of Git's specialties is making branching and merging simple and efficient. This encourages you as a developer to branch often. In this case, we're branching for each module version, but in complex projects you may want to branch every time you start work on any independent chunk of code.

In this recipe, before we branch, we use "git pull" to make sure we're in sync with the latest code in the remote repository. This command is a convenient single step way of issuing a "git fetch", that pulls down the latest code, and a "git merge", that merges that code with our local branch.

From there, we create a new branch, and check it out, so that any changes we make are to the branch rather than the master. We do our editing and adding, and then get ready to commit our changes. Git helps us identify our changes using the "git status" command, that identifies which files we have made changes to, and which new files we have created.

When you're ready to preserve your changes, you commit to the repository. First, we need to tell Git which of the modified or newly created files will be part of the commit. We do this using the "git add" command. Then, we issue the "git commit" itself. If we omit the -m flag, Git will open up an editor for us to enter a commit message.

Your Module and the Community

When we have finished making changes on a branch, we will eventually want to merge it back into the master branch. This process involves checking out the master branch. After doing the checkout, it will appear that all of our changes have vanished! However, there is no need to panic—Git is tracking all of our changes. To get our code back, we could simply check out our version 1.1 branch again, or, alternatively merge those changes into the master branch. In this recipe, we merge the version 1.1 branch into the master branch.

All of the changes we've made thus far are in our local repository. If we want to share these changes, we need to push them to the remote repository. This is where the "`git push`" command comes in; we tell it which remote repository we wish to push it to, and which branch. If we omit the remote branch, our push will default to the master branch.

There's more...

Git has many commands and operations, and this recipe just scratches the surface of what you can do with it.

> For in-depth Git documentation, refer to the documentation online (http://www.kernel.org/pub/software/scm/git/docs/user-manual.html) or read through the official Git tutorial (http://www.kernel.org/pub/software/scm/git/docs/gittutorial.html).

Here are a few other commands that you might find useful in day-to-day work:

- `git log`—displays the commit messages for a given file
- `git diff`—displays differences between a working file and the committed version (or between versions)
- `git rm`—removes a file in the current branch
- `git clone`—copies a public repository to a local filesystem
- `git tag`—labels a snapshot of the current state

Handling conflicts in Git

If there is parallel development going on with your project, you will be forced to merge changes when pushing to the remote repository. That's what we were doing when we issued the "git pull origin" before pushing our copy. Normally, this process is painless, and Git is able to cleanly merge the changes in the code.

However, situations can arise where multiple people make changes in the exact same lines of code, and the Git can't know which version is correct. In the case of a conflict, the pull will fail:

```
samuelg$ git pull origin master
remote: Counting objects: 5, done.
remote: Compressing objects: 100% (2/2), done.
```

```
remote: Total 3 (delta 1), reused 0 (delta 0)
Unpacking objects: 100% (3/3), done.
From git@git.cmsmadesimple.org:ajaxmaps
 * branch            master     -> FETCH_HEAD
Auto-merged action.generate_coords.php
CONFLICT (content): Merge conflict in action.generate_coords.php
Automatic merge failed; fix conflicts and then commit the result.
```

At this point, you have to manually resolve the conflict. If you edit the file, you will see diff-style markers in the code where Git ran into problems, and you can figure out how to resolve the issue. You can also use the Git "`mergetool`" command, that will open your choice of programs to help you visually resolve the conflict.

`git mergetool`

Using opendiff, your results may look something like:

`$counter +=1;`
`list($lat,$lon) = explode(',',$thisCoord);`
`// fixed wrong latitude for Tropic of Cancer`
`if ($lat == 23.5)`
`{`
`    $tropic = 'Cancer';`
`}`
`else if ($lat == -23.5)`
`{`
`    $tropic = 'Capricorn';`
`}`
	→	`$counter +=1;`
		`list($lat,$lon) = explode(',',$thisCoord);`
		`if ($lat == 23.5)`
		`{`
		`    $tropic = 'Cancer';`
		`}`
		`else if ($lat == -23.5)`
		`{`
		`    $tropic = 'Capricorn';`
		`}`

Using the tool, you can easily see where the conflict occurred, and resolve it. Then, you re-add your merged version, commit it, do another pull from the origin just to be sure, and then finally push your version:

```
samuelg$ git commit -m "Merged changes"
Created commit 35ca79e: Merged changes

samuelg$ git pull origin master
From git@git.cmsmadesimple.org:ajaxmaps
 * branch            master     -> FETCH_HEAD
Already up-to-date.

samuelg$ git push origin master
Counting objects: 10, done.
Compressing objects: 100% (4/4), done.
Writing objects: 100% (6/6), 620 bytes, done.
```

Your Module and the Community

```
Total 6 (delta 2), reused 0 (delta 0)
To git@git.cmsmadesimple.org:ajaxmaps.git
   340e5d2..35ca79e  master -> master
```

Now the conflict is resolved, and development can continue.

See also

- *Creating an account on the CMS Made Simple Developer's Forge* recipe
- *Adding your module to the Forge* recipe
- *Creating your Git repository* recipe

Deciding on Git versus Subversion

In this chapter, there are recipes using two different revision control systems: Git and Subversion. For a given project, however, you are not going to use both systems, which means you need to decide which to use.

This recipe will help you evaluate which system will be best for you.

How to do it...

- Consider the following table. For each row, decide which column better meets your needs.

A	B
Single Central Repository	Distributed Repository Copies
Branches are actual directories on the filesystem	Branches are maintained by the Software
Download only current versions of files on checkout	Download entire history of all files on checkout
Viewing history requires contacting server over the network	History is available locally
Branching and merging is an involved process	Branching and merging is easy
Excellent GUI tools for most Operating Systems	Fair GUI tools for most Operating Systems
Integration into most IDEs	Integrates into some IDEs
Easily supported by the CMS Made Simple Translation Center	Not easily supported by CMS Made Simple Translation Center
Widely used in Open Source Projects	Rapidly being adopted by Open Source Projects
Older, more established, and understood by more programmers	Younger, new kid on the block, being learned by many programmers

- If you selected Column A more than Column B, you should use Subversion
- If you selected Column B more than Column A, you should use Git

How it works...

The previous table tries to weigh the comparative features of the two revision control systems. Let's examine each point.

- Centralized versus Distributed Repository. Subversion has a single canonical repository, and everyone who works with the code keeps a subsidiary copy. Git is distributed, and each copy of a repository is equally authoritative.
- Organization of branches. Subversion makes physical directories for each branch, which means you can explore them on your local filesystem like any other files. Git manages branches internally, so you need to check out a branch to directly see the files.
- What gets copied on a checkout of a working set? With Subversion, you check out a specific revision (the most current version, unless you specify otherwise). When you clone a repository in Git, you copy the entire history of the project. When doing day-to-day commits and updates, Subversion transfers them to/from the central server, while Git only moves changes over the network when you tell it to.
- Where is the history? With Subversion, you need to contact the central repository to view file history. Git keeps it all locally, so you can access history even when you're offline.
- Branching and Merging. Subversion makes branching easy but merging has traditionally been more difficult, requiring that you remember which revision you branched from. With Subversion 1.5 and later, this has improved, but does not maintain some metadata across merges. Git is designed from the ground up to make branching and merging very simple.
- GUI Tools. Subversion has a number of excellent GUI tools on various platforms. While there are GUI tools for Git, they're not (yet) up to the overall quality level of the Subversion tools.
- IDE integration. Like GUI tools, there is generally excellent support for Subversion in programmers' IDEs, while support for Git is slowly catching up.
- The CMS Made Simple Translation Center was implemented using Subversion externals, and the integration is seamless. As yet, there is no equivalent integration for projects using Git.
- Popularity in Open Source projects. Subversion was released in 2000, and rapidly replaced the CVS revision control system. A huge number of projects use Subversion. Git was first released in 2005, and has been quickly gaining in acceptance.

- Subversion is older and more established than Git. There are more programmers who are familiar with Subversion than with Git. Both are popular projects with vibrant communities backing them.

There's more...

It probably goes without saying that a list of ten features cannot offer a comprehensive comparison of two complex systems. There are numerous benefits and annoyances with either system that are not detailed here. If you're interested, you can read many a discussion on the Internet where people argue the finer points of these systems (often with a religious fervor).

What's more, there is a svn-git bridge, which allows you to use a local Git repository while still committing to and checking out from a remote Subversion repository, so if you simply cannot make a decision, this is a possible approach. Still, experience would lead to the recommendation that you choose one system, and learn to use it. Both systems are powerful, and either will work for maintaining code and making it easy to collaborate with other programmers.

See also

- *Creating your Subversion Repository* recipe
- *Using Subversion while developing your module* recipe
- *Creating your Git repository* recipe
- *Using Git while developing your module* recipe

8
Creating Useful Admin Panels

In this chapter, we will cover:

- Creating an admin panel for your module
- Creating multiple tabs for your admin module
- Creating and enforcing new permissions for your module's administration
- Displaying a page in the CMS Admin without the surrounding theme
- Writing a line to the CMS Admin Log
- Displaying a message after installation
- Creating an admin-side input element from your module using a `ContentModule` block
- Hiding your module from Administrators who don't have permission to use it
- Creating a module-specific preference and admin panel to set it
- Displaying an alert in the CMS Admin from a module

Introduction

In the previous chapters, we have explored how modules can interact with the user side of your website. For many applications, your module will want to interact with the administrator of the site as well. Whether it is to allow the admin to update module-specific templates, to moderate user-side input, or simply to set module preferences, you will need to create interfaces for the site admin.

Creating Useful Admin Panels

In this chapter, we will cover creating and organizing admin-facing interfaces, will look at how to control access to those interfaces, and will explore a few approaches to communicating important messages to admin users.

> These recipes all require access to your site's Administration area with permission to "Modify Modules", as well as write access to the filesystem of the server where your CMS is installed. Several recipes require access to your site's Administration area with a less privileged account, such as an account that's part of the "Editor" group.

Creating an admin panel for your module

Before you can create an elaborate tabbed admin-side panel with forms and other feedback mechanisms, you need to take the basic step of creating an admin panel in the first place. The CMS Made Simple module API provides a number of methods for this purpose.

This recipe introduces the steps required to create an admin panel.

How to do it...

1. Using any of the methods described in *Chapter 4, Getting Started with Modules* create a new plugin type module stub for your Gift List Registry module, and call it `"GiftList"`.

2. Using your favorite editor, add the following method to `GiftList.module.php`:

   ```
   function HasAdmin()
     {
     return true;
     }
   ```

3. Create a new file in your editor, and type in the following:

   ```
   <?php
   if (!isset($gCms)) exit;

   echo "This is the Gift List Admin Area";
   ?>
   ```

4. Save this file as `"action.defaultadmin.php"` in your `modules/GiftList` directory.

5. Log in to your CMS Administration area. Using the top menu, go to "**Extensions**" and select "**Modules**".

6. Find "**GiftList**" in the module list, and click on the "**install**" link.

7. Using the top menu, go to "**Extensions**" and select "**GiftList**"

8. You will see the placeholder Admin panel.

| CMS | Content | Layout | Users & Groups | Extensions | Site Admin |

Extensions » GiftList

GiftList

This is the Gift List Admin Area

« Back to Menu

How it works...

For modules to appear in the Admin menu, they need to tell the CMS that they have an admin panel. This is accomplished in the `HasAdmin()` method, that, by default, returns `false`. When you override the method in your module and return a value of `true`, your module will appear in the "**Extensions**" menu.

If the admin clicks on this link, the CMS admin will call your module's default admin method. If you don't separate your module into multiple files, this call goes to your module's `DoAction()` method where the `$action` variable will be set to `"defaultadmin"`. Or, more typically, if your module is separated into multiple files, the CMS will load and execute your `action.defaultadmin.php`.

As shown in the example code, the first thing you'll want to do in your `action.defaultadmin.php` is verify that you are being called by the CMS. We do that by making sure that the `$gCms` reference to the `CmsObject` is in scope. After that, we are free to implement any code we want for our admin panel.

There's more...

When your module returns `true` for the `HasAdmin()` method, your module will automatically appear in the Admin menu. If you have specified a friendly name for the module (by overriding the `GetFriendlyName()` method to return a human-readable name), that name will appear in the menu; otherwise, the module's class name will appear. By default, the module will appear in the "**Extensions**" menu. You can change this, however, by overriding the default `GetAdminSection()` method.

This method simply needs to return a string telling the CMS which menu section it wants to be in. Valid values are:

- `main`—the Main menu tab.
- `content`—the Content menu
- `layout`—the Layout menu
- `usersgroups`—the "Users and Groups" menu
- `extensions`—the Extensions menu (this is the default)
- `siteadmin`—the "Site Admin" menu
- `myprefs`—the "My Preferences" menu
- `ecommerce`—the "E-Commerce" menu (if the e-commerce suite is installed)

See also

- *Chapter 4, Breaking a module into multiple files* recipe
- *Create and enforce new permissions for your module's administration* recipe
- *Hiding your module from Administrators who don't have permission to use it* recipe

Creating multiple tabs for your admin module

As anyone who has used the CMS Made Simple News module knows, a module can have a large number of configuration and management options available to the site administrator. To minimize confusion for the site administrator, it is important to organize those options in a clean, orderly fashion.

By dividing the admin panel into multiple tabs, your module can selectively hide or reveal collections of forms or other controls. This allows your interface to be less cluttered, and (one hopes) less confusing.

This recipe shows you how to create multiple tabs in your module admin, and how to place content into them.

How to do it...

1. Using any of the methods described in *Chapter 4, Getting Started with Modules* create a new plugin type module stub for your Movie Collection module, and call it "`Movies`".

2. Using your favorite editor, add a `HasAdmin()` method to `Movies.module.php` that returns a Boolean value of "true".

3. Create a new file in your editor, and type in the following:

```php
<?php
if (!isset($gCms)) exit;

$tab = '';
if (!empty($params['active_tab']))
  {
  $tab = $params['active_tab'];
  }
$smarty->assign('tab_headers',
  $this->StartTabHeaders().
  $this->SetTabHeader('movies','Movies', ('movies' == $tab)).
  $this->SetTabHeader('categories','Categories',
     ('categories' == $tab)).
  $this->SetTabHeader('settings','Settings',
     ('settings' == $tab)).
  $this->EndTabHeaders().
  $this->StartTabContent()
  );
$smarty->assign('start_movies_tab',
  $this->StartTab('movies', $params));
$smarty->assign('start_categories_tab',
  $this->StartTab('categories', $params));
$smarty->assign('start_settings_tab',
  $this->StartTab('settings', $params));

$smarty->assign('tab_end',$this->EndTab());
$smarty->assign('tab_footer',$this->EndTabContent());

echo $this->ProcessTemplate('admin_panel.tpl');
?>
```

4. Save this file as "`action.defaultadmin.php`" in your `modules/Movies` directory.

5. Create a new file in your editor, and type in the following:

```
{$tab_headers}
   {$start_movies_tab}
      This shows up in the Movies Tab
   {$tab_end}
   {$start_categories_tab}
    This shows up in the Categories Tab
```

Creating Useful Admin Panels

```
            {$tab_end}
            {$start_settings_tab}
             This shows up in the Settings Tab
            {$tab_end}
        {$tab_footer}
```

6. Save this file as "admin_panel.tpl" in your modules/Movies/templates directory.
7. Log in to your CMS Administration area. Using the top menu, go to "**Extensions**" and select "**Modules**".
8. Find "**Movies**" in the module list, and click on the "**install**" link.
9. Using the top menu, go to "**Extensions**" and select "**Movies**"
10. You will see your Admin panel, with the first tab open:

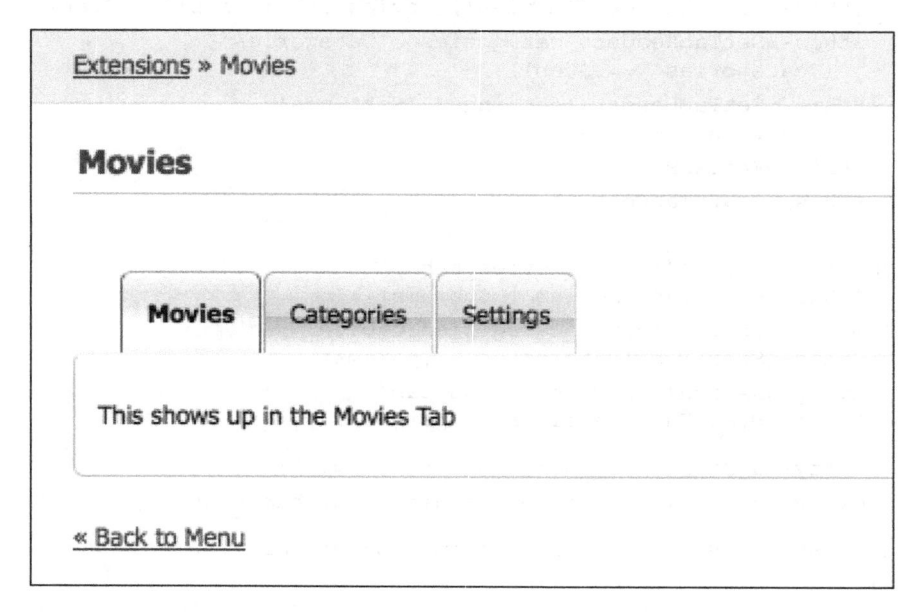

> Extensions » Movies
>
> **Movies**
>
> | **Movies** | Categories | Settings |
>
> This shows up in the Movies Tab
>
> « Back to Menu

11. Click on the "**Categories**" tab, and confirm that the panel's content area shows that tab's content:

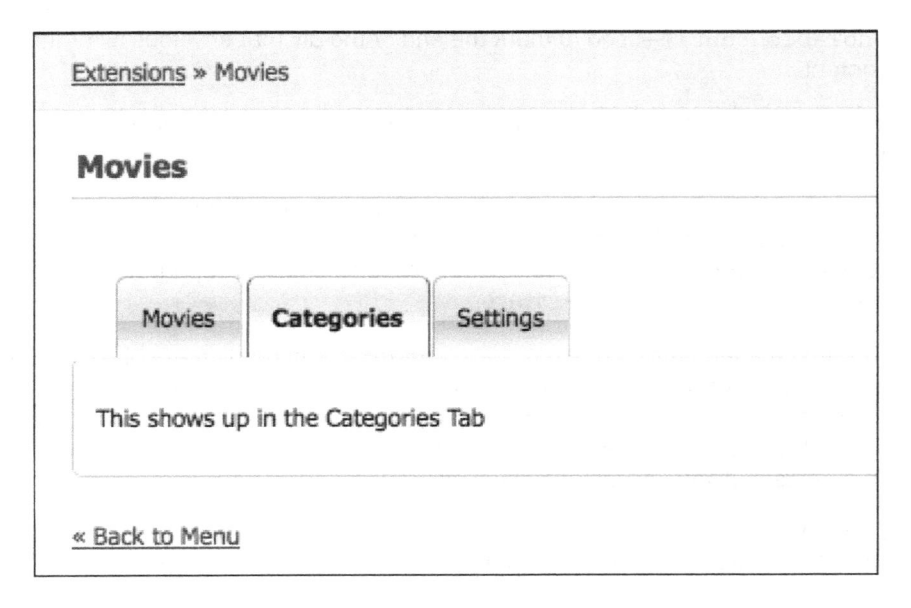

[Screenshot: Movies admin panel with Movies, Categories, Settings tabs; Categories tab shows "This shows up in the Categories Tab"; "« Back to Menu" link below.]

How it works...

The needs of modules tend to be fairly consistent, so CMS Made Simple provides APIs to fulfill some of these needs. These APIs reduce the work required for implementing features, while simultaneously creating informal standards. Why reinvent the wheel (or the jet-pack, for that matter)?

Many modules need a way of organizing their admin panels into multiple functional groups. The module API has built-in methods for creating JavaScript-based tabbed interfaces, as demonstrated in this recipe. Specifically, there are seven methods, that are used to create the tab system:

- StartTabHeaders()—used to open the divs used by the tab section.
- SetTabHeader()—called to define an individual tab. It takes three parameters: the internal tab name, the label for the tab, and a Boolean to indicate whether this is the active tab.
- EndTabHeaders()—used to mark the end of the tab, and close the divs opened by StartTabHeaders().
- StartTabContent()—used to open the divs that envelop all of the tabs' content.
- StartTab()—used to mark the beginning of a specific tab's content. It takes two parameters: the name of the tab being opened, and an array of parameters.
- EndTab()—used to mark the end of the most recent tab's content.

Creating Useful Admin Panels

> ▸ `EndTabContent()`—used to mark the end of the div that envelops all of the tabs' content.

These methods all return strings, that could be output directly, or, as in this recipe, assigned to Smarty variables.

We create a single Smarty variable "`tab_headers`" that combines the output of `StartTabHeaders()`, our three tabs that are each created by a call to `SetTabHeader()`, `EndTabHeaders()`, and `StartTabContent()`. We also create a separate Smarty variable for each tab, which is the call to `StartTab()`.

As you can see in the template, we output `tab_headers`, and then create blocks of output surrounded by their specific start tab tag and an end tab tag (for example, `{$start_movies_tab}` and `{$end_tab}`). The block of output that's within the tab area can contain any markup that will validate. Typically, these blocks contain forms, help text, or other interface elements, but you can include anything you want.

Since the output of `EndTab()` is not specific to a tab, we reuse it for each tab's content block. We also close the entire tab content area with the output from `EndTabContent()`.

Earlier, we asked "Why reinvent the wheel?" Sometimes, though, there is a good reason for doing so. If you're using some of the fancier jQuery interfaces, you might choose to use custom code rather than these built-in API methods.

There's more...

This recipe also demonstrates a mechanism for having your interface automatically open to a specific tab, using the "`active_tab`" parameter. If you had a form in your "settings" tab, for example, you'd want the user returned to that tab after saving a change. To do so, your code for handling the change would set the `active_tab` parameter to "settings".

If you want to display a message to the user in your active tab, you can do this by setting the "`tab_message`" parameter. Using the tab message involves a bit of a trick, however, as the parameter does not contain the text of the message, but the key to a string in your language file. So instead of setting:

```
$params['tab_message']=$this->Lang('message');
```

you simply set:

```
$params['tab_message'] = 'message';
```

See also

> ▸ *Create an admin panel for your module* recipe

Creating and enforcing new permissions for your module's administration

Permissions, in CMS Made Simple, are used for two major and related purposes: enforcing security via access control, and interface simplification. Access control is mostly self-explanatory: you only allow users to take actions that they are authorized to perform. Interface simplification is the related process of only displaying interface elements to users who will need to use them. If someone performs the role of an editor, there's no point in showing them interfaces for updating templates.

CMS Made Simple has a built-in group-based permission system for implementing both purposes. This recipe demonstrates how to use it.

How to do it...

1. Using any of the methods described in *Chapter 4, Getting Started with Modules* create a new plugin type module stub for your Mad Science module, and call it "MadScience".

2. Using your favorite editor, add a `HasAdmin()` method to `MadScience.module.php` that returns a Boolean value of "true".

3. Create a new file in your editor, and type in the following:

   ```php
   <?php
   if (!isset($gCms)) exit;
   
   $this->CreatePermission('MadScience','Authorized to do Mad Science');
   
   ?>
   ```

4. Save this file as "method.install.php" in your modules/MadScience directory.

5. Create a new file in your editor, and type in the following:

   ```php
   <?php
   if (!isset($gCms)) exit;
   
   $tab = '';
   if (!empty($params['active_tab']))
     {
     $tab = $params['active_tab'];
     }
   $tabs = $this->StartTabHeaders().
     $this->SetTabHeader('ideas','Perfectly Innocent Ideas',
     ('ideas' == $tab));
   $smarty->assign('start_ideas_tab',
   ```

Creating Useful Admin Panels

```
            $this->StartTab('ideas', $params));
    if ($this->CheckPermission('MadScience'))
        {
        $tabs .= $this->SetTabHeader('devices',
            'World Domination',($tab=='devices'));
        $smarty->assign('start_devices_tab',
            $this->StartTab('devices', $params));
        $devices = array('Planetary Death-Ray',
            'Heat-seeking Ferrets','Lizards with Lasers');
        $smarty->assign
            ('devices','<ul><li>'.implode('</li><li>',$devices).
            '</li></ul>');
        }
    else
        {
        $smarty->assign('start_devices_tab','');
        }
    $tabs .= $this->EndTabHeaders(). $this->StartTabContent();
    $smarty->assign('tab_headers',$tabs);
    $smarty->assign('tab_end',$this->EndTab());
    $smarty->assign('tab_footer',$this->EndTabContent());
    echo $this->ProcessTemplate('admin_panel.tpl');
    ?>
```

6. Save this file as "`action.defaultadmin.php`" in your `modules/MadScience` directory.

7. Create one more new file in your editor, and type in the following:

```
{$tab_headers}
    {$start_ideas_tab}
     <ul>
        <li>Fuzzy, glow-in-the-dark Kittens</li>
        <li>Rainbow-colored Bunnies</li>
        <li>Hot cocoa and blankies</li>
     </ul>
    {$tab_end}
    {if $start_devices_tab!=''}
     {$start_devices_tab}
        {$devices}
     {$tab_end}
    {/if}
{$tab_footer}
```

8. Save this file as "`admin_panel.tpl`" in your `modules/MadScience/templates` directory.
9. Log in to your CMS Administration area. Using the top menu, go to "**Extensions**" and select "**Modules**".
10. Find "**MadScience**" in the module list, and click on the "**install**" link.
11. Using the top menu, go to "**Users & Groups**" and select "**Group Permissions**" to confirm that the Editor group does not have the "Authorized to do Mad Science" permission checked.

Permission	Admin	Editor	Designer
Add Global Content Blocks	✓	☐	✓
Add Groups	✓	☐	☐
Approve News For Frontend Display	✓	☐	☐
Clear Admin Log	✓	☐	☐
Delete News Articles	✓	☐	☐
Authorized to do Mad Science	✓	☐	☐

12. Log out of your CMS Administration area, then log in again using an editor account.
13. Using the top menu, go to "**Extensions**" and select "**MadScience**".

Creating Useful Admin Panels

14. View the module's admin panel:

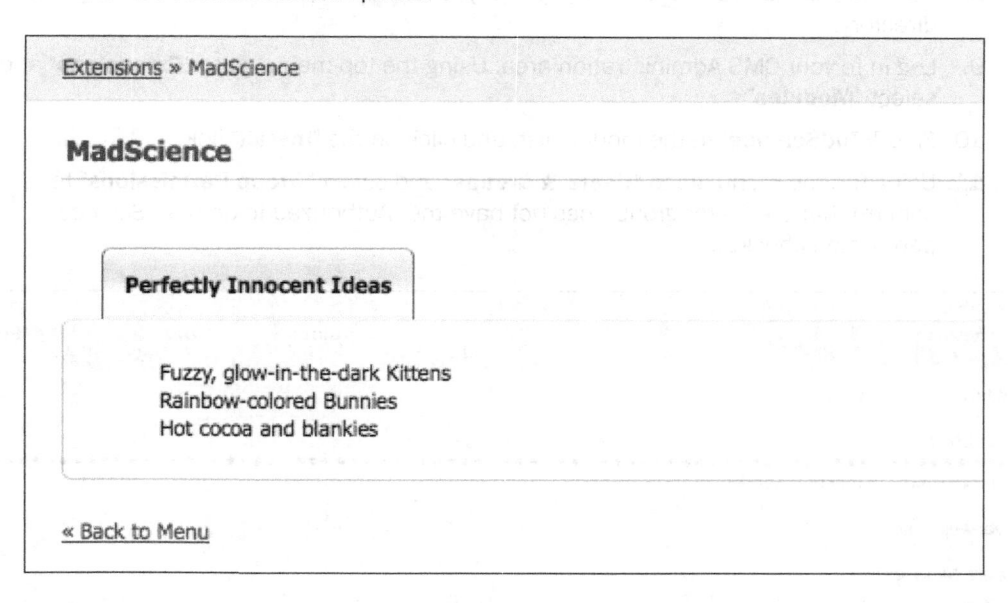

> Extensions » MadScience
>
> **MadScience**
>
> **Perfectly Innocent Ideas**
>
> Fuzzy, glow-in-the-dark Kittens
> Rainbow-colored Bunnies
> Hot cocoa and blankies
>
> « Back to Menu

15. Log out of your CMS Administration area, then log in again using your admin account.
16. Using the top menu, go to "**Extensions**" and select "**MadScience**".
17. View the module's admin panel. You can click on the previously hidden tab to see the protected area.

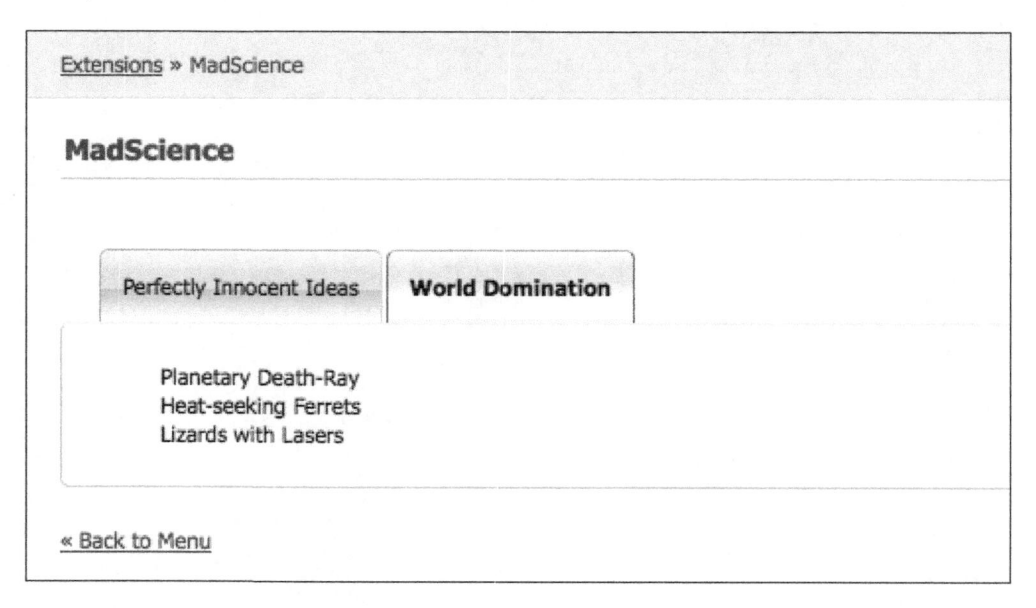

> Extensions » MadScience
>
> **MadScience**
>
> **Perfectly Innocent Ideas** | **World Domination**
>
> Planetary Death-Ray
> Heat-seeking Ferrets
> Lizards with Lasers
>
> « Back to Menu

How it works...

Access controls in the CMS Made Simple admin system are built upon group-based permissions. Individual content pages may be given edit control on a user-by-user basis, but access to the rest of the admin area is restricted by the group permissions, effectively yielding a role-based permission model. When you implement a module, you can choose to neglect permissions altogether, opt to use existing permissions (such as "Manage All Content"), or create new permissions.

This recipe uses a custom permission ("Authorized to do Mad Science") to determine whether or not to allow the logged-in user to view the "World Domination" tab in the Mad Science module's admin panel. In your own modules, you're much more likely to use permissions to divide your module's functions according to the typical roles set by the default groups, for example, Admin, Editor, or Designer. For example, you might set it up so that a full admin has permissions to set low-level module configurations, an admin in the Editor group only has permission to add records or approve user-submitted content from the module, and an admin in the Designer group would have permission to alter the module's templates.

In this recipe, we create the new "Authorized to do Mad Science" permission in our `method.install.php`. This is done by a call to the `CreatePermission()` method. The first parameter to this method is the internal name of the permission; the second is a more descriptive label for the permission. New permissions are only granted to the full Admin group. To grant these permissions to other groups, you need to do it through the "Group Permissions" panel under "Users & Groups" in the admin.

In the `method.defaultadmin.php`, we call the `CheckPermission()` method, passing the permission name as a parameter. `CheckPermission()` evaluates whether or not the currently logged in user belongs to a group that is granted the permission in question, and returns a Boolean `true` or `false`.

This recipe demonstrates an Administration panel that alters its behavior based upon a single permission—there's no reason, however, that you can't use multiple permissions to control access to various actions within your module. Similarly, this recipe uses access control to display or hide an entire tab of the admin area, but it could use the permission check for individual items within a single admin panel.

There's more...

You might look at the way this recipe implements access control, and wonder why it makes things so complicated. It actually generates different tab headers and Smarty variables for the content of the different tabs based on the permission. Why not simply set a flag to Smarty to hide or display the contents of a tab?

Creating Useful Admin Panels

The fact is, in a module like this one, you could easily use the simpler approach. There are a number of things to weigh when deciding how to approach your permission implementation. How strongly do permissions need to separate users? What degree of trust are you putting in your less-trusted users?

This recipe uses the joking example of a mad scientist's module for a reason: sometimes even knowledge of the existence of certain information presents a security issue. Perhaps a more real-world example would be the keeping of personal identifying information, such as credit card numbers, passport numbers, social security numbers in the US, and so on. You may have relatively untrusted editors who are authorized to make changes to portions of user records, but who are not authorized to access the sensitive information. Hiding the fact that the sensitive data is in the system is one measure that can be used to protect the data.

This also brings up why the more complicated security approach is taken by not even setting variables that contain potentially sensitive information unless the user has permission to see that data; you add a layer of protection against accidental exposure of the data. Since many modules allow the admin to modify Smarty templates, they could be vulnerable to an overcurious or malicious editor if the restricted information is assigned to Smarty variables and merely hidden.

Whether or not you will be facing this kind of security threat, it's preferable to err on the side of caution. Even if your application doesn't need strong enforcement of permissions, implementing robust enforcement will make your module useful to others who may need it. In the end, of course, you will need to balance your security and access control requirements against any extra efforts that the stronger implementation would impose.

See also

- *Creating an admin panel for your module* recipe
- *Creating multiple tabs for your admin module* recipe
- *Hiding your module from Administrators who don't have permission to use it* recipe

Displaying a page in the CMS Admin without the surrounding theme

Anything your module outputs to its admin panel will be displayed to the logged-in user wrapped nicely within the selected admin theme. This is desirable for numerous reasons: the admin theme handles display of the main navigational menu, the module name is automatically displayed to help orient the administrator, and any pending alerts or messages are displayed.

You may, however, have cases where you wish to have total control over an admin page. This recipe shows you how to do that.

How to do it...

1. Using any of the methods described in *Chapter 4, Getting Started with Modules* create a new plugin type module stub for your Chart module, and call it `"Chart"`.
2. Make sure your `Chart.module.php` has a `HasAdmin()` method that returns a Boolean value of `"true"`.
3. Create a new file in your editor, and type in the following:

    ```php
    <?php
    if (!isset($gCms)) exit;

    $vals = array('bg,lg,270,EFEFEF,0,BBBBBB,1',
       'chxs=0,676767,12.5','chxt=x','chs=400x225','cht=p','chd=s:fMJGD',
       'chdl=Procrastinating|Meetings|Coding|Debugging|Documenting',
       'chl=50%25|20%25|15%25|10%25|5%25&chma=35,10,23,10',
       'chtt=Development+Time');

    echo '<h1>Research Data</h1>';
    echo '<img src="http://chart.apis.google.com/chart?chf=';
    echo implode($vals,'&');
    echo '" alt="chart" />';

    ?>
    ```

4. Save this file as `"action.defaultadmin.php"` in your `modules/Chart` directory.
5. Log in to your CMS Administration area. Using the top menu, go to "**Extensions**" and select "**Modules**".
6. Find "**Charts**" in the module list, and click on the "**Install**" link.

Creating Useful Admin Panels

7. Using the top menu, go to "**Extensions**" and select "**Charts**" to view the output of your module.

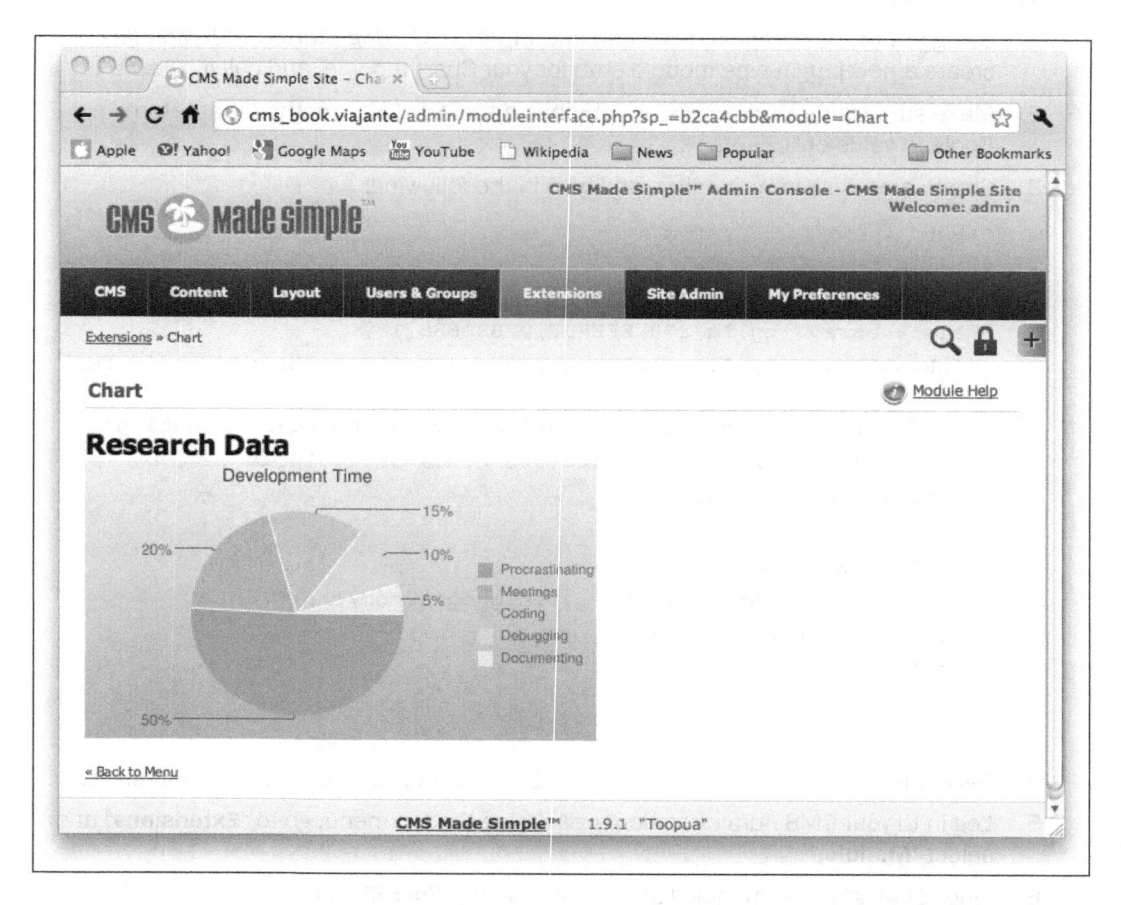

8. Using your favorite editor, add the following method to your `Chart.module.php`:

    ```
    function SuppressAdminOutput()
    {
    return true;
    }
    ```

9. Using the top menu, go to "**Extensions**" and select "**Charts**" to view the output of your module again:

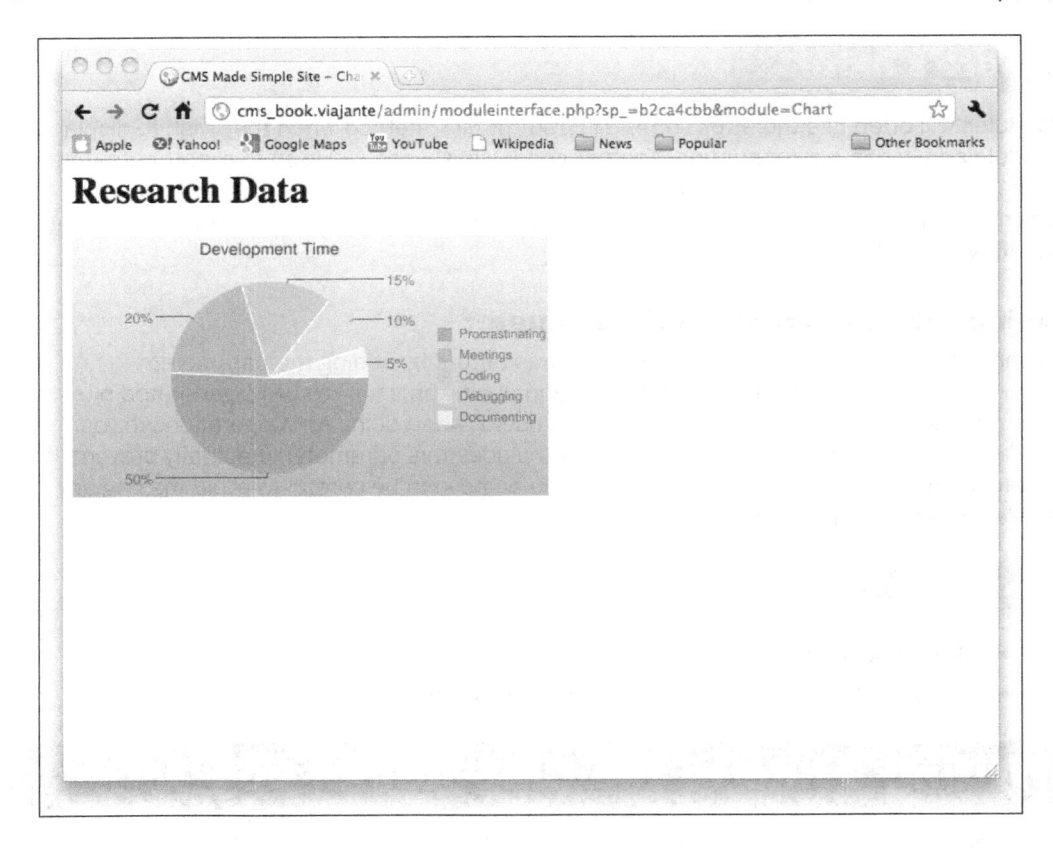

How it works...

This entire recipe is based upon a single method in the Module API, `SuppressAdminOutput()`. This method returns a Boolean value, and unless you override it, will return `false`. While the method's name suggests that it prevents all output from the admin area, it really only suppresses the admin theme output.

There are a few important considerations to keep in mind when suppressing the admin theme output. When you turn off display of the theme, you are now responsible for the entire page output, meaning that instead of outputting arbitrary code snippets, you probably will want to output an entire, validating HTML page. If you only output code snippets (as we did in this recipe), most browsers will still display something, but it may not be what you expected.

For usability, you should provide your users with a link or some other way of getting back to the admin area. Since the theme is no longer displaying a menu or breadcrumb trail, your admin user could become disoriented.

Creating Useful Admin Panels

There's more...

Modules will often use the `SuppressAdminOutput()` method when they wish to display module admin content for printing. Another good use is when you wish to export data from your module for download rather than display in a browser. To force the user's browser to download the data, you would use `SuppressAdminOutput()` in conjunction with setting a MIME-type header.

Using the "showtemplate" parameter

In some cases, you can also suppress the admin output by adding the parameters `"showtemplate=false"` to your URL. This approach works for any URLs generated by your module that calls module actions, and is useful when doing AJAX operations in your module's administration area. If your module includes this parameter, it actually prevents the instantiation of the admin theme object, so you do have to be careful to avoid making any references to the admin theme.

See also

- *Creating an admin panel for your module* recipe
- *Chapter 10, Outputting a downloadable CSV file from your module output* recipe

Writing a line to the CMS Admin Log

Modules provide several kinds of information to CMS Made Simple site administrators. For most modules, there's the module's administration panel, where the various site administrators can interact directly with the module. There are alert messages that the module displays in the admin panel. There is debug information, where the module can output internal state information to help diagnose problems. There is also audit information. This is where the module writes messages to the Admin Log to record when significant events have occurred.

The Admin log is useful to record things that are important from both a diagnostic and organizational standpoint. If you're encountering a new behavior from a module, for example, it would be useful to see in the log that the module was recently upgraded. Similarly, there could be module actions where it would be useful to know who performed the action: who added or modified a database record, for example.

This recipe shows how you can write such audit messages from your module.

How to do it...

1. Using any of the methods described in *Chapter 4, Getting Started with Modules* create a new plugin type module stub for your Fantasy League tracking module, and call it "FantasyLeague".
2. Open "`method.install.php`" in your editor (or create a new install file), and add the following line:

    `$this->Audit(0,'Fantasy League Module',$this->Lang('install_log',$this->GetVersion()));`
3. Save the file.
4. Edit modules/FantasyLeague/lang/en_US.php, and add the following line:

    `$lang['install_log'] = 'Fantasy League Module version %s has been installed';`
5. Log in to your CMS Administration area. Using the top menu, go to "**Extensions**" and select "**Modules**".
6. Find "**FantasyLeague**" in the module list, and click on the "**install**" link.
7. Using the top menu, go to "**Site Admin**" and select "**Admin Log**" to view the log.

Admin Log

Download

User	Item ID	Item Name	Action	Date
admin	0	Fantasy League Module	Fantasy League Module version 0.1 has been installed	12/11/10 18:08:54
admin	1	admin	User Login	12/11/10 18:07:35

How it works...

To write a line to the Admin Log is quite simple: make a call to the `Audit()` method. The method takes three parameters:

- `item id`—an optional numerical ID. This is useful for pointing to a specific record ID in a database table.
- `item name`—the name of the item upon which the action was taken. This is a string of up to 50 characters.
- `action`—the action that was taken. This is a string of up to 255 characters.

Creating Useful Admin Panels

The key to making the most of the Admin log is to give as much useful information in as few characters as possible. In our recipe, we placed a log message specifying that the module had been installed, and giving the version that was installed. In a module upgrade method, it's helpful to place a line in the log telling you not only that the module was upgraded, but which versions it was upgraded from and to.

> Writing lines to the Admin Log is useful not only for module installations, removals, and upgrades. Depending on the module, you might consider logging when the configuration changes, or when records are created, edited, or deleted. It can also be useful for security audits to put a line in the log when someone attempts to use the module but lacks permission.

See also

- *Chapter 4, Making a module localizable* recipe
- *Displaying a message after installation* recipe
- *Creating a module-specific preference and admin panel to set it* recipe

Displaying a message after installation

Administrators install modules for a CMS Made Simple installation in one of a few ways: they can use the `ModuleManager` module, they can upload a module XML file through the Module admin panel, or they can extract a file archive on the filesystem and perform the installation via the Module admin panel. Each of these methods gives the administrator an opportunity to read something about the module before they do the installation, and modules can provide a help facility, that is visible in the admin area.

Modules can also display a message immediately after installation. This is useful to give a confirmation of successful installation, or to give the administrator brief usage hints. This recipe shows you how to display this post-installation message.

How to do it...

1. Using any of the methods described in *Chapter 4, Getting Started with Modules* create a new plug-in type module stub for your Fantasy League tracking module, and call it "ColorPicker".
2. Open "ColorPicker.module.php" in your editor, and add the following method:
   ```
   function InstallPostMessage()
   {
   return $this->Lang('post_install');
   }
   ```

3. Edit `modules/ColorPicker/lang/en_US.php`, and add the following line:

   `$lang['post_install'] = 'Color Picker Module has been installed. You can now use the color picker by clicking on the "Color" button when you edit pages.';`

4. Log in to your CMS Administration area. Using the top menu, go to "**Extensions**" and select "**Modules**".

5. Find "**ColorPicker**" in the module list, and click on the "**install**" link:

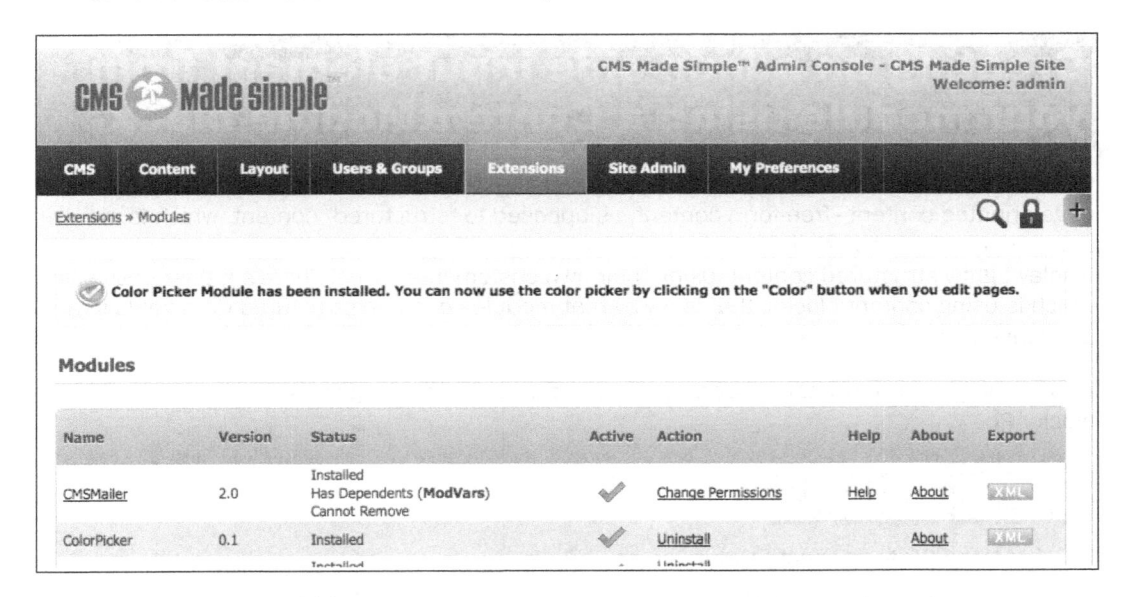

How it works...

This recipe demonstrates the `InstallPostMessage()` method. The method is extremely simple: any string returned by this method will be displayed on the Modules admin panel after the module is installed.

There's more...

There are two other related messages that your module can use to display this kind of informational messages to the administrator: `UninstallPreMessage()` and `UninstallPostMessage()`. These, as their names indicate, allow you to pass messages to the administrator before they uninstall a module, and after a module has been uninstalled.

By default, when the administrator clicks on the "**uninstall**" link, a dialog box will pop up to confirm whether or not they really intend to uninstall the module. You can provide your own text to this message by overriding the `UninstallPreMessage()` method to return a string containing your customized message.

Creating Useful Admin Panels

Similarly, if you'd like to show a message to the administrator after the module has been uninstalled, override `UninstallPostMessage()` to return that message.

See also

- *Chapter 4, Making a module localizable* recipe
- *Writing a line to the CMS Admin Log* recipe

Creating an admin-side input element from your module using a ContentModule block

CMS Made Simple is designed primarily for managing what is known as "unstructured" page-oriented content—free-form content, as opposed to "structured" content, which is more strictly controlled, record-oriented data. Still, modules allow you to create, manage, and display tightly structured content, using their own custom interfaces. There's a third possibility, which is using content blocks, that is a way that modules can add structured data fields to an otherwise unstructured page.

This recipe gives an example of adding two structured fields to pages using the content block API.

How to do it...

1. Use SSH to connect to your server.
2. Change your working directory to the modules directory of your CMS Made Simple installation directory, for example:

   `cd /var/www/mysite-root/modules`

3. Create a top level module directory:

   `mkdir DreamCars`

4. Open your favorite text editing program, and create a new file.
5. Type the following code:

```php
<?php
class DreamCars extends CMSModule
  {
  var $colors =
    array('Red'=>'red','Yellow'=>'yellow','Silver'=>'silver');
  var $marques = array('Select
    One'=>'','BMW'=>'BMW','Bentley'=>'Bentley',
    'Ferrari'=>'Ferrari','Jaguar'=>'Jaguar',
    'Lamborghini'=>'Lamborghini');
```

```php
function GetName()
  {
  return 'DreamCars';
  }

function GetVersion()
  {
  return '0.1';
  }

function SetParameters()
  {
  $this->RegisterModulePlugin();
  }
function IsPluginModule()
  {
  return true;
  }

function HasCapability($capability,$params = array())
  {
  if ($capability == 'contentblocks')
    return true;
  return false;
  }

function GetContentBlockInput($blockName,$value,$params,
  $adding = false)
  {
  switch ($blockName) {
    case 'marque':
      return $this->CreateInputDropdown('',$blockName,
        $this->marques,-1,$value);
    case 'color':
      return $this->CreateInputDropdown('',$blockName,
        $this->colors,-1,$value);
    default:
      return 'Unknown block '.$blockName;
    }
  }
```

```
        function
          GetContentBlockValue($blockName,$blockParams,$inputParams)
          {
          if (isset($inputParams[$blockName]))
             return $inputParams[$blockName];
          }

        function
          ValidateContentBlockValue($blockName,$value,$blockparams)
          {
          if ($blockName == 'marque' && empty($value))
             return 'Must specify a Marque!';
          }
        }
     ?>
```

6. Save this file as "`DreamCars.module.php`" in your `modules/Cars` directory
7. Create a new file in your editor, and type in the following:
    ```
    <?php
    if (!isset($gCms)) exit;

    $contentops = $gCms->GetContentOperations();
    $content_obj = $contentops->getContentObject();

    echo "This car is a ".$content_obj->GetPropertyValue('color').
      " ".$content_obj->GetPropertyValue('marque').'.';

    ?>
    ```
8. Save this file as "`action.default.php`" in your `modules/DreamCars` directory.
9. Log in to your CMS Administration area. Using the top menu, go to "**Extensions**" and select "**Modules**".
10. Find "**DreamCars**" in the module list, and click on the "**install**" link.
11. Using the top menu, go to "**Layout**" and select "**Templates**".
12. Click on the "**Add New Template**" button.
13. In the "**Name**" field enter "**DreamCars**", and in the content area enter the following:
    ```
    {process_pagedata}
    <!DOCTYPE html PUBLIC "-//W3C//DTD XHTML 1.0 Transitional//EN"
    "http://www.w3.org/TR/xhtml1/DTD/xhtml1-transitional.dtd">
    <html xmlns="http://www.w3.org/1999/xhtml" xml:lang="en" >
    <head>
    <title>{sitename} - {title}</title>
    ```

```
{metadata}
{cms_stylesheet}
</head>
<body>
<div id="header"><h1>{sitename}</h1></div>
<div id="menu">{menu collapse=1}</div>
<div id="content">
  <h1>{title}</h1>
  {Cars}
  {capture}
    {content_module module='DreamCars' block='marque'
      label='Marque'}
    {content_module module='DreamCars' block='color'
      label='Color'}
  {/capture}
  {content}
</div>
</body>
</html>
```

14. Click on the "**Submit**" button.
15. Using the top menu, go to "**Content**" and select "**Pages**". Click on the "**Add New Content**" button.
16. Click on the "**Options**" tab, and select "**DreamCars**" from the "**Template**" drop-down.
17. Enter "**My Car**" into the "**Title**" and "**Menu Text**" fields. Enter a short description into the "**Content**" area.

Creating Useful Admin Panels

18. Click on "**Submit**".

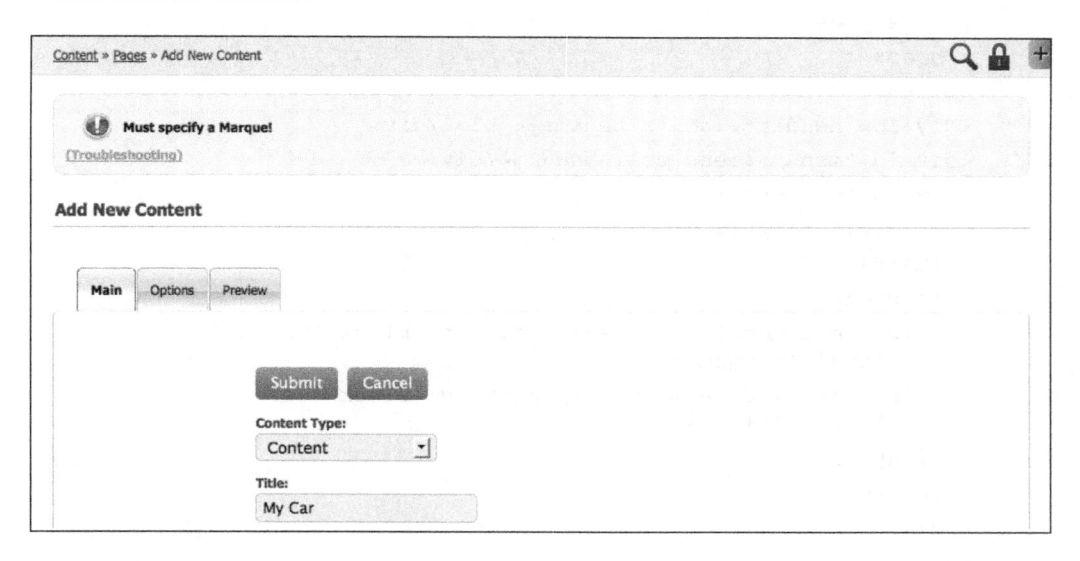

19. Scroll down to the bottom of the page, and select a Marque for the car:

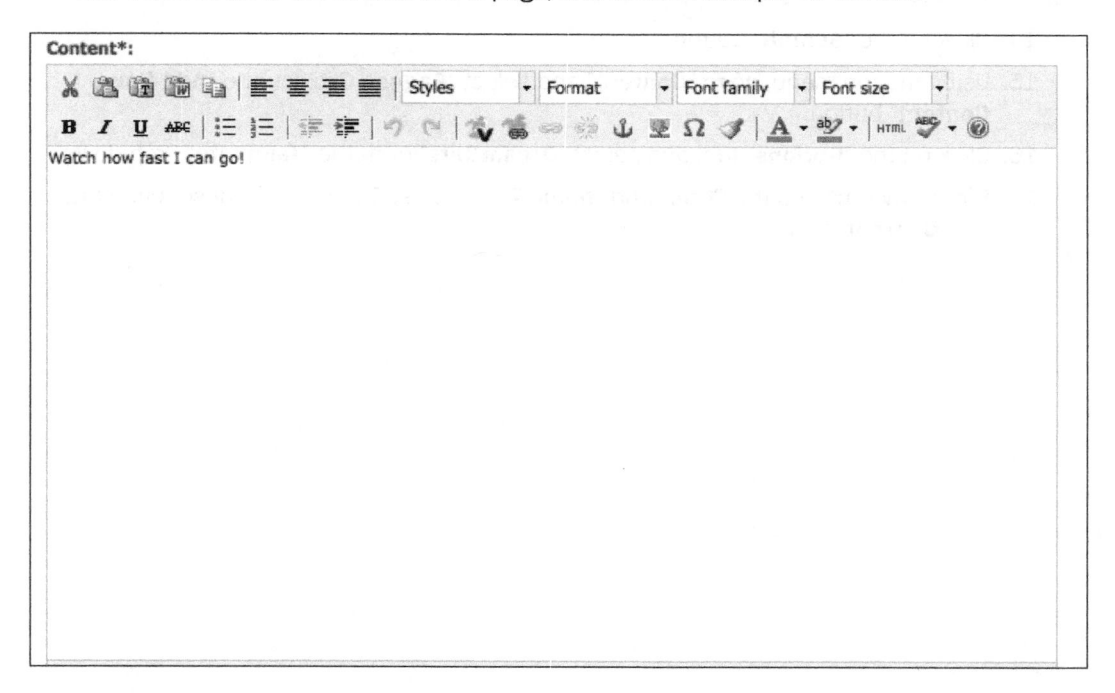

20. Click the "**Submit**" button.

21. On the user side, go to your new "**My Car**" page.

CMS Made Simple Site

- Home
- How CMSMS Works
- Default Templates Explained
- Default Extensions
- My Car

My Car

This car is a red Ferrari. Watch how fast I can go!

How it works...

> This recipe uses the content blocks feature introduced to the module API in CMSMS version 1.8. A content block is a rudimentary implementation of structured data management, or a way of creating a custom content type whose value gets associated with a page. The module may create any kind of input for populating that value. Since the value is associated with the page rather than the module, the page may be copied and the value will be copied along with it.

For a module to support content blocks, it must do three things: it must report that it supports content blocks, it must create inputs for those content blocks, and it must return the values for a named content block. Optionally, it may also validate content block values (which only works in CMSMS versions later than 1.9.2).

For a module to report that it supports content blocks, it needs to implement that code in the `HasCapability()` method. This method is intended to be an interface by which modules can report various capabilities that they implement (such as WYSIWYG editors, and so on). At the time of this writing, however, the only capability checked by the CMSMS core is content blocks. So, to report that our module supports content blocks, we override the `HasCapability()` method to return `"true"` when called to test the `"contentblocks"` capability.

Creating Useful Admin Panels

Next, our module needs to create inputs for its new content blocks. This is done in the `GetContentBlockInput()` method. The method is called when content is edited, and has four parameters: `$blockName`, `$value`, `$params`, and `$adding`. `$blockName` contains the name of the block being requested, a name which is taken from the Smarty tag that includes the content block. The `$value` parameter is populated with the current value of the content block (if any). The `$params` parameter is an associative array of parameters that originate in the Smarty tag that includes the current content block. Lastly, the `$adding` parameter is set to `true` if the page is being created rather than edited.

Let's examine the first of our example Smarty tags in our module's "DreamCars" template:

    {content_module module='Cars' block='marque' label='Marque'}

When a page containing this tag is edited, the CMS will call the `GetContentBlockInput()` method of the module specified ("DreamCars") with the `$blockName` coming from the `'block'` designation ("marque"). It will use the "`label`" parameter to provide the administrator with a description of what the field is used for. Any additional name/value pairs in the Smarty tag would be passed to `GetContentBlockInput()` in the `$params` array.

So in our `DreamCars` module, we have two custom content blocks, `marque` and `color`. When the `GetContentBlockInput()` method is called, we identify which content block is being requested, and render an input for that particular block.

The content block values will be saved automatically with the assets for the page. But the CMS needs to know how to interpret the form values it receives, which is where the `GetContentBlockValue()` method comes in. This method needs to understand how to translate the value submitted by the form control for a content block into a value to save. The parameters it takes are:

- `$blockName` – which block is being handled
- `$blockParams` – name/value pairs that are specified in the content block's Smarty tag
- `$inputParams` – an associative array of the submitted form values

In this module, we generated drop-downs for our two content blocks, and each drop-down used the content block's name. So, for our `GetContentBlockValue()` method, we can simply use the content block name as a key to the `$inputParams` array, and return that element's value.

If you're using a version of CMSMS later than 1.9.2, you can also have validation rules on your content block inputs. This is implemented with the `ValidateContentBlockValue()` method. The method takes three parameters, `$blockName` (which block is being handled), `$value` (the value submitted by the form for that block), and `$blockparams` (name/value pairs that are specified in the content block's Smarty tag). The method confusingly returns a blank string, a Boolean `false`, or no value at all to signal success, or the text of an error message if validation fails.

There's more...

Normally, content blocks are displayed to the end user as the block's value (as would be returned by the `GetContentBlockValue()` method). When the page is rendered, the Smarty tag specifying the content block is simply replaced by that value.

In this recipe, however, we do something a little trickier since we want to format the values (of course, we could do that formatting in the template, but there may be cases where the logic would be too complex for Smarty). To achieve this, we place our content block Smarty tags within a capture block, which is a simple way of keeping the Smarty tags in the page while suppressing output when the page is rendered. We need to keep the tags in the page, so that the CMS admin knows to get input for them when editing the page.

Then, we place our module tag in the page, so that the `action.default.php` gets called. In this method, we retrieve our content block values by getting the page's content object, and retrieving the property values corresponding to our content blocks.

This approach is particularly useful if you're using a content block as a complex interface. For example, if you're integrating databases, the `GetContentBlockInput()` method might query names and keys from a database table, and the saved value might just be the key value. The page display may involve fetching multiple records based upon the key. The approach taken by this recipe will work well in complicated cases such as this.

See also

- *Chapter 3, Using the current content object in a User-Defined Tag* recipe
- *Chapter 6, Creating a basic form in a module* recipe

Hiding your module from Administrators who don't have permission to use it

Permissions are used for access control in CMS Made Simple, but are also very useful for task-specific interface simplification. If an administrator has no use for a given function, it's often advantageous to hide that function. It reduces the clutter of the interface, removes distractions, and prevents confusion. Similarly, from an access-control standpoint, there is no point in revealing functionality to a user who does not have the permission to use those functions.

This recipe shows you how to hide the existence of an entire module from an admin user who lacks permission to use the module.

Creating Useful Admin Panels

How to do it...

1. Using any of the methods described in *Chapter 4, Getting Started with Modules* create a new plugin type module stub for your `Superuser` module, and call it "Superuser".

2. Open "`Superuser.module.php`" in your editor, and add the following methods:

   ```
   function HasAdmin()
   {
   return true;
   }

   function GetAdminSection()
   {
   return 'content';
   }

   function VisibleToAdminUser()
   {
   return $this->CheckPermission('Superuser Access');
   }
   ```

3. Edit (or create) `modules/Superuser/method.install.php`, and add the following line:

   `$this->CreatePermission('Superuser Access','Access Superuser Module');`

4. Log in to your CMS Administration area. Using the top menu, go to "**Extensions**" and select "**Modules**".

5. Find "**Superuser**" in the module list, and click on the "**install**" link.

6. Using the top menu, go to "**Content**" and confirm that your "**Superuser**" module shows up in the menu.

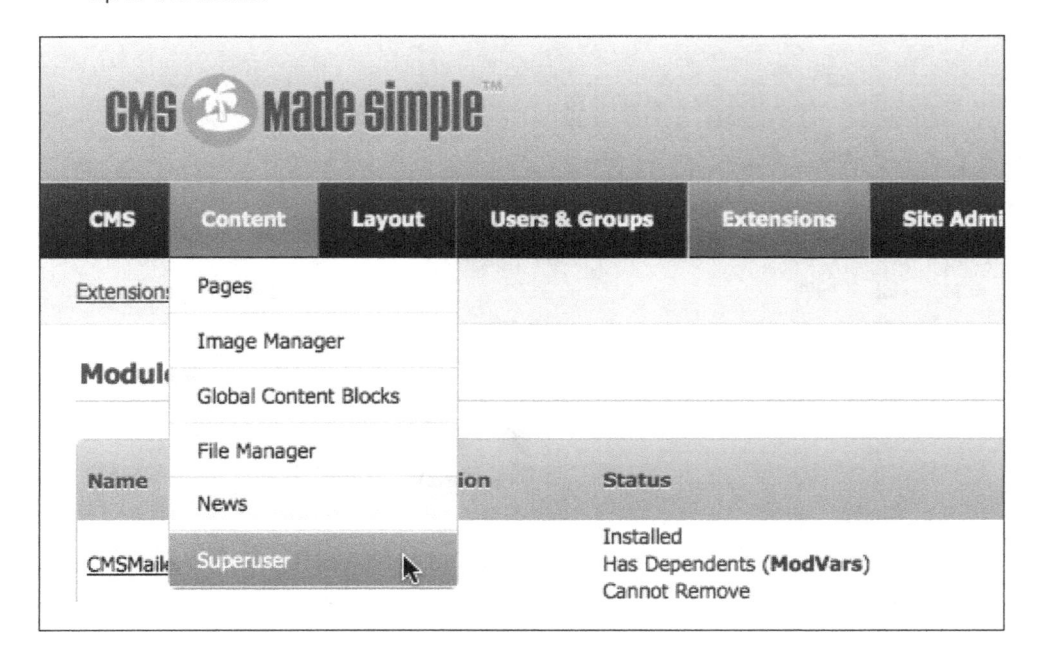

7. Log out of the CMS Administration area, and the log in again using an Editor account or other account that lacks full admin privileges.

Creating Useful Admin Panels

8. Using the top menu, go to "**Content**" and confirm that your "**Superuser**" module is not visible in the menu.

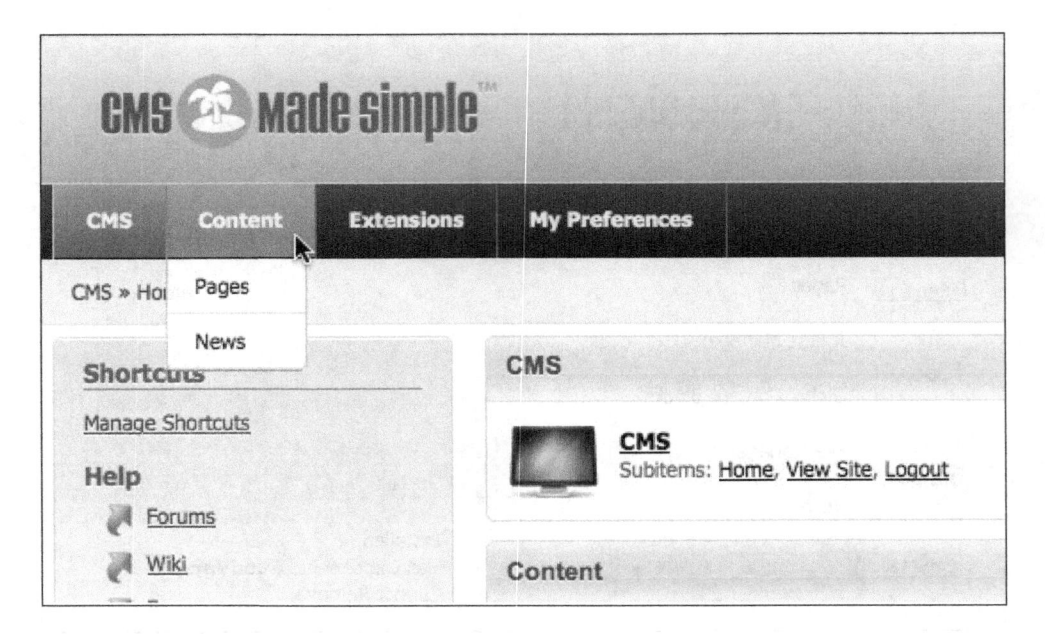

How it works...

This recipe demonstrates the use of the `VisibleToAdminUser()` method. The method returns a `true` or `false` value, which determines whether or not the module appears to the currently-logged in CMS Admin user.

In this recipe, we create a new permission to "Access Superuser Module" to determine whether or not a user may access the module. We test this permission in the `VisibleToAdminUser()` method. If the user has this permission, we allow them to see the module, if they don't have the permission, we hide it from them.

In our initial test, logged in as the primary Admin user, we see the menu item for the module, even though we haven't granted the permission. This occurs because the primary Admin user is granted all permissions automatically. When we log in as an editor or any other account that has not been granted the permission, the module is not visible.

There's more...

Making a module invisible to unprivileged admin users is an important step in setting up permissions, but it should not be confused with truly securing the module. A carefully crafted URL would enable any logged in admin account to access the module's admin panel, whether or not it is visible to them.

For robust security, your module can enforce permissions by performing the check in its admin methods. For example, placing the following code at the top of every admin action file (for example, `action.defaultadmin.php`) will guarantee that only admins with suitable permission will be able to access the module:

```
if (! $this->CheckPermission('Access Superuser')) exit;
```

Depending on the degree of security you need, you could also display warnings and/or write a line to the Admin Log in the event of an attempted unauthorized access.

See also

- *Creating an admin panel for your module* recipe
- *Creating and enforcing new permissions for your module's administration* recipe
- *Writing a line to the CMS Admin Log* recipe

Creating a module-specific preference and admin panel to set it

Modules often need a way to have multiple options available for customization. That way, a single module can be used in different ways on different websites, and a site administrator can configure the module to suit their needs without having to modify the module's code.

To have such options, it would be an advantage if there were a standard approach to setting and retrieving persistent preference settings. Not surprisingly, the CMS Made Simple module API provides just that standard. This recipe gives an example of using that API, and wraps it into a form that allows the site administrator to update the preference.

How to do it...

1. Using any of the methods described in *Chapter 4, Getting Started with Modules* create a new plug-in type module stub for your Weather Report tracking module, and call it "`WeatherReport`".

2. Open "`method.install.php`" in your editor (or create a new install file), and add the following line:

   ```
   $this->SetPreference('seasonal_templates', 1);
   ```

3. Open your method.defaultadmin.php in an editor, and replace the contents with the following:

   ```
   <?php
   if (!isset($gCms)) exit;
   ```

```
    $message = '';
    if (isset($params['seasonal_templates']))
    {
      $this->SetPreference('seasonal_templates', $params['seasonal_
templates']);
      $message='Settings Updated';
    }
    $smarty->assign('message',$message);
    $smarty->assign('form_start',
      $this->CreateFormStart($id, 'defaultadmin', $returnid));
    $smarty->assign('input_seasonal',
       $this->CreateInputHidden($id,'seasonal_templates',0).
       $this->CreateInputCheckbox($id, 'seasonal_templates', 1, $this-
>GetPreference('seasonal_templates',0)).
       $this->CreateLabelForInput($id, 'seasonal_templates', 'Change
weather template based on season?'));
    $smarty->assign('submit',
       $this->CreateInputSubmit($id, 'submit', 'Submit'));
    $smarty->assign('form_end', $this->CreateFormEnd());
    echo $this->ProcessTemplate('form.tpl');
    ?>
```

4. Create a new template file in modules/WeatherReport/templates called "form.tpl" that contains the following code:

```
{if $message!=''}<p class="pagemessage">{$message}</p>{/if}
{$form_start}
  <p>{$input_seasonal}</p>
  <p>{$submit}</p>
{$form_end}
```

5. Log in to your CMS Administration area. Using the top menu, go to "**Extensions**" and select "**Modules**".

6. Find "**WeatherReport**" in the module list, and click on the "**install**" link.

7. Using the top menu, go to "**Extensions**" and select "**WeatherReport**" to view your module:

[CMS Made Simple admin interface showing WeatherReport module with "Change weather template based on season?" checkbox checked, and a Submit button]

8. Uncheck the preference, and hit the "**Submit**" button.

How it works...

The bulk of this recipe is Admin-side Form API code, which is necessary to demonstrate the Admin Preference system. The key methods for handling preferences, however, are the straightforward `SetPreference()` and `GetPreference()`.

The `SetPreference()` method takes two parameters: a name for the preference, and a value to set it. The name can be any string up to 255 characters and the value can be a string up to 64k characters, although for performance reasons, it's advisable to keep both names and values shorter.

The `GetPreference()` method also takes two parameters: preference name and an optional default value. It returns the stored value of the named preference, or, if no such preference is set, the value specified in by the default value.

Preferences are persisted in the database, but are cached upon retrieval. This caching makes the CMS much more efficient: no matter how many times you check a preference in a module action, only one database query is executed.

Creating Useful Admin Panels

The default value specified in the `GetPreference()` method call makes it entirely possible to simply start adding `GetPreference()` calls to your module without worrying about initializing the preference. For consistency's sake, this recipe sets an initial value for the preference in its install method. If you do the same in your modules, you may omit the optional default value when you call `GetPreference()`, although, some people find that specifying a default value at the time of the method call is more legible.

There's more...

You'll notice that the form code in this recipe is virtually identical to the form code that is used in the User side form recipes in *Chapter 6, Using the Module Form API*. The module Form API is designed to work the same way, whether on the Admin or the User side. There are a few differences to keep in mind, however:

- Parameter sanitizing does not affect the Admin side
- Forms on the Admin side ignore the `$returnid` variable in the `CreateFormStart()` method
- Some methods have specialized versions depending on whether they're intended for User side or Admin side use, for example, `CreateFrontendLink()` versus `CreateLink()`

See also

- *Chapter 6, Creating a basic form in a module* recipe
- *Create an admin panel for your module* recipe

Displaying an alert in the CMS Admin from a module

In one of the previous recipes, we have seen how to save important messages from a module to the Admin Log. Sometimes, however, we may need to actively communicate important messages to the administrator.

This recipe demonstrates how to place a message on the Admin alert queue.

How to do it...

1. Using any of the methods described in *Chapter 4, Getting Started with Modules* create a new plug-in type module stub for your Store Inventory Manager module, and call it "`StoreManager`".

2. Open "`method.install.php`" in your editor (or create a new install file), and add the following lines:

```
$db = $gCms->GetDb();

$dict = NewDataDictionary( $db );

$flds = "
    item_id I KEY,
  title C(80),
  description X,
  inventory I";

$sqlarray = $dict->CreateTableSQL( cms_db_prefix()."module_shopmanager",
            $flds,
            $taboptarray);
$dict->ExecuteSQLArray($sqlarray);
```

3. Open your `StoreInventory.module.php` in an editor, and add the following method:

```
function GetNotificationOutput($priority=2)
  {
  $gCms = cmsms();
  $db = $gCms->GetDb();
  $rcount = $db->GetOne('select count(*) from '.cms_db_prefix().'module_shopmanager');
     if ($priority < 4 && $rcount == 0 )
     {
     $ret = new stdClass;
     $ret->priority = 2;
     $ret->html='You have not added any items to your inventory. '.
       $this->CreateLink('', 'defaultadmin', '', 'Click here to add items');
     return $ret;
     }
  return '';
  }
```

4. Log in to your CMS Administration area. Using the top menu, go to "**Extensions**" and select "**Modules**".

5. Find "**StoreManager**" in the module list, and click on the "**install**" link.

Creating Useful Admin Panels

6. Note that there is the "You have one unhandled notification" message at the top of your page. Click on the plus sign button to view the notification:

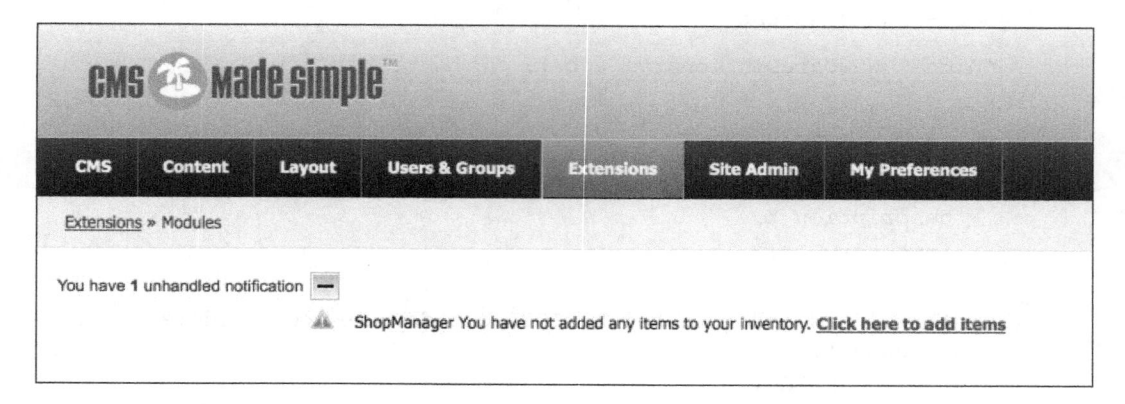

How it works...

The module API provides a method for adding messages to the notification queue atop admin pages. These notifications are intended for high-priority notices, like version upgrades, security issues, un-configured modules, and much more, however, your module can create notifications whenever it's necessary. Be careful, though, because presenting the admin with too many notifications will result in all of them being ignored (or turned off in the preferences).

Modules add messages to the notification queue using the `GetNotificationOutput()` method. This method takes a priority number as a parameter; the priority is not yet used, but future versions of the CMSMS admin may perform filtering based on them. This method normally returns an empty string, which means that it has no messages to display. While the natural assumption is that returning a non-empty string will display a notification, this is not how it's actually implemented. Instead, the method needs to return a standard PHP object with two attributes, "`priority`" and "`html`".

In this recipe, we perform a database query to determine if there are any records in the Shop Manager module database. If there is not, we wish to alert the admin and provide a helpful link to the admin panel where records can be added. So if the count is less than one, we create a `StdClass()` and assign it a priority of 2, and provide our message and link. Returning this object then displays the message to the admin.

There's more...

When should a module display messages? In addition to the cases mentioned earlier, a few possibilities include:

- When specific module actions have not been taken in a given time window (for example, no one has checked the orders in an e-commerce module in the last week)
- To provide low-level system information (for example, server disk space warnings)
- When the module has detected security violations (for example, unauthorized admin users attempting to use the module)

See also

- *Displaying a message after installation* recipe
- *Writing a line to the CMS Admin Log* recipe

Using Events

In this chapter, we will cover:

- Attaching a User-Defined Tag to an event
- Finding what parameters an event passes using a User-Defined Tag
- Generating an event from a module
- Handling an event with a module
- Use an event to send an e-mail when an Administrator Account is added or deleted

Introduction

In previous chapters, we have primarily explored the use of different types of tags and modules when they are embedded in pages. The code is linked to a specific place in the site; it's part of a page that the user views, or part of a panel used by the administrator. There is an entirely different class of use cases for tags and modules, which are not tied to pages but to events.

CMS Made Simple has a framework for triggering and handling events, that is used extensively in the core. Modules have the ability to both generate and separately handle events. User-Defined Tags can be bound to events either programmatically or by site administrators via the Event Manager.

Events are very powerful and flexible. Unlike direct calls to other module instances, event generation and handling creates a sort of ad-hoc interface that can be used by other modules or tags. By providing your module with a well-designed set of events, you are essentially saying to other developers "I don't know what uses you'll have for my code, but I'm going to make it possible for you to do things I may not have even imagined."

Using Events

This chapter will show you how to use the Event Manager to associate a User-Defined Tag (UDT) with an event, and how to generate and handle events with modules. The chapter also has two applications for the event system that might inspire you to think of new and novel uses for it.

> For most of the recipes in this chapter, you will need login access to your site's Administration area with permission to "Modify Events" and "Modify User-defined Tags." Some recipes will also require filesystem access to the server where your CMS is installed, or read access to your server's PHP error logs.

Attaching a User-Defined Tag to an event

One way of using the CMS Made Simple event system is to create User-Defined Tags that handle events. This approach is very powerful, and can be used for a huge range of applications. For example, to improve the content of your site, you might want to know not just what keywords people are searching for, but how many results they are getting. This is an application that can be implemented with a UDT that handles events from the Search module.

This recipe combines such a UDT with module events to write search details to the Admin log. It demonstrates how an administrator can associate a UDT with an event triggered by the Search module using the Event Manager.

How to do it...

1. Log in to your CMS Administration area. Using the top menu, go to "**Extensions**" and select "**User Defined Tags**".
2. Click on the "**Add User Defined Tag**" button.
3. Type "search_logger" into the "**Name**" field, and the following snippet into the "**Code**" area:

   ```
   audit(-1,'Search','User searched for '.$params[0].' and
     got '.count($params[1]).' results');
   ```

4. Click on the "**Submit**" button.
5. Using the top menu, go to "**Extensions**" and select "**Event Manager**".
6. In the "**Filter by Module**" drop-down, select "**Search**" and click the "**Submit**" button.
7. Click on the "**SearchCompleted**" event.

Originator	Event	Description		
Search	SearchAllItemsDeleted	Sent when all items are deleted from the index.		
Search	SearchCompleted	Sent when a search is completed.		
Search	SearchInitiated	Sent when a search is started.		
Search	SearchItemAdded	Sent when a new item is indexed.		
Search	SearchItemDeleted	Sent when an item is deleted from the index.		

Filter By Module: Search — Submit

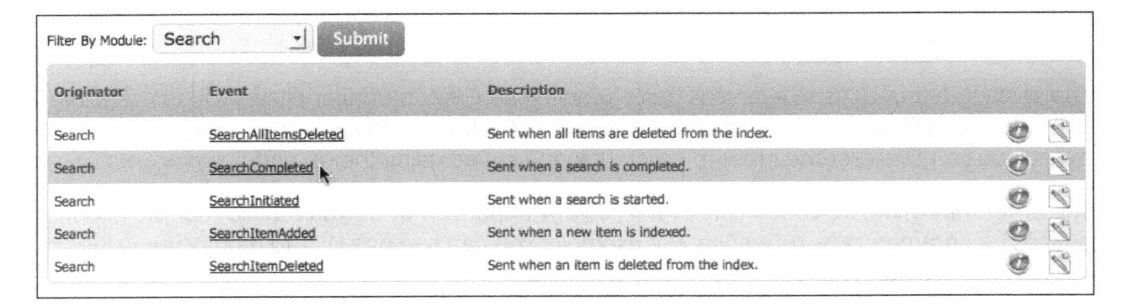

8. From the drop-down, select "`search_logger`" and click the "**Add**" button.
9. View your site from the user side.
10. Enter "**news**" into the search box, and hit return.
11. Return to the CMS Administration area. Using the top menu, go to "**Site Admin**" and select "**Admin Log**".
12. See your event-triggered log message:

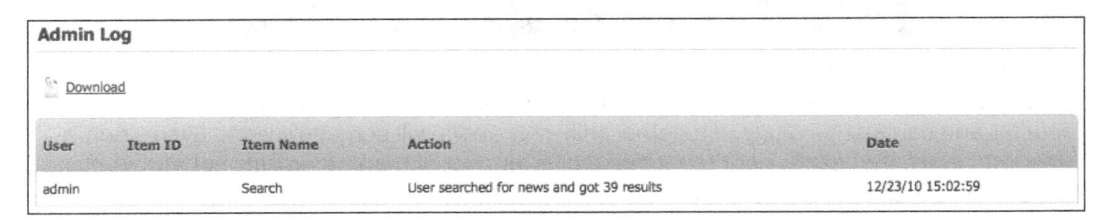

Admin Log

Download

User	Item ID	Item Name	Action	Date
admin		Search	User searched for news and got 39 results	12/23/10 15:02:59

How it works...

The User-Defined Tag used by this recipe is quite simple. It calls the core `audit()` function, that is used to write a line to the Admin log (this is the function that underlies the module API's `Audit()` method). Once the UDT has been created, we go through the simple process of using the Event Manager to add this UDT to the `SearchCompleted` event triggered by the Search Module.

Looking at the UDT code, you'll notice that it references a `$params` variable, that, it assumes, is an array with at least two elements. If you click on the information icon next to the **SearchCompleted** event in the Event Manager listing, you will see that the event passes two parameters: text that was searched for, and an array of the results. So our UDT creates a string that includes the search term and the count of the elements in the second array, and writes that to the Admin Log.

Using Events

There's more...

The assignment of UDTs to events is quite simple. The Event Manager allows you to associate one or more UDTs for any event registered to the CMS. If you add more than one UDT to an event, you can even set the order in which they are called using the up and down arrows.

The order that UDTs are called can be particularly important when you realize that the event passes its parameters by reference. For example, you can use one UDT to modify the values of the parameters before another UDT handles them.

See also

- *Finding what parameters an event passes using a User-Defined Tag* recipe
- *Handling an Event with a module* recipe

Finding what parameters an event passes using a User Defined Tag

The Event Manager is an area of the CMS Made Simple admin area that new users often find confusing. New users sometimes get the impression that Events and UDTs are completely modular and can just be plugged together willy-nilly and it will somehow work. Even when users are aware that each event transmits a different set of parameters, it's not always clear to them what those parameters are.

This recipe gives some pointers for identifying event parameters and their data structures. To fully utilize this recipe, you'll need read access to your server's PHP error logs.

How to do it...

1. Log in to your CMS Administration area. Using the top menu, go to "**Extensions**" and select "**Event Manager**".
2. Click on the Information icon next to the **LoginPost** event.

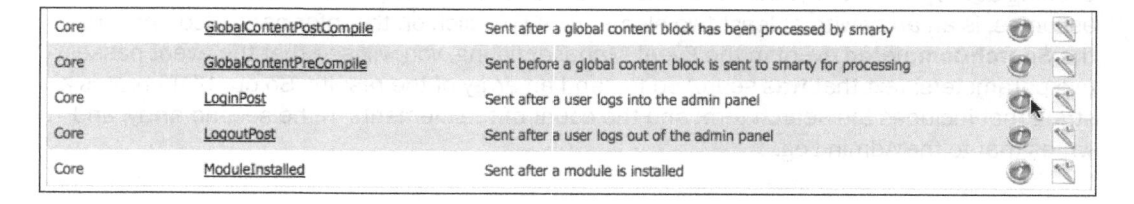

Core	GlobalContentPostCompile	Sent after a global content block has been processed by smarty
Core	GlobalContentPreCompile	Sent before a global content block is sent to smarty for processing
Core	LoginPost	Sent after a user logs into the admin panel
Core	LogoutPost	Sent after a user logs out of the admin panel
Core	ModuleInstalled	Sent after a module is installed

3. View the provided help:

> **Event Manager**
>
> **LoginPost**
>
> Sent after a user logs into the admin panel.
>
> **Parameters**
>   'user' - Reference to the affected user object.
>
> « Back to Menu

4. Using the top menu, go to "**Extensions**" and select "**User Defined Tags**".
5. Click on the "**Add User Defined Tag**" button.
6. Type "**dumper**" into the "**Name**" field, and the following snippet into the "Code" area:
   ```
   error_log(print_r($params, true));
   ```
7. Click on the "**Submit**" button.
8. Using the top menu, go to "**Extensions**" and select "**Event Manager**".
9. Click on the "**LoginPost**" event.
10. From the drop-down, select "**dumper**" and click the "**Add**" button.
11. Log out from the CMS Administration area, and then log in again.
12. View the PHP error log on your server.
    ```
    [24-Dec-2010 01:23:14] Array
    (
        [user] => User Object
            (
                [id] => 1
                [username] => admin
                [password] => 7a495904a8c0b3e6aabe27440b436c28
                [firstname] => Samuel
                [lastname] => Goldstein
                [email] => sjg@cmsmodules.com
                [active] => 1
                [adminaccess] => 1
            )

    )
    ```

Using Events

How it works...

This recipe goes through the typical steps that one takes when determining exactly what parameters are passed to handlers by an event. The first step is to view the help page. In our recipe, we're looking at the `LoginPost` event, and when we view the help, it tells us that the parameter is a "reference to the affected user object".

Now, if we are conversant with this particular object, that's all we need to know. We can go and start coding. However, if we are not, there are a couple of things we can do. One approach would be to find where this object is defined in the source (which turns out to be in `lib/classes/class.user.inc.php`), and read the definition to figure out how to use the class. In this recipe, we use a less involved approach that will get us less complete information but will get it to us faster: we create a User Defined Tag that dumps the object to the error log, and attach that UDT to the event.

Once we have triggered the event, we can look at the PHP error log, and see all of the attributes available to us in the object. We then write whatever it is we were going to use to handle the event, remembering to remove the "dumper" UDT from the event's handler.

See also

- Chapter 1, *Using CMS in debug mode* recipe
- Chapter 6, *How to use debug_display to see what parameters your module is receiving* recipe

Generating an Event from a module

In *Chapter 7, Your Module and the Community* we explored some of the community-related aspects of developing modules for CMS Made Simple. Using a public code repository and maintaining a presence on the CMS Developer's Forge are both ways to leverage the power of Open Source software. Another way that modules can encourage collaboration and interoperability is in the code itself. By generating events at key points, your module can allow other modules or User-defined tags to hook in and take advantage of your module's functionality.

Generating events is a lot like creating an open-ended or inverse API, that gives other code an opportunity to step in and interact with what your code is doing. This allows unprecedented opportunities for combining modules in novel ways to achieve functionality far beyond the original design of your module.

This recipe gives an example of generating events from a simple voting module.

How to do it...

1. Using any of the methods described in *Chapter 4, Getting Started with Modules* create a new plugin type module stub for your vote tracking module, and call it "Voter".

2. Edit "method.install.php" (or create a new install file), and add the following lines:

   ```
   $this->CreateEvent('OnVoteFormDisplayed');
   $this->CreateEvent('OnVoteFormSubmitted');
   ```

3. Edit "Voter.module.php" and add the following two methods:

   ```
   function GetEventDescription($eventname)
     {
     if ($eventname == 'OnVoteFormDisplayed')
       return 'Called when a Voter Form is displayed.';
     else if ($eventname == 'OnVoteFormSubmitted')
       return 'Called after a Voter Form is submitted.';
     }
   function GetEventHelp($eventname)
     {
     $help = $this->GetEventDescription($eventname) .
       '<br>Parameters: <ul>';
     if ($eventname == 'OnVoteFormDisplayed')
       $help .= '<li>ip -  the IP address of the person viewing
         the form</li>';
     else if ($eventname == 'OnVoteFormSubmitted')
       $help .= '<li>ip -  the IP address of the person
         voting</li>' .
         '<li>vote -  the vote that was submitted</li>';
     $help .= '</ul>';
     return $help;
     }
   ```

4. Create a new "action.default.php" file containing the following:

   ```
   <?php
   if (!isset($gCms)) exit;
   $votes = array('Aye'=>'yes', 'Nay'=>'no');
   $event_params = array('ip'=>$_SERVER['REMOTE_ADDR']);
   if (isset($params['vote']))
     {
     $event_params['vote'] = $params['vote'];
   ```

```
            $this->SendEvent('OnVoteFormSubmitted', $event_params);
            echo 'Your opinion has been
              received: '.array_search($params['vote'],$votes);
            return;
            }
        $this->SendEvent('OnVoteFormDisplayed', $event_params);
        $smarty->assign('form_start',
            $this->CreateFormStart($id, 'default', $returnid));
        $smarty->assign('input_vote',
            $this->CreateInputRadioGroup($id, 'vote', $votes));
        $smarty->assign('submit',
            $this->CreateInputSubmit($id, 'submit', 'Submit'));
        $smarty->assign('form_end', $this->CreateFormEnd());
        echo $this->ProcessTemplate('form.tpl');
        ?>
```

5. In your modules/Voter/templates directory, create a template named "form.tpl" containing the following:

```
<h2>What Say You?</h2>
{$form_start}
  <p>{$input_vote}</p>
  <p>{$submit}</p>
{$form_end}
```

6. Log in to your CMS Administration area. Using the top menu, go to "**Extensions**" and select "**Modules**".
7. Find your "**Voter**" module and click on the "**install**" link.
8. Using the top menu, go to "**Extensions**" and select "**Event Manager**".
9. Select "**Voter**" from the drop-down menu, and click on the "**Submit**" button:

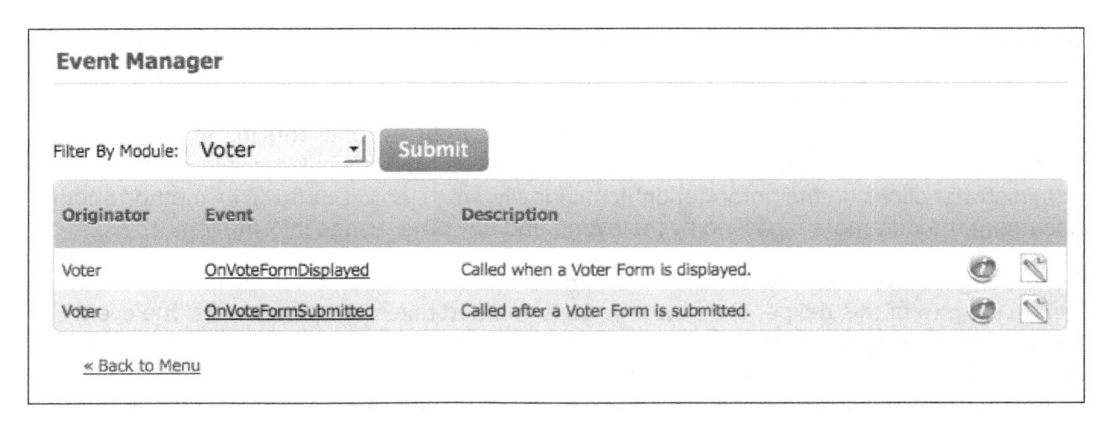

Event Manager

Filter By Module: Voter ▼ [Submit]

Originator	Event	Description		
Voter	OnVoteFormDisplayed	Called when a Voter Form is displayed.		
Voter	OnVoteFormSubmitted	Called after a Voter Form is submitted.		

« Back to Menu

10. Click on the Information icon next to the **OnVoteFormSubmitted** event:

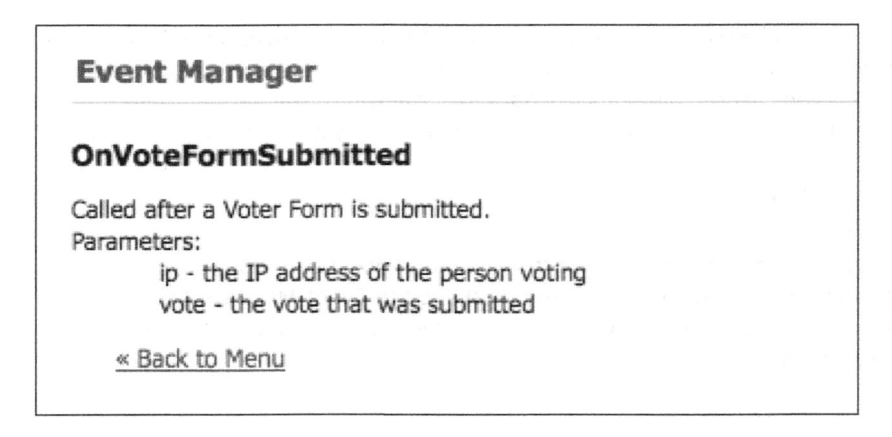

Event Manager

OnVoteFormSubmitted

Called after a Voter Form is submitted.
Parameters:
　　　ip - the IP address of the person voting
　　　vote - the vote that was submitted

« Back to Menu

How it works...

To create events from a module, there are only two mandatory steps: calling the `CreateEvent()` method in the module's `method.install.php`, and calling the `SendEvent()` method. This recipe goes a bit deeper, however, and shows how to create module events that will be both user-friendly for site administrators, and usable by other modules and UDTs.

The first step, as mentioned, is creating the events via the `CreateEvent()` method. This method takes the event name as a parameter. The convention is to use a single word, in "camel case" for the name. Use as descriptive a name as possible: you have 200 characters, so feel free to be verbose.

Using Events

While not strictly required, it's strongly recommended to override `GetEventDescription()` and `GetEventHelp()` methods for your new events. Both of these methods are very simple: they receive the event's name as a parameter, and return strings. The string from `GetEventDescription()` is what is displayed in the list of events in the Event Manager, while the string from the `GetEventHelp()` method is what is displayed when the administrator clicks on the "information" icon. Ideally, your `GetEventHelp()` method should document the parameters passed by the event, and any other usage information.

Generating the event itself is done via the `SendEvent()` method, as shown in the `action.default.php` of this recipe. The `SendEvent()` method takes two parameters: the event name, and an array of parameters. The association between events and event handlers is stored in the database; however, the event handler code in the CMS core maintains a cache, so the only real performance cost of sending an event is the cost of the handlers that process the event. Sending an event that is not being handled by a module or UDT has virtually zero performance impact.

Also note, when we send the events, particularly the **OnVoteFormSubmitted** event—the event is triggered before the value is used by our module. This is by design. If some code that handles the event needs to modify the data in some way, it will happen before we use it. That way, we're allowing the event handler to interact directly with how our vote module works.

There's more...

To see these events in action, we use the technique described elsewhere in this chapter. We create a "dumper" User-defined Tag, and then use the Event Manager to associate this UDT with our two new events. Then, we add our module's tag to a page, and visit that page on the user side of the site:

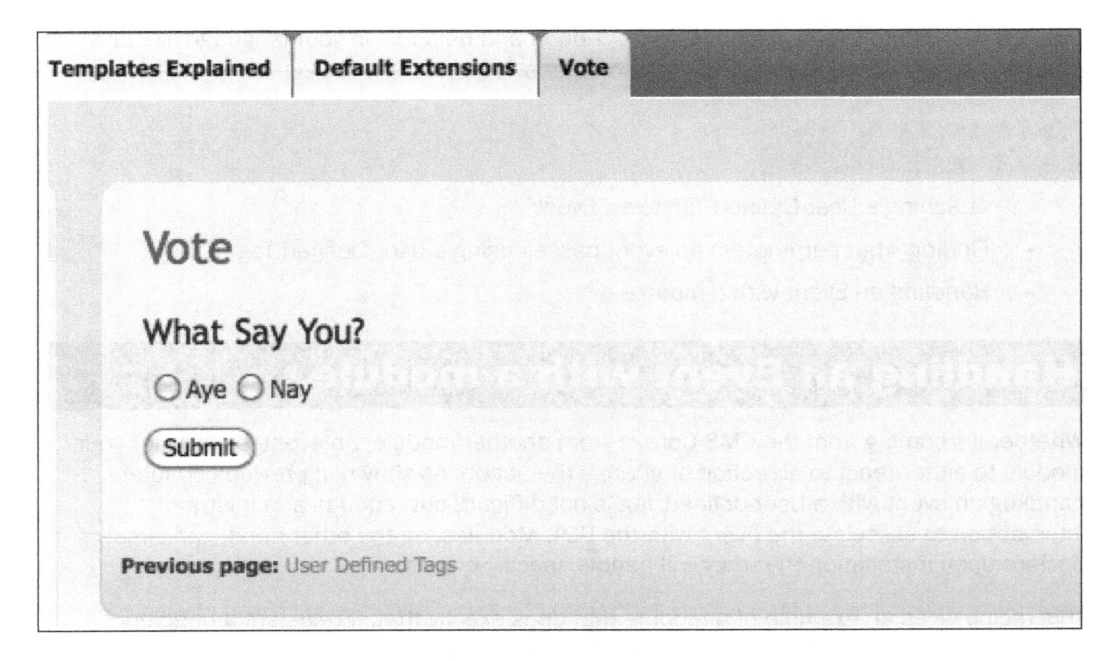

Looking at the PHP error log, we see the following:

```
[31-Dec-2010 17:21:15] Array
(
    [ip] => 198.81.128.15
)
```

Choosing an option, we submit the form. This results in the following addition to the PHP error log:

```
[31-Dec-2010 17:25:44] Array
(
    [ip] => 198.81.128.15
    [vote] => yes
)
```

Event help-text conventions

One helpful convention for the `GetEventHelp()` and `GetEventDescription()` methods is to simply use the event name as part of a localization string, for example:

```
function GetEventDescription($eventname)
{
   return $this->Lang('event_description_'.$eventname);
}
```

Using Events

This enables you to simply define your description and help text in your language file, and avoid any conditional code at all in these methods.

See also

- Attaching a User Defined Tag to an Event
- Finding what parameters an event passes using a User Defined Tag
- Handling an Event with a module

Handling an Event with a module

Whether it's coming from the CMS Core or from another module, an event is a way for your module to either react to an action or change the action. As shown in previous chapters, handling an event with a User-defined Tag is not difficult, but requires administrator intervention to associate the event with the UDT. Modules, on the other hand, can simply declare upon installation that they will handle specific events.

This recipe gives an example of a module that does exactly that. It registers a handler for an event generated by the CMS Core—AddStylesheetPre—that is generated when someone adds a stylesheet to the system. This handler is used for the hypothetical case where company policy mandates that all stylesheets have a comment containing copyright information: it checks to see if such a copyright notice exists in the stylesheet, and adds one if needed.

How to do it...

1. Using any of the methods described in *Chapter 4, Getting Started with Modules* create a new module stub for your copyright declaration module, and call it "Copyrighter".

2. Edit "method.install.php" (or create a new install file), and add the following line:
   ```
   $this->AddEventHandler('Core', 'AddStylesheetPre', true);
   ```

3. Edit your "Copyrighter.module.php" file, and add the following method:
   ```
   function DoEvent($originator, $eventname, &$params)
     {
     if ($originator == 'Core' && $eventname ==
       'AddStylesheetPre')
       {
       if (stripos($params['stylesheet']->value,'copyright') ===
         false)
         {
   ```

```
          $params['stylesheet']->value .= "\n/*\n".
            "Stylesheet: ".$params['stylesheet']->name."\n".
            "Copyright (C) ".date('Y')." by
              cmsmodulefactory.com\n*/";
        }
      }
    }
```

4. Log in to your CMS Administration area. Using the top menu, go to "**Extensions**" and select "**Modules**".

5. Find your "**Copyrighter**" module and click on the "**install**" link.

6. Using the top menu, go to "**Layout**" and select "**Stylesheets**".

7. Click on the "**Add a Stylesheet**" button.

8. Enter "**embolden**" into the "**Name**" field, and type the following into the "**Content**" area:

   ```
   body {font-weight: bold;}
   ```

9. Check "**all : Suitable for all devices**" for the Media Type, and click the "**Submit**" button.

10. In the stylesheet list, click on the title link for your "**embolden**" stylesheet to edit it. Note the added copyright notice:

    ```
    body {font-weight: bold;}
    /*
    Stylesheet: embolden
    Copyright (C) 2011 by cmsmodulefactory.com
    */
    ```

How it works...

Just as modules can register new events with the CMS Core, they can also register event handlers. This tells the CMS that this module has code that should be called when a specific event is triggered. To register an event handler, the `AddEventHandler()` method is used. This method takes three parameters:

- The source of the event. This could be "Core" or the name of a module that generates events.
- The name of the specific event.
- Whether or not this handler may be removed. If this is true, the administrator may remove the association between the module and the event using the Event Manager.

Using Events

In this recipe, we register that we will be handling the "`AddStylesheetPre`" event generated by the Core. This event is sent after an administrator adds a new stylesheet, but is called before that stylesheet is saved to the database.

Unlike some systems where you specify a `callback` method for event handlers, CMS Made Simple uses a single method for modules that process events. This method, `DoEvent()`, is called any time an event is triggered that matches one of the events for which the module registered a handler using the `AddEventHandler()`.

The `DoEvent()` module is passed a set of parameters to allow the module author to figure out what event has been received: `$originator` tells where the event came from, `$eventname` tells which event it is, and `$params` is an array of event parameters. Since the `$params` are passed by reference, we can modify the contents in our handler, as we do in this recipe.

For this particular application, we search to see if the body of the stylesheet contains the word "Copyright," and, if not, we add a copyright comment to the end. Since our handler gets called before the stylesheet is stored in the database, our modifications to the stylesheet will be saved.

There's more...

If your module handles a large number of events, the `DoEvent()` method could get awkward. Likewise, if your event handlers are overly complex, the method could grow unwieldy. Fortunately, there is a way of splitting out event handlers, similar to how module actions can be broken out into separate files.

For each event your module handles, you can use a file with the naming convention of "`event.$originator.$eventname.php`". So, for example, this recipe could omit the `DoEvent()` method, and move all of its code into a file named "`event.Core.AddStylesheetPre.php`" in the `modules/Copyrighter` directory. You will still have to register the event handler to the CMS, but this can make the event handling code easier to organize and maintain.

See also

- *Finding what parameters an event passes using a User Defined Tag* recipe
- *Use an event to send an e-mail when an Administrator Account is added or deleted* recipe

Use an event to send an e-mail when an Administrator Account is added or deleted

Event handlers often fall into one of the two major categories: using events to change the operation of a process, or using events to trigger notifications of some sort. This recipe is an example of the latter sort.

Consider the case of a CMS site that has a relatively large number of users who have access to the CMS admin area, whether as administrators, editors, or designers. It might be useful to keep the various users apprised of the new users or of the users who are no longer given access.

This recipe demonstrates one way of providing this kind of functionality. It shows you how to create a module that handles user creation and deletion events, and generates e-mails to site administrators to notify them of these events.

How to do it...

1. Using any of the methods described in *Chapter 4, Getting Started with Modules* create a new module stub for your administrator notification module, and call it "AdminNotifier".

2. Edit "method.install.php" (or create a new install file), and add the following lines:

   ```
   $this->AddEventHandler('Core', 'AddUserPost', true);
   $this->AddEventHandler('Core', 'DeleteUserPre', true);
   ```

3. Edit your "AdminNotifier.module.php" file, and add the following two methods:

   ```
   function GetDependencies()
     {
     return array('CMSMailer'=>'1.73');
     }

   function NotifyAllAdmins($message='',$subject='CMS Admin
       Notice',$exclude_user_id)
     {
     $db = $this->GetDb();
     $result = $db->Execute('select * from
       '.cms_db_prefix().'users where active=1 and user_id <>?',
       array($exclude_user_id));
     if ($result)
       {
       $mail = $this->GetModuleInstance('CMSMailer');
   ```

Using Events

```
                if ($mail != FALSE)
                {
                $mail->reset();
                $mail->SetSubject($subject);
                $mail->SetBody($message);
                }
            while ($row = $result->FetchRow())
                {
                $mail->AddAddress($row['email'],
                    $row['first_name'].' '.$row['last_name']);
                }
            $sent = $mail->Send();
            }
        }
```

4. Create a new event handler file in your modules/AdminNotifier directory called "event.Core.AddUserPost.php" containing the following code:

```
<?php
if (!isset($gCms)) exit;

$message = 'FYI: A new CMS admin user "'.$params['user']-
    >firstname.' '.$params['user']->lastname.'"
    ('.$params['user']->username.
    ') has been added.';

$this->NotifyAllAdmins($message,'CMS New Admin',$params['user']-
>id);
?>
```

5. Create a new event handler file in your modules/AdminNotifier directory called "event.Core.DeleteUserPre.php" containing the following code:

```
<?php
if (!isset($gCms)) exit;

$message = 'FYI: CMS admin user "'.$params['user']->firstname.
    ' '.$params['user']->lastname.'"
    ('.$params['user']->username.
    ') has been terminated.';

$this->NotifyAllAdmins($message,'CMS Admin
Deleted',$params['user']->id);
?>
```

6. Log in to your CMS Administration area. Using the top menu, go to "**Extensions**" and select "**Modules**".
7. Find your "**AdminNotifier**" module and click on the "**install**" link.
8. Using the top menu, go to "**Users & Groups**" and select "**Users**".
9. Add and/or remove a user. You should receive an e-mail notifying you of the changes.

How it works...

This recipe demonstrates the creation of a module that handles two standard Core system events, and uses those events to keep site administrators apprised of changes to the list of authorized users. This is just one example of a potentially very useful class of modules that keep site users informed of system status changes.

By handling the `AddUserPost` and `DeleteUserPre` events, the module is able to track when a user has been added or deleted. It registers the fact that it will handle these events by calling `AddEventHandler()` in the `method.install.php`. As described elsewhere in this chapter, the `AddEventHandler()` method takes three parameters: the source of the event, the event name, and whether the administrator may remove the module's event handler.

This recipe generates two different kinds of e-mail messages with otherwise identical requirements. The e-mail needs to go to all active site administrator accounts, but also needs to exclude the user whose changes are being described. The commonality makes this a natural candidate for separating out into a general method, which we call `NotifyAllAdmins()` and place in the main module file.

The `NotifyAllAdmins()` method performs a number of tasks. It gets a database reference using the `GetDb()` method, and queries the database for a list of all active administrators excluding the user whose `user_id` is provided in the `$exclude_user_id` parameter. It gets a reference to the CMSMailer module using the `GetModuleInstance()` method. It then generates an e-mail to each of the people in that list. The body of the e-mail and the subject are both provided to the `NotifyAllAdmins()` method as parameters.

To actually call the `NotifyAllAdmins()` method when the module receives one of the two registered events, we create the two event handler files, `event.Core.AddUserPost.php` and `event.Core.DeleteUserPre.php`. These handlers both work the same way. They start with enforcing proper usage by checking that they have been called by the CMS rather than directly from a user's browser. They then construct a message using the user object that `AddUserPost` and `DeleteUserPre` events both pass as a parameter. They then call `NotifyAllAdmins()` to actually send the notifications.

There's more...

The CMS Made Simple Core generates a lot of events that could extend a module of this nature. A little imagination should suggest a lot of opportunities for improvements. Some additions you might consider are:

- Using the `ChangeGroupAssignPre` event to notify administrators when a user's group assignment is changed
- Using the `EditUserPost` event to conditionally notify administrators when a user updates their profile (you might want to notify on a change of e-mail address but not on a change of password, for example)
- Use the `AddGroupPre` and `DeleteGroupPre` events to send notification on added or removed groups
- Use the `LoginPost` and `LogoutPost` events to drive all of your administrators crazy by telling them every time someone uses the system

PreSave versus PostSave events

You might wonder why the module uses the post-save event when looking for an added user and a pre-save event when looking for a deleted user. Examining the parameters when those events are called might help clarify. When a user is added, the user object has no ID set until after it is stored in the database, since the ID contains the unique identifier for the database record. In this particular recipe, that ID is not used, but there are numerous circumstances where it might be (for example, if the e-mail were to list which groups the new user is assigned to).

Similarly, the user record in a post-save user deletion event turns out to be an empty user object—after all, the user has already been deleted! So, if you want to get any information on that user, you need to do it before the deletion has been finalized, so the pre-save event is the one to use.

In general, pre-save events are useful if you wish to modify an object before it's saved or if the saving of the object will be destructive. Post-save events are useful if you want a complete object that includes the database ID of the saved object, or if the saving of the object is non-destructive.

See also

- *Handling an Event with a module* recipe
- *Chapter 4, Calling methods on other Modules and specifying module dependencies* recipe
- *Chapter 5, Making a database query from a module* recipe

10
Advanced Module Tricks and SEO

In this chapter, we will cover:

- Overriding Module strings or layout
- Making your module's data available to Site Search
- Output a downloadable CSV file from your module
- Using a module and `ContentPostRender` to automatically append META KEYWORDS tags
- Setting special diagnostic messages for debug mode
- Using Pretty URLs in your module
- Custom URLs for module records in CMS Made Simple version 1.9+

Introduction

In the previous chapters, we have explored a lot of practical examples of creating CMS Tags and Modules. This chapter covers a number of module-related features that didn't fit neatly into any of the other chapters. These tips and tricks include ways to customize modules without making upgrading impossible, ways to control the output of templates, so that your module can provide downloadable content, and how to give enhanced debug output.

This chapter also covers a few tricks to help with **Search Engine Optimization** (**SEO**). We demonstrate the automatic generation of Meta tags using the `ContentPostRender` event, and two separate ways to make better, search-engine friendly links to module calls.

Advanced Module Tricks and SEO

Most of the recipes in this chapter will require login access to your site's Administration area with permission to "Modify Modules", and may also need write access to the filesystem of the server where your CMS is installed.

Overriding Module strings or layout

If you use CMS Made Simple to build websites for customers, you will sometimes get into the frustrating situation where the functionality of a module is perfect for that customer's needs, but the name of the module confuses them. A common example of this is when a customer wants to publish a post-only blog on their site: the News module does exactly what they want, but they find the name "News" misleading.

There's a great solution, however, that works for everyone. You simply override the strings used by the module, so it calls itself "Blog" instead of "News." This recipe will show you how to override strings and even layouts of a CMS module.

How to do it...

1. Using your FTP client or a login shell, find your base installation directory.
2. In your base installation directory, create a directory named "`module_custom`".
3. Inside the `module_custom` directory, create a directory named "`News`"
4. Inside the "`module_custom/News`" directory create a directory named "`lang`".
5. Create a file in "`module_custom/News/lang`" containing the following:

   ```
   <?php
   $lang['news'] = 'Blog';
   $lang['addnewsitem'] = 'Add Blog Posting';
   $lang['description'] = 'Add, edit and remove Blog Postings';
   ?>
   ```

6. Save this file as "`en_US.php`".
7. Log in to your CMS Administration area.
8. Using the top menu, click on "**Content**" and observe that the News module now shows the updated module strings:

Pages

Pages
This is where we add and edit pages and other content.

Image Manager

Image Manager
Upload/edit and remove images.

Global Content Blocks

Global Content Blocks
Global Content Blocks are chunks of content you can place in your pages or templates.

Blog

Blog
Add, edit and remove Blog Postings

How it works...

As we have seen in *Chapter 4, Getting Started with Modules*, the CMS Made Simple localization system abstracts strings that are displayed by modules: within the code, a string name (key) is used instead of the string itself, and that name is used in conjunction with files of translated strings. For example, the name of the News module is labeled in the code using the key "news", that may be almost identical to the translation in the English language file, but could map to anything.

When the CMS loads the language strings for a module, it looks for the special directory "`module_custom/modulename/lang`", where `modulename` is the name of the module. If there is a file named for the language where customizations will take place, it will be used to override the module language strings. The file naming convention is the two-letter ISO 639-1 language code (in lowercase) followed by an underscore followed by the two-letter ISO 3166-1 country code. If there is no language specified for the module, it will default to US English, or `en_US.php`.

So in this case, we override the module name, module description, and an example string. The only tricky part of this is identifying which keys we wish to override. While there are a few conventions for string names, in general, the best way to identify the keys is to look at the original language file.

There's more...

Just as you can override strings from a module, you can override the templates the module uses. For any template in the `modules/modulename/templates` directory, you can create your own version in the `module_custom/moduleame/templates` directory. You simply create a copy of the Smarty template, making sure it has the same name.

As with customizing language strings, you will need to refer to the original template file to determine what Smarty variables are available (and how they're used). However, this can take more trial and error than the replacing of language strings. You can override the way the module displays logic, but this doesn't alter the way the module works internally. So, if a module requires an input field that you wish to be hidden, simply removing it from the template isn't going to work. Unless you're prepared to do complicated search and replace logic in Smarty (or go through some trial and error to find what fields are actually required by the module), you should probably limit your changes to the templates to be layout-related.

Why not change modules directly?

You might wonder why you would both override module strings and templates in the `module_custom` directory. After all, you have to identify the keys for the strings in the original language files in order to override them, and look at the variables that are available in the templates in order to re-organize them. It seems like extra work to create the `module_custom` files.

Why not just make your changes in the original files? You could easily edit the language file or templates directly. This would work, of course, but a bit of thought will show you that it's not a good idea.

The primary problem with editing files directly is that the next time you upgraded the module, all of your changes would get clobbered. Selectively upgrading files quickly becomes a management nightmare. By keeping your changes in a `module_custom` file, they are preserved through the upgrade process, and you don't have to remember every detail of where you've made changes.

Chapter 10

See also

- *Chapter 2, Renaming the "extra" content fields in the CMS Admin* recipe
- *Chapter 4, Making a module localizable* recipe
- *Chapter 2, Seeing what Smarty variables are available to your template* recipe

Making your module's data available to CMS Site Search

Content search is one of the outstanding features that comes with even the most minimal installation of CMS Made Simple. Without any user intervention, the page content of a site is indexed and can be searched by end users. What about module content?

Many modules extend the content of a CMS Made Simple site by adding structured data and ways of browsing it. You probably already know that site search works for the core News module, but what about other modules? It turns out that for your module to participate in the site search, there are some steps as a module author that you need to take.

This recipe uses a dictionary module example to show you how to add your module's content to the site search.

How to do it...

1. Using any of the methods described in *Chapter 4, Getting Started with Modules* create a new plugin type module stub for your dictionary module, and call it "Dictionary".

2. Edit "method.install.php" (or create a new install file), and add the following lines:

   ```
   <?php
   if (!isset($gCms)) exit;

   $db = $gCms->GetDb();

   $taboptarray = array('mysql' => 'TYPE=MyISAM');
   $dict = NewDataDictionary($db);

   $fields = "
     word_id I KEY AUTOINCREMENT,
     word C(255),
     definition X";
   ```

287

Advanced Module Tricks and SEO

```
    $sqlarray =
      $dict->CreateTableSQL(cms_db_prefix()."module_dictionary",
      $fields, $taboptarray);
    $dict->ExecuteSQLArray($sqlarray);

    $insert_sql = 'insert into '.cms_db_prefix().
      'module_dictionary (word,definition) values (?,?)';

    $res = $db->Execute($insert_sql,array('aciniform','Having the
      form of a cluster of grapes; clustered like grapes'));
    $res = $db->Execute($insert_sql,array('biloquist','Person with
      the power of speaking in two distinct voices'));
    $res = $db->Execute($insert_sql,array('cledonism','Using
      convoluted language to avoid unlucky words'));
    $res = $db->Execute($insert_sql,array('deasil','Clockwise, or a
      clockwise motion'));
    $res = $db->Execute($insert_sql,array('ebrious','Intoxicated,
      or inclined to consume alcohol to excess'));
    $res = $db->Execute($insert_sql,array('fulminate','Thunder,
      explode. Rant loudly or speak with great power'));
    $res = $db->Execute($insert_sql,array('galimatias','Nonsense or
      gibberish'));
    ?>
```

3. Edit "Dictionary.module.php" and add the following two methods:

```
    function SearchReindex(&$module)
      {
      $db = $this->GetDb();
      $result = $db->Execute('select * from '.
        cms_db_prefix().'module_dictionary');
      while ($result && $row=$result->FetchRow())
        {
        $module->AddWords($this->GetName(), $row['word_id'], '',
          $row['word'].' '.$row['definition']);
        }
      }

    function SearchResult($returnid, $id, $attr = '')
      {
      $result = array();
      $db = $this->GetDb();
      $dbresult = $db->Execute('select word
        from '.cms_db_prefix().
```

```
                'module_dictionary where word_id=?', array($id));
            if ($dbresult && $row=$dbresult->FetchRow())
            {
            $result[0] = 'Dictionary';
            $result[1] = $row['word'];
            $result[2] = $this->CreateLink('cntnt01', 'default',
                $returnid, '',
                array('word_id' => $id) ,'', true);
            }
        return $result;
        }
```

4. Create a new "action.default.php" file containing the following:

```
<?php
if (!isset($gCms)) exit;

if (isset($params['word_id']))
    {
    $db = $this->GetDb();
    $dbresult = $db->Execute('select * from '.cms_db_prefix().
        'module_dictionary where word_id=?',
          array($params['word_id']));
    if ($dbresult && $row=$dbresult->FetchRow())
        {
        echo '<dl><dt>'.$row['word'].'</dt>';
        echo '<dd>'.$row['definition'].'</dd></dl>';
        }
    }
?>
```

5. Log in to your CMS Administration area. Using the top menu, go to "**Extensions**" and select "**Modules**".
6. Find your "**Dictionary**" module and click on the "**install**" link.
7. Using the top menu, go to "**Extensions**" and select "**Search**".
8. Click on the "**Options**" tab.
9. Scroll down to the bottom of the page, and click on the "**Reindex All Content**" button.
10. View your site from the user side.
11. Enter "**Power**" into the Search box, and click on the search icon.

Advanced Module Tricks and SEO

12. See your module's output in the search results:

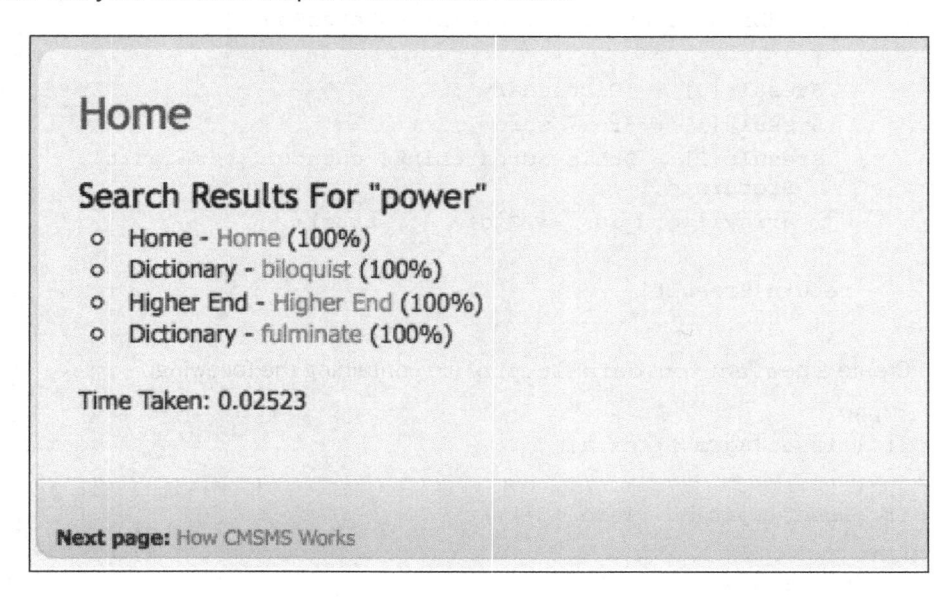

   Home

   Search Results For "power"
   - Home - Home (100%)
   - Dictionary - biloquist (100%)
   - Higher End - Higher End (100%)
   - Dictionary - fulminate (100%)

   Time Taken: 0.02523

   Next page: How CMSMS Works

13. Click on the link for "**fulminate**" and confirm the result is from your module and contains your search term:

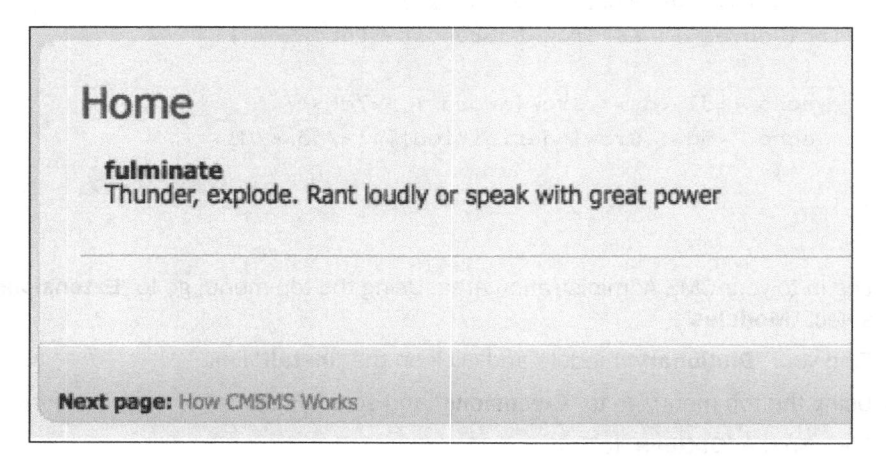

   Home

   fulminate
   Thunder, explode. Rant loudly or speak with great power

   Next page: How CMSMS Works

How it works...

For this recipe, we start with a fairly straightforward `method.install.php`, where we create a database table and load it up with our dictionary words and definitions. We will want both the words and their definitions to be added to the site search.

The site search for CMS Made Simple is managed entirely by the core Search module. The Search module maintains an index of search terms, and links to the pages that contain those terms. Modules may also add search terms to the index, but must implement a few methods to help the Search module display the proper links for those terms.

The simplest way to add terms to the Search module is to get a reference to the Search module instance, and call its `AddWords()` method. This method takes five parameters:

- `$module`—the name of the module that will handle the formatting of this content if it shows up in the search results
- `$id`—any unique record identifier for the content being indexed
- `$attr`—an optional descriptive attribute for the content being indexed (useful if your module manages multiple kinds of indexed content)
- `$content`—the text to be indexed
- `$expires`—the date this content is to be removed from the index (or null, for non-expiring content)

If your module allows dynamic addition of records that you want searchable, you can call `AddWords()` directly as part of the record creation process.

The Search module also provides a way of adding all records when the site is reindexed. That is how we added our terms to the search index in this recipe. The Search module will call a `SearchReindex()` method in your module if you implement it. This method gets called with a reference to the Search module. We use this method to query all of our words and definitions, and add them to the index. Note that we prepend the word to the definition, so that both the word and its definition are indexed and linked as a reference to the `word_id`.

Because we didn't add our terms dynamically to the search index, we were required to reindex the whole site. If we had added the words to the index at the same time we loaded them into our module's database, we would not have needed that extra step. But even if we add the records to the search index dynamically, it's important to implement the `SearchReindex()` method—when the Search module performs a reindex, it starts by removing all records from the index. If you don't add your terms back in with a `SearchReindex()` method, your search terms will be lost if and when the site is reindexed.

Advanced Module Tricks and SEO

The other half of making your module content searchable is implementing your `SearchResult()` method. This is the method that gets called by the Search module when your content is included in the search results. Because the Search module has no knowledge of how your module organizes its information, it needs you to tell it how to create a link to view a specific record from your module.

The `SearchResult()` method is called with three parameters:

- `$returnid`—the `content_id` of the page containing the Search module (this is the standard variable used by forms, and available to module actions)
- `$id`—the unique ID of the record that contains the match
- `$attr`—the optional descriptive attribute for the matching record

This method needs to return an array with three elements. The first element is a high-level description of the content—typically this would be your module's name. The second element is a title for the record, which matched the search. This second element will be displayed as the text of the link displayed to the end user as a search hit. To determine this second element, we need to use the `$id` provided by the search module to look up that record in the database. The last element of the return array is an URL to our Dictionary module's action to view the full record identified by `$id`.

This last element is highly dependent upon your module. In this recipe, we use the module's default action to display words and their definitions, based upon a `word_id` parameter. So we use the module API's `CreateLink()` method to create a link to the default action. The `CreateLink()` method is one of the API methods that takes an inordinate number of parameters; specifically of interest in this instance are: `$id` is the module identifier for the link target, `$action` is our default method, `$returnid` is passed along from the Search module, `$params` contains our `word_id` for use by the default method, and `$onlyhref` tells the method to create the link URL but not the full HTML for a link.

There's more...

To remove words from the search index, the Search module has a `DeleteWords()` method. It takes the same first three parameters as the `AddWords()` method. If your module allows dynamic addition and removal of records, and you are making those records searchable, you should make certain to delete terms from the index when their corresponding records are deleted.

See also

- *Chapter 5, Making a database query from a module* recipe
- *Chapter 4, Calling methods on other Modules and specifying module dependencies* recipe
- *Chapter 5, Creating a database table when a module gets installed* recipe

Outputting a downloadable CSV file from your module

If your module handles a lot of structured data, you will eventually get the requirement to generate reports on that data (particularly if the data is user-entered). There are several tacks you could take to meet this requirement. You could write code with elaborate calculations and various graphing libraries to present fancy reports, or, alternatively, you could give your site users the ability to export the data to a spreadsheet or other tool that's designed specifically for processing data and making reports.

As is obvious from the title of this chapter, this recipe is a demonstration of the latter approach. We export some sample data in Comma Separated Value (CSV) format, that is recognized by thousands of programs ranging from spreadsheets to databases to reporting packages.

How to do it...

1. Using any of the methods described in *Chapter 4, Getting Started with Modules* create a new plugin type module stub for your Author Data module, and call it "Authors".
2. Verify that the module returns a Boolean true from the IsPluginModule() and HasAdmin() methods.
3. Make sure the module overrides SetParameters(), and this method makes a call to RegisterModulePlugin().
4. Add the following two methods to Authors.module.php:

```
function &CreateData()
  {
  $genres = array('Action-adventure',
    'Crime','Detective','Fantasy',
    'Horror','Mystery','Romance','Science fiction',
      'Western','Inspirational');
  $fnames =
    array('Mary','James','Patricia','John','Linda',
'Robert','Barbara','Michael','Elizabeth','William');   $lnames =
    array('Smith','Johnson','Williams','Jones',
    'Brown','Davis','Miller','Wilson','Moore',
    'Taylor','Anderson','Murakami');
  $out = array();
```

```php
      array_push($out,array('Ranking','Author First Name',
        'Author Last Name',
        'Primary Genre','Books Published','Total Sales'));
    $sales = 10000000;
    for ($i=0;$i<10;$i++)
      {
      $rec = array();
      $sales -= rand(10000,999999);
      $rec[0] = ($i + 1);
      $rec[1] = $fnames[array_rand($fnames)];
      $rec[2] = $lnames[array_rand($lnames)];
      $rec[3] = $genres[array_rand($genres)];
      $rec[4] = rand(1, 10);
      $rec[5] = $sales;
      array_push($out,$rec);
      }
    return $out;
    }

  function SuppressAdminOutput(&$request)
    {
    if (strpos($_SERVER['QUERY_STRING'],'export') !== false)
      {
      return true;
      }
    return false;
    }
```

5. Create an `action.default.php` that contains the following code:

```php
<?php
if (!isset($gCms)) exit;

echo $this->CreateLink($id, 'export', $returnid, 'Export Data', array('showtemplate'=>'false'));
?>
```

6. Create an `action.export.php` file that contains the following code:

```php
<?php
if (!isset($gCms)) exit;

$data = $this->CreateData();
```

```
   @ob_clean();
   @ob_clean();
   header('Pragma: public');
   header('Expires: 0');
   header('Cache-Control: must-revalidate, post-check=0,
     pre-check=0');
   header('Cache-Control: private',false);
   header('Content-Description: File Transfer');
   header('Content-Type: text/csv; charset=iso-8859-1');
   header('Content-Disposition: attachment; filename=export.csv');
   $f=fopen('php://output','w');
   foreach ($data as $oneRow)
      {
         fputcsv($f, $oneRow);
      }
   fclose($f);
   exit;
   ?>
```

7. Create an action.admindefault.php that contains the following code:

    ```
    <?php
    if (!isset($gCms)) exit;

    echo $this->CreateLink($id, 'export', $returnid, 'Export Data');
    ?>
    ```

8. Log in to your CMS Administration area. Using the top menu, go to "**Extensions**" and select "**Modules**".

9. Find your "**Authors**" module and click on the "**install**" link.

10. Using the top menu, go to "**Extensions**" and select "**Authors**".

11. Click on the "**Export Data**" link, and view your sample download:

    ```
    Ranking,"Author First Name","Author Last Name","Primary
    Genre","Books Published","Total Sales"
    1,Michael,Brown,Mystery,5,9851468
    2,James,Williams,Western,10,9593013
    3,James,Miller,Horror,9,9337703
    4,Elizabeth,Williams,Romance,5,8728139
    5,Mary,Murakami,Romance,7,8476173
    6,Elizabeth,Jones,Horror,3,8420664
    7,Mary,Anderson,Romance,8,8356969
    8,Robert,Smith,Detective,9,7753422
    ```

Advanced Module Tricks and SEO

```
        9,William,Moore,Western,9,7499956
        10,Michael,Brown,Action-adventure,7,6954796
```

12. Using the top menu, go to "**Content**" and select "**Pages**".
13. Click on the "**Add new Content**" button.
14. Enter "**Authors**" into the "**Name**" and "**Menu Text**" fields.
15. Enter "**{Authors}**" into the "**Content**" area, and click on the "**Submit**" button.
16. View your site from the user side, and click on the menu to go to the "**Authors**" page.
17. Click on the "**Export Data**" link, and view your sample download.

How it works...

This recipe starts with the `CreateData()` method, which is a placeholder for whatever you will be using to provide the data, which you will be exporting from your module. This placeholder method uses a few arrays of common names from the 2000 U.S. Census, a list of book genres, and the random number generator to create plausible records for exporting. The only thing of note in this method is the structure of the data. Each record is an array, where each field is in a consistent index position from record to record. It returns these arrays within a containing array.

When providing data for downloading, your module needs to tell the user's browser that the content being provided is a file rather than displayable content. This is done by setting a collection of headers, that you can observe in `action.export.php`. Many of these headers are redundant and/or browser-specific to prevent caching or misinterpretation. Long and painful experience has gone into the identification of this collection, but happily these headers work for the vast majority of browsers that are in use.

The last two headers are the most important from a module's perspective, and the most likely to be changed. The "Content-Type" header optionally provides the character set. In this case, we specify ISO-8859-1 (without actually enforcing it in our data, which we should do if we anticipate any characters outside of the US-ASCII range). RFC 4180 suggests that the CSV standard should be US-ASCII unless specified otherwise. In the real world, most systems assume ISO-8859-1 because that's what Microsoft uses. Similarly, the filename provided in the "Content-Disposition" header is not guaranteed to be honored by browsers, but using a "`csv`" extension tends to be helpful especially with Microsoft browsers.

As HTTP headers must be the first thing output by a program, we issue two `@ob_clean()` commands before the headers. This will clear out any output that was buffered before this point. We issue the headers, and then we use PHP's built-in `fputcsv()` function to handle the actual formatting of the data we export.

In addition to setting HTTP headers and outputting the formatted data, there is something else we need to do—we need to prevent the CMS from wrapping our output in a template. This suppression of the template is accomplished differently depending on whether the module is being called on the user side or on the admin side. This recipe demonstrates both.

For the user side, there's a magic parameter that suppresses templates. As you can see in `action.default.php`, the link that's created includes a parameter called "showtemplate", which is set to "false". This parameter is all that it takes!

On the admin side, omitting the template is not so easy. There is the `SuppressAdminOutput()` method, that returns a Boolean value. You will get no surrounding template if you return "true" from this method, however, the method is called before your module has any opportunity to know which action is being called. You can't set a variable or test for the action in this method, because it gets called very early in the page processing. The solution is to look at the server `$_SERVER` query string supervariable, where you can look for your download action, and use that to determine the method's return value.

In both the user side and the admin side, the `action.export.php` explicitly calls the PHP "exit" function once the output is complete. If it didn't do this, control would return to the CMS, that could possibly output additional headers, cookie information, footers, or other content that would spoil our export.

There's more...

The CSV format described in RFC 4180 is quite simple, but a surprising number of implementations don't adhere to the proposed standard. The de-facto standard is often defined as "what will work in Microsoft Excel." For example, a significant number of spreadsheet programs will be more successful on import if you create a tab-delimited data file and identify it as a CSV file. If you find that your output is not working with a specific application, you can try providing the `fputcsv()` command with the optional delimiter and enclosure values. The tab is a good alternative delimiter, and some older programs seem to favor single quotes as their enclosure symbol.

See also

> ▸ Chapter 8, *Displaying a page in the CMS Admin without the surrounding theme* recipe,

Advanced Module Tricks and SEO

Setting special diagnostic messages for debug mode

During the debugging of a particularly knotty problem, you often want to display the immediate content of variables, but on a temporary basis. That is to say, you put a line into your code that displays your troubleshooting details, and then, once the problem is solved, you edit the code to remove that line because it's no longer needed.

There is also diagnostic information that may be useful in general debugging. That's why CMS Made Simple displays all SQL queries when in debug mode, for example. Your module may also have generally useful diagnostic data that should be pushed into the debug output whenever the site is in debug mode. This recipe will show you how to do that.

How to do it...

1. Using any of the methods described in *Chapter 4, Getting Started with Modules* create a new plug-in type module stub for your debug module, and call it `"Diagnostic"`.

2. Make sure that the `SetParameters()` method makes a call to `RegisterModulePlugin()`.

3. Paste the following code into the `action.default.php`:

   ```
   <?php
   if (!isset($gCms)) exit;

   debug_buffer('', 'Entering Diagnostic Module');
   $var = array();
   for ($i=0;$i<25000;$i++)
     {
     $var[$i]=str_repeat('x',$i);
     if ($i % 5000 == 0)
       {
       debug_buffer($i,'Allocating array data');
       }
     }
   debug_buffer('', 'Leaving Diagnostic Module');
   ?>
   ```

4. Log in to your CMS Administration area.
5. Using the top menu, go to "**Extensions**" and select "**Modules**".
6. Find your Diagnostic module, and click on the "**install**" link next to it.

7. Using the top menu, go to "**Content**" and select "**Pages**".
8. Click on the link to edit your home page.
9. In the content, insert the tag `{Diagnostic}`.
10. Go to the user side of your site, and verify that it works (you may experience out-of-memory condition if you haven't allocated a lot of memory to the PHP process).
11. Edit the `config.php` for your site, and set `$config['debug']` to "`true`".
12. Reload your home page, and observe the debug output:

```
Debug display of 'Entering Diagnostic Module':(3.946277) - (usage: 3723264) - (peak: 3723264)
Debug display of 'Allocating array data':(3.946836) - (usage: 3821568) - (peak: 3821568)
Debug display of 'Allocating array data':(4.085743) - (usage: 17915904) - (peak: 17915904)
5000
Debug display of 'Allocating array data':(4.259971) - (usage: 57241600) - (peak: 57241600)
10000
Debug display of 'Allocating array data':(4.591811) - (usage: 121638912) - (peak: 121638912)
15000
Debug display of 'Allocating array data':(4.837023) - (usage: 211210240) - (peak: 211210240)
20000
Debug display of 'Leaving Diagnostic Module':(5.11523) - (usage: 325824512) - (peak: 211210240)
```

How it works...

When CMS Made Simple is in debug mode, it maintains an internal diagnostic log, that gets output after the complete processing and output of each page. In practice, this means it will be output after the closing `</html>` tag for the page—this will display in most browsers, even if it does prevent the page from validating.

The `debug_buffer()` function allows you to add lines to this log. The function accepts a variable and a title for that variable.

Reading the log is fairly straightforward. Each record starts with the word "**Debug**", which is followed by "display of X" where X is a title (if a title was provided). Then there are three numbers, each in its own set of parenthesis. The first is the number of seconds since execution began, the next, labeled "**usage**" is the amount of memory that PHP reports as being in use, and the last, labeled "**peak**" is the maximum amount of memory that PHP reports as being used during the processing of the page. The following line is the variable that was passed to the `debug_buffer` function.

This recipe demonstrates debug logging in a nasty memory-eating loop. Because the loop consumes a lot of memory, you may need to decrease the number of iterations for it to work in your particular PHP installation. It's a good demonstration, however, because you can see the amount of memory used increasing, as well as the delay caused when the web server runs out of real memory and the virtual memory starts swapping.

Advanced Module Tricks and SEO

There's more...

As we saw in *Chapter 6, Using the Module Form API* you can call `debug_display()` for immediate, unconditional display of variables. There are a number of other, related functions that you can use for outputting information:

- `debug_output($var, $title)`—works like `debug_display()` to output data immediately, but will suppress output unless the site is in debug mode
- `debug_to_log($var, $title)`—works like `debug_display()` to output data, but appends the output to a file called "`debug.log`" in your site's `tmp/cache` directory
- `debug_bt()`—generates and outputs an immediate backtrace by calling the PHP `debug_backtrace()` function
- `debug_bt_to_log()`—works like `debug_bt()` but appends the output to a file called "`debug.log`" in your site's `tmp/cache` directory

See also

- *Chapter 1, How to use CMS debug mode* recipe
- *Chapter 6, Using debug_display to see what parameters your module is receiving* recipe

Using Pretty URLs in your module

When people first build a site using CMS Made Simple, they are often excited by how easy it is to make page URLs search-engine friendly. But then, sometimes, they are surprised or disappointed when they add a module, and see links that contain all sorts of opaque identifiers and control strings. People quickly learn to turn on "Pretty URLs", that make those module links look a lot less ugly.

When you implement a module, you might think that using the API to create links will automatically create Pretty URLs for you. Unfortunately, it's not that simple. The good news is that it's not hard to create Pretty URLs, but you do need to know which steps to take. This recipe shows you exactly what you need to do.

How to do it...

1. Using any of the methods described in *Chapter 4, Getting Started with Modules* create a new plug-in type module stub for your hiker's guide module, and call it "`Hikes`".
2. Add the following method to `Hikes.module.php`:

```php
    function SetParameters()
    {
    $this->RegisterModulePlugin();
    $this->RegisterRoute('/hike\/cat\/(?P<returnid>
        [0-9]+)\/(?P<category_id>[0-9]+)$/',
        array('action'=>'category'));
    $this->RegisterRoute('/hike\/hike\/(?P<returnid>
        [0-9]+)\/(?P<hike_id>[0-9]+)$/',
        array('action'=>'hike'));
    }
```

3. Create a method.install.php containing the following:

```php
<?php
if (!isset($gCms)) exit;

$taboptarray = array('mysql' => 'TYPE=MyISAM');
$dict = NewDataDictionary($db);

$fields = "
    hike_id I KEY AUTOINCREMENT,
    category_id I,
    name C(255),
    difficulty I,
    view I,
    description X";

$sqlarray =
    $dict->CreateTableSQL(cms_db_prefix().'module_hikes_hike',
    $fields, $taboptarray);
$dict->ExecuteSQLArray($sqlarray);

$fields = "
    category_id I KEY AUTOINCREMENT,
    name C(255),
    description X";

$sqlarray = $dict->CreateTableSQL(
    cms_db_prefix().'module_hikes_category',
    $fields, $taboptarray);
$dict->ExecuteSQLArray($sqlarray);

$insert_cat_sql = 'insert into '.cms_db_prefix().
    'module_hikes_category (category_id,name,description) values
(?,?,?)';

$res = $db->Execute($insert_cat_sql,array(1,'Easy Hikes',
    'Nice strolls'));
```

Advanced Module Tricks and SEO

```
    $res = $db->Execute($insert_cat_sql,array(2,'Famous Trails',
      'Treks with a reputation'));
    $res = $db->Execute($insert_cat_sql,array(3,'Weekends in
      Malibu','Trails in Topanga State Park'));

    $insert_hike_sql = 'insert into '.cms_db_prefix().
      'module_hikes_hike (category_id,name,difficulty,view,descripti
    on) values
      (?,?,?,?,?)';

    $res = $db->Execute($insert_hike_sql,array(1,'Palisades
      Park',1,9,
      'A park on the top of the Santa Monica bluffs with a view of
        the beach and pier'));
    $res = $db->Execute($insert_hike_sql,array(1,'Venice Canals
      Walk',1,7,
      'Wander between canals, over bridges, and between million dollar
    homes'));
    $res = $db->Execute($insert_hike_sql,array(2,'Sam Merrill
      Trail',9,10,'Walk up to historic Mt. Lowe to the former site
      of the Echo Mountain hotel'));
    $res = $db->Execute($insert_hike_sql,array(2,'Mount Wilson Toll
      Road',8,7,'Go from Eaton Canyon to the famous Mt. Wilson
      Observatory'));
    $res = $db->Execute($insert_hike_sql,array(3,'Temescal
      Gateway',5,5,'Follow the creek up to the waterfall, or climb
      up to the ridge'));
    $res = $db->Execute($insert_hike_sql,array(3,'Corral
      Canyon',3,8,'Strange rock formations and great views are
      found on both sides of this fire road'));
    $res = $db->Execute($insert_hike_sql,array(3,'Passeo
      Miramar',6,10,'Climb up to Parker Mesa overlook, and see the
      whole sweep of the city and Santa Monica bay'));
    ?>
```

4. Create an `action.default.php` containing the following:

```
<?php
if (!isset($gCms)) exit;

$db= $this->GetDb();
$cats = array();
$res = $db->Execute('select * from
  '.cms_db_prefix().'module_hikes_category');
while ($res && $row=$res->FetchRow())
  {
  $prettyurl = 'hike/cat/'.$returnid.'/'.$row['category_id'];
```

```php
    $row['link'] = $this->CreateLink($id, 'category', $returnid,
      $row['name'],
      array('category_id'=>$row['category_id']), '', false,
        false, '', false,
      $prettyurl);
    array_push($cats,$row);
    }
$smarty->assign('cats',$cats);
echo $this->ProcessTemplate('display_cats.tpl');
?>
```

5. Create an `action.category.php` containing the following:

```php
<?php
if (!isset($gCms)) exit;

$db= $this->GetDb();
$hikes = array();
$res = $db->Execute('select * from '.cms_db_prefix().
  'module_hikes_hike where category_id=?',
  array($params['category_id']));
while ($res && $row=$res->FetchRow())
  {
  $prettyurl = 'hike/hike/'.$returnid.'/'.$row['hike_id'];
  $row['link'] = $this->CreateLink($id, 'hike', $returnid,
    $row['name'], array('hike_id'=>$row['hike_id']), '', false,
    false, '', false, $prettyurl);
  array_push($hikes,$row);
  }
$cat = $db->GetOne('select name from '.cms_db_prefix().
    'module_hikes_category where category_id=?',
    array($params['category_id']));
$smarty->assign('hikes',$hikes);
$smarty->assign('category',$cat);
echo $this->ProcessTemplate('display_hikes.tpl');
?>
```

6. Create an `action.hike.php` containing the following:

```php
<?php
if (!isset($gCms)) exit;

$db = $this->GetDb();
$hikes = array();
$res = $db->Execute('select * from '.cms_db_prefix().
  'module_hikes_hike where hike_id=?',
```

Advanced Module Tricks and SEO

```
      array($params['hike_id']));
if ($res && $row=$res->FetchRow())
  {
  $smarty->assign('hike',$row);
  }
echo $this->ProcessTemplate('hike_detail.tpl');
?>
```

7. In your `modules/Hikes/templates` directory, create a template called `display_cats.tpl` that contains the following:

   ```
   <h2>Hike Categories</h2>
   <ul>
   {foreach from=$cats item=category}
     <li>{$category.link}</li>
   {/foreach}
   </ul>
   ```

8. In the same templates directory, create a template called `display_hikes.tpl` that contains the following:

   ```
   <h2>{$category}</h2>
   <ul>
   {foreach from=$hikes item=hike}
     <li>{$hike.link}</li>
   {/foreach}
   </ul>
   ```

9. Create one last template, called `hike_detail.tpl`, that contains the following:

   ```
   <h2>{$hike.name}</h2>
   <div>Hike: {$hike.name}</div>
   <div>Difficulty rating (1-10): {$hike.difficulty}</div>
   <div>View rating (1-10): {$hike.view}</div>
   <div>Description: {$hike.description}</div>
   ```

10. Log in to your CMS Administration area.

11. Using the top menu, go to "**Extensions**" and select "**Modules**".

12. Click on the "**install**" link next to your Hikes module.

13. Using the top menu, go to "**Content**" and select "**Pages**".

14. Click on the "**Add New Content**" button.

15. Enter "**Hikes**" into the "**Name**" and "**Menu Text**" fields.

16. Enter "**{Hikes}**" into the "**Content**" text area, and click on the "**Submit**" button.

17. On the user side of your site, go to your new "**Hikes**" page. Click around in the hike categories and details, noting the URLs in your browser's address bar.

    ```
    http://yourdomain.com/index.php?mact=Hikes,cntnt01,hike,0&cntnt01h
    ike_id=6&cntnt01returnid=91
    ```

18. Edit your site's `config.php`, and change the URL rewriting option to internal pretty URLs:

    ```
    $config['url_rewriting'] = 'internal';
    ```

19. On the user side of your site, go back to your new "**Hikes**" page. Click around in the hike categories and details, noting the new pretty URLs in your browser's address bar.

    ```
    http://yourdomain.com/index.php/hike/hike/91/6
    ```

How it works...

This recipe establishes a database application with three different actions, each of which is a fairly straightforward database query and formatting of data for output. The basic module follows the examples of database API as explored in Chapter 5, Using the Database API. Where this recipe diverges from these earlier examples is in how the links from one action to another are formed and handled.

The implementation of pretty URLs requires additional code in two different places. First, the module's `SetParameters()` method needs to establish the means of interpreting the pretty URLs, and next, those pretty URLs need to be passed to the API link-creation method every time the module generates a link.

We start by defining what our pretty URLs will look like. This is done in `SetParameters()` by calling the `RegisterRoute()` method. The `RegisterRoute()` method takes only two parameters: a regular expression defining the route, and a set of parameters that will be passed when this regular expression matches. Let's look at this in detail, using the first route defined in `Hikes.module.php`.

The regular expression used is:

```
/hike\/cat\/(?P<returnid>[0-9]+)\/(?P<category_id>[0-9]+)$/
```

Translating this into English, the first portion looks for an URL string that starts with `/hike/cat`. The next clause,

```
(?P<returnid>[0-9]+)
```

is what is called a "named group substring match". The parenthesis delimits the group, and the `?P<name>` assigns any matches of the group to a variable `<name>`. So this clause matches any string of one or more digits, and assigns them to the variable "`returnid`". Similarly, the next clause matches a forward slash, followed by another string of digits, which get assigned to the variable "`category_id`".

Advanced Module Tricks and SEO

As you probably anticipated, these variables get passed to the CMS as if they were part of the standard $params array. The second parameter to the RegisterRoute() method is an array that also gets merged into the standard $params array, in this case setting our $params['action'] to be 'category'.

So, given the route definition

```
$this->RegisterRoute('/hike\/cat\/(?P<returnid>[0-9]+)\/(?P<category_id>[0-9]+)$/', array('action'=>'category'));
```

an incoming URL of the form

```
/hikes/cat/12/5
```

would be interpreted like a call to the action "category" with the $returnid equal to 12 and the $params['category_id'] equal to 5. You'll note that the special CMS variables $action and $returnid are available directly, while the category_id gets placed into the $params array—it turns out that all of the variables coming in from a registered route will be placed into the standard $params array, but the system also knows to look for the two special variables "action" and "returnid".

Knowing how to handle the pretty URL routes is only half of the equation, however. When creating links, the API needs to be provided with the pretty version of the URL. Because there could be many similar pretty URL mappings (involving the same actions and even some parameters), the API can't create the link side on its own. As you can see in action.default.php and action.category.php, a pretty URL is assembled as a string and passed as a parameter to the API's CreateLink() call. As the module author, you will know how to create the appropriate pretty URL string to match the routes that you created in the SetParameters() method. The API does know enough to use the pretty URL if the site is configured to use "internal" pretty URLs, or fall back to the uglier collection of parameters otherwise.

See also

- *Chapter 5, Creating a database table when a module gets installed* recipe
- *Chapter 4, Making a database query from a module* recipe
- *Chapter 4, Using Smarty variables and templates with a module* recipe
- *Custom URLs for module records in CMS Made Simple version 1.9+* recipe

Custom URLs for module records in CMS Made Simple version 1.9+

As shown in the previous recipe, CMS Made Simple can be set up to use Pretty URLs that hide some of the uglier parameter strings that scare Search-Engine Optimization experts. As of version 1.9, CMS Made Simple adds the ability to create custom URLs for both pages and for module data. A custom URL allows you to specify the path part of the URL (the portion after the "`index.php`"), and uniquely assign it to a module call.

Custom URLs are immensely powerful—they make it possible to use any URL to refer to your module. You can create virtual hierarchies with module records, or even map multiple URLs to a given resource. This recipe shows you two ways to use Custom URLs.

How to do it...

1. Using any of the methods described in *Chapter 4, Getting Started with Modules* create a new plugin type module stub for your pie reference module, and call it "`Pies`".

2. Add the following method to `Pies.module.php`:

```php
function SetParameters()
  {
  $this->RegisterModulePlugin();
  $gCms = cmsms();
  $contentops = $gCms->GetContentOperations();
  $returnid = $contentops->GetDefaultContent();
  $parms = array('action'=>'default','returnid'=>$returnid);
  $parms['pie_id'] = 1;
  $route = new CmsRoute('apple/pie/is/the/best',
    $this->GetName(),$parms,TRUE);
  cms_route_manager::register($route);
  $db = $this->GetDb();
  $res = $db->Execute('select pie_id, name from
    '.cms_db_prefix().'module_pies');
  while ($res && $row=$res->FetchRow())
    {
    $parms['pie_id'] = $row['pie_id'];
    $route = new CmsRoute('pie/'.strtolower($row['name']),
      $this->GetName(),$parms,TRUE);
    cms_route_manager::register($route);
    }
  }
```

Advanced Module Tricks and SEO

3. Create a new `method.install.php` that contains the following code:

```php
<?php
if (!isset($gCms)) exit;

$taboptarray = array('mysql' => 'TYPE=MyISAM');
$dict = NewDataDictionary($db);

$fields = "
  pie_id I KEY AUTOINCREMENT,
  name C(255),
  description X";

$sqlarray =
  $dict->CreateTableSQL(cms_db_prefix().'module_pies',
  $fields, $taboptarray);
$dict->ExecuteSQLArray($sqlarray);

$insert_sql = 'insert into '.cms_db_prefix().
  'module_pies (pie_id,name,description) values (?,?,?)';

$res = $db->Execute($insert_sql,array(1,'Apple',
  'Delectable and tart, Apple is always a favorite.'));
$res = $db->Execute($insert_sql,array(2,'Strawberry-Rhubarb',
  'Tangy and sweet, this is good with whipped cream.'));
$res = $db->Execute($insert_sql,array(3,'Cherry',
  'Most versions are far too sweet, but outstanding when done
  right'));
$res = $db->Execute($insert_sql,array(4,'Key-Lime',
  'Great with strong dark coffee.'));
$res = $db->Execute($insert_sql,array(5,'Pumpkin',
  'Worth eating all year, not just for Thanksgiving.'));
?>
```

4. Create a new `action.default.php` that contains the following code:

```php
<?php
if (!isset($gCms)) exit;

$db= $this->GetDb();
$res = $db->Execute('select * from '.cms_db_prefix().
  'module_pies where pie_id=?', array($params['pie_id']));
if ($res && $row=$res->FetchRow())
  {
  echo '<h2>'.$row['name'].'</h2>';
  echo '<p>'.$row['description'].'</p>';
  }
else
```

```
    {
      echo "[unknown pie]";
    }
?>
```

5. Edit your site's `config.php`, and change the URL rewriting option to internal pretty URLs:

    `$config['url_rewriting'] = 'internal';`

6. Log in to your CMS Administration area. Using the top menu, go to "**Extensions**" and select "**Modules**".

7. Click on the "**install**" link next to your Pies module.

8. Go to the user-side of your website. Change the URL in the address bar to be:

    `http://yourdomain.com/index.php/apple/pie/is/the/best`

9. Observe that you have gone to the appropriate page:

    # Home

    ## Apple

    Delectable and tart, Apple is always a favorite.

    Next page: How CMSMS Works

10. Enter the following into your browser address bar:

    `http://yourdomain.com/index.php/pie/apple`

11. Note that you have gone to the same page. Now try:

    `http://cms_book.viajante/index.php/pie/strawberry-rhubarb`

12. See that you have gone to the appropriate page:

> **Home**
>
> **Strawberry-Rhubarb**
>
> Tangy and sweet, this is good with whipped cream.
>
> **Next page:** How CMSMS Works

How it works...

In this recipe, we see how we can associate an arbitrary path portion of an URL with a specific call to a module. We with a fairly standard module that creates and populates a database table in its install method, and displays individual records with its default action. Now, to improve our search-engine rankings, we want to avoid URLs that have arbitrary record ID numbers in them, and use custom, relevant URLs instead.

Custom URLs are accomplished entirely in your module's `SetParameters()` method, by creating new `CmsRoute` objects, and registering them with the CMS. A `CmsRoute` object defines a custom URL string, and maps it to a module call, as well as specifying a collection of parameters. The constructor for a `CmsRoute` takes four parameters:

- `$term`—this is the URL string that will be mapped.
- `$dest`—name of the module that will handle requests that match the term.
- `$defaults`—an array of parameters. This array has two mandatory parameters: `action`, and `returnid`. These match the usual variables of the same name. Any other parameters will be available to the called module action as part of the `$params` array.
- `$is_absolute`—Boolean indicating whether or not the URL string must be an exact match (if `false`, a partial match will work).

Once we have a `CmsRoute` object, we need to register it with the CMS. This is done by making a static call to the `register()` method of the `cms_route_manager` class:

```
cms_route_manager::register($route);
```

So, in our recipe, we start by creating a standard array of parameters that we will use. First, we need to come up with a `returnid`. Remember that the `returnid` is the `page_id` of the page, which will be used to display module output—essentially, the specified page will have its content area replaced by our module's output. Many modules, like News, have a specific default page, that they use for displaying output. If our module had such a page, we would use that `page_id` for the `returnid`. Since we don't have a specific page, we will use the site's default page. To do so, we get the `ContentOperations` object, and retrieve the default site `page_id` using its `GetDefaultContent()` method. We use this `page_id` for our `returnid`.

To our standard set of parameters, we add an action specification, and the `pie_id` of 1, which we know corresponds to "Apple." Then we create the route by specifying our desired URL string (`"apple/pie/is/the/best"`), the name of our module, our parameter array, and a Boolean `true` to state that it's an absolute URL.

In addition to making one URL to map to the long `"apple/pie/is/the/best"` URL, we want the other pies to have their own individual URLs. So we query the database for all our records, and create routes based on their names, registering each route after creating it. In an actual production system, we'd want to be a little more careful about converting the names to URLs, so we could avoid characters like spaces.

There's more...

What happens if you register two routes that conflict? One kind of conflict occurs if you use the same URL string twice (for example, mapping `"apple/pie/is/the/best"` to the Pies module's action to display Apple Pie, and also to the Opinions module's action for displaying how many people prefer apple pie.) In this case, the first route that was registered is the one that wins out when there is a match.

Another possible conflict occurs if you're not using absolute URLs and two different routes will partially match the user's URL. Again, the first route that was registered that would match is the one that will be called.

See also

- *Chapter 5, Creating a database table when a module gets installed* recipe
- *Chapter 5, Making a database query from a module* recipe
- *Using Pretty URLs in your module* recipe

Index

Symbols

$action parameter 190
$action variable 227
$adding parameter 252
$attr parameter 291, 292
$blockName parameter 252
$blockParams parameter 252
$category parameter 103
$content parameter 291
$db variable 146
$enctype parameter 190
$end_time parameter 103
$exclude_user_id parameter 281
$expires parameter 291
$extra parameter 190
$icon parameter 103
$id parameter 190, 291, 292
$idsuffix parameter 190
$id variable 176
$inline parameter 190
$inputParams parameter 252
$invert_case parameter 106
$mail->send() method 141
$message variable 176
$method parameter 190
$module parameter 291
$params parameter 190, 252
$params variable 267
$returnid parameter 190, 292
$returnid variable 176, 260
$_SERVER variable 73
$smarty
   versus $this->smarty 136

$smarty->_current_page variable
   about 110
   values 110
$start_time parameter 103
$status parameter 103
$summary parameter 103
$taboptarray 146
$text parameter 103
$this reference 24
$this->smarty
   versus $smarty 136
$title parameter 103
$value parameter 252
{$variable|uppercase} modifier 9, 11
{Absurdists} tag 190
{assorted_variables} tag 77
<body> tag 77, 79
{content} tag 96, 190
{get_template_vars} tag 65, 66
<head> tag 79
.htaccess file 46, 118
{ldelim} tag 52
{literal} tag 52
-m flag 205
.module.php extension 116
@ob_clean() commands 296
{page_attr} tag 75
.php extension 117
{rdelim} tag 52
-r flag 211
.tar file 214
{translator} tag 96
{user_ip} tag 72
--username flag 206
.zip file 214

A

about text function 20
access control 233
account
   creating, on Developer's Forge 200-202
action.action_name.php file 127
action.admindefault.php file 295
action.defaultadmin.php file 226
action.defaultadmin.php stub 125
action.default.php file 156, 173, 176,
      253, 289
action.default.php stub 125
action.export.php file 296
action parameter 243
action.YOUR_ACTION.php stub 125
action.YOUR_ADMIN_ACTION.php stub 125
active_tab parameter 232
ActiveX Database Objects. *See* ADO
AddColumnSQL() method 165
AddEventHandler() method 277, 281
AddGroupPre event 282
additional indexes
   creating, for tables 149-151
AddNewsArticle() method 102
AddUserPost event 281
AddWords() method
   about 291
   parameters 291
Admin alert queue
   message, placing on 260-263
admin.inc.php file 38, 39
administrators
   module, hiding from 253-256
Admin log 242
admin module
   multiple tabs, creating for 228-231
admin panel
   about 204
   creating 257-260
   creating, for module 226, 227
admin_panel.tpl file 230
admin-side input element
   creating, ContentModule block used 246-252
ADO 145
ADOdb
   about 146

   high-level datatypes 147
   versus ADOdb-lite 148
ADOdb-lite
   versus ADOdb 148
ADODB Lite 81
article
   posting, to News Module 100-103
assign_by_ref() method 79
assign() method 79
attributes
   getting, page_attr used 75, 76
audit() function 267
Audit() method
   about 243, 267
   parameters 243
auto-increment 160, 161
average_rating field 146

B

Babelfish
   about 95
   translation of current page, displaying with
      UDT 95-98
basic form
   creating, in module 172-178
block
   displaying, for Home page 56-59
BookmarkOperations object 75
bug reports (BRs) 200

C

caching 20
changefreq attribute 49, 50
ChangeGroupAssignPre event 282
ChangeTableSQL() method 165
character encoding 50
Chart.module.php file 239
checkboxes
   creating 195-197
checkout command 211
CheckPermission() method 237
CLEAN_FILE type code 182
CLEAN_FLOAT type code 182
CLEAN_INT type code 182
CLEAN_NONE type code 182
CLEAN_STRING filter 183

CLEAN_STRING type code 182
CMS
  about 143
  Extra Page Attributes, renaming in 36-38
  page number, displaying with UDT 80-82
  structured system 143
  unstructured system 143
  using, in debug mode 24, 26
CMS Admin
  page, displaying in 238-241
cms_db_prefix() function 82, 86, 156
CMS Made Simple
  about 7, 143
  basic form, creating in module 172-178
  benefits 70
  caching pages mechanism 17
  file structure, creating for 114-116
  module, breaking into multiple files 125-127
  module, creating for 21-24
  module dependencies, specifying 136-140
  module, localizing 128-130
  new module stub, creating with ModuleMaker module 122-125
  new module stub, creating with Skeleton module 118-121
  Smarty variables, using with module 132-135
  Smarty variables, using with templates 132-135
  tag, creating for 17-20
  UDT, creating for 14-16
CMS Made Simple Module API 113, 114
CMS Made Simple version 1.9+
  custom URLs, for modules 307-310
CMS Mailer 137
CMSModule object 136
cmsms() function 74, 78, 82
CmsObject
  about 78, 82
  using, in UDT 73, 74
CmsRoute object 310
CMS Site Search
  module data, making available to 287-292
CMS_VERSION 24
ColorPicker.module.php file 244
color set
  creating, in stylesheet 28-31

commands, Git
  about 220
  git clone 220
  git diff 220
  git log 220
  git rm 220
  git tag 220
commands, Subversion
  about 210
  svn copy 210
  svn log 210
  svn merge 210
  svn mv 210
  svn revert 210
  svn rm 210
Comma Separated Value (CSV) format 293
computer program 171
config.php file 25
conflicts
  about 209
  handling, in Git 220, 222
content:block_name 110
content_en property 98
ContentModule block
  admin-side input element, creating 246-252
ContentOperations object
  about 74, 75, 98, 194
  using, in UDT 74
ContentPostRender event 283
content search feature 287
content tag 70
count(*) command 82, 157
count_words modifier 63
crackers 83
CreateData() method 296
created attribute 45
CreateEvent() method 273
CreateFieldsetEnd() method 177
CreateFieldsetStart() method 176
CreateFileUploadInput method 178
CreateFormEnd() method 177
CreateFormStart() method
  about 176, 190, 260
  parameters 190
CreateFrontendFormStart method 178
CreateFrontendLink() method 260
CreateIndexSQL() method 151

CreateInputCheckbox() method 177
CreateInputDropdown method 178
CreateInputFile method 178
CreateInputHidden method 178
CreateInputPassword method 178
CreateInputRadioGroup() method 177
CreateInputReset method 178
CreateInputSelectList method 178
CreateInputText method 178
CreateInputTextWithLabel() method 176
CreateLabelForInput() method 177
CreateLink() method 260, 292, 306
CreateParameter() method 182
CreatePermission() method 237
CreateSequence() method 159
CreateTableSQL() method 147, 151, 159
CreateTooltipLink method 178
CreateTooltip method 178
criteria, for tag 11
cURL
  using 93, 94
curl_exec() method 93
cURL library 92
CURLOPT_HTTPHEADER 99
CURLOPT_POST 98
CURLOPT_POSTFIELDS 98
CURLOPT_RETURNTRANSFER 93, 99
custom URLs 307

D

database abstraction layer 114
database index
  advantages, demonstrating 151, 153
  creating, during table creation 148-151
database query
  creating, from module 153-157
database sequence
  creating 157-159
  using 157-159
database table
  altering, during module upgradation 161-164
  cleaning up, during module uninstallation 166-168
  creating, during module installation 144-147
datastore 145
Db 75

dbrescue module 207
debug_bt() method 300
debug_bt_to_log() method 300
debug_buffer() function 299
debug_display() function 185
debug_display() method 104, 300
  using 183-185
debug mode
  about 26
  CMS, using in 24, 26
  diagnostic messages, setting for 298, 299
debug_output() method 300
debug_to_log() method 300
defeats field 151
DeleteGroupPre event 282
Delete() method 103
DeleteUserPre event 281
DeleteWords() method 292
description field 146
Developer's Forge
  about 200
  account, creating on 200-202
  module, adding to 202, 203
diagnostic messages
  setting, for debug mode 298, 299
dictionary module
  example 288-292
Dictionary.module.php file 288
diff command 208
disqualifying questions, for tag 12
disqualifying questions, for UDT 10
distributed system 92
DoAction() method 24, 126, 127, 136, 141, 227
DoEvent() method 278
downloadable CSV file
  outputting, from module 293-297
DropTableSQL() method 168

E

echo() function 185
EditUserPost event 282
e-mails
  generating, for site administrator notification 279-281
EndTabContent() method 232

EndTabHeaders() method 231
EndTab() method 231
entity encoding 183
en_US.php file 117
error_log() function
  using 183-185
evaluated template 110
event
  about 265
  e-mails, generating for site administrator notification 279-281
  generating, from module 270-274
  generating, simple voting module 270-274
  handling, with module 276-278
  notifications, triggering 279-281
  UDT, attaching to 266, 267
event handlers 279
event help-text conventions 275
Event Manager
  about 266, 268
  UDT, attaching, to event 266, 267
event parameters
  identifying 268-270
Execute() method 82, 86, 156
ExecuteSQLArray() method 147, 151, 159, 165
ext directory 117
extensions 8
Extra Page Attributes
  renaming, in CMS 36-38

F

FetchRow() method 86, 156
file command 92
filespec 110
file structure
  creating, for module 114-116
first_name field 150
foreach command
  about 55
  parameters 55
form_start tag 178
fputcsv() command 297
fputcsv() function 296

G

GCB 8, 20, 43
GetAdminSection() method
  about 227
  menu sections 228
GetAuthorEmail() method 120
GetAuthor() method 120
GetContentBlockInput() method 252, 253
GetContentBlockValue() method
  parameters 252
GetDefaultContent() method 311
GetDependencies() method 140
GetEventDescription() method 274, 275
GetEventHelp() method 274, 275
GetFriendlyName() method 227
GetModuleInstance() method 102, 140, 281
GetName() method 23, 116, 117, 120
GetNotificationOutput() method 262
GetOne() method 82, 157
GetPreference() method 259, 260
get_template_vars() method 89
GetVersion() method 24, 120, 165
GiftList.module.php file 226
Gift List Registry module 226
Git
  about 215, 217
  commands 220
  conflicts, handling in 220, 222
  module, developing with 217-220
  using 217
  versus Subversion 222, 223
git add command 219
git clone command 220
git commit command 219
git diff command 220
git fetch command 219
git-gui 216
GitHub 217
git init command 216
git log command 220
git merge command 219
git pull command 219
git push command 216, 220

Git repository
  creating 215, 216
git rm command 220
git status command 219
git tag command 220
Global Content Block. *See* **GCB**
globalcontent:block_name 110
GlobalContentOperations object 75
global declaration 76
Google Sitemap
  creating, with Menu Manager 46, 48
GroupOperations object 75

H

HasAdmin() method 227, 229, 233, 293
HasCapability() method 251
haschildren attribute 45
Hello World module
  creating 21-24
Hello World tag
  creating 17-20
Hello World UDT
  creating 14-16
help text function 20
hierarchy attribute 45
HierarchyManager object 75
high-level datatypes, ADOdb
  about 147
  C 147
  C2 147
  D 147
  F 147
  I 147
  1 147
  I2 147
  I8 147
  L 147
  N 147
  T 147
  TS 147
  X 147
  X2 147
  XL 147
Hikes.module.php file 300
Home page
  block, displaying for 56-59

html_entity_decode() method 183
htmlspecialchars() function 87

I

image attribute 45
images
  naming conventions 45
individual localization files 117
Install() method 126, 127, 135
InstallPostMessage() method 245
IsPluginModule() method 23, 156, 293
isset() function 177, 198
item id parameter 243
item name parameter 243

J

JavaScript
  embedding, in template 51, 52
  Smarty variables, using in 52

K

knight_id field 150

L

lang directory 117
Lang() method 176
lastmod attribute 49
last_name field 150
layouts
  overriding, of CMS module 284-286
loc attribute 49
LoginPost event 270, 282
LogoutPost event 282
looping capabilities 53

M

MadScience.module.php file 233
MailDemo module 139
mashups 89
Menu Manager
  basic Google Sitemap, creating with 46, 48
  personnel directory, creating with 39-44
menu sections, GetAdminSection() method
  content 228

ecommerce 228
extensions 228
layout 228
main 228
myprefs 228
siteadmin 228
usersgroups 228
mergetool command 221
message
   auditing, from module 242, 243
   displaying, after CMS Made Simple installation 244, 245
   placing, on Admin alert queue 260-263
method.defaultadmin.php file 237
method.install.php file 125, 144, 146, 164, 172, 176, 237
method.uninstall.php file 125
method.upgrade.php file 125, 127, 165
modified attribute 45
modifiers 104
module
   about 8, 13, 14, 114, 265
   adding, to Developer's Forge 202, 203
   admin panel, creating for 226, 227
   basic form, creating in 172-178
   breaking, into multiple files 125-127
   creating 21-24
   database query, creating from 153-157
   developing, Git used 217-220
   developing, Subversion used 206, 208
   downloadable CSV file, outputting from 293-297
   event, generating with 270-274
   event, handling with 276-278
   file structure, creating for 114-116
   hiding, from administrators 253-256
   layouts, overriding 284-286
   localizing 128-130
   localizing, without Subversion 132
   messages, auditing from 242, 243
   output, displaying 186-190
   parameters, restricting to 179-182
   Pretty URLs, using in 300-305
   qualifying questions 13, 14
   Smarty variables, using with 132-135
   strings, overriding 284-286
Module API 8

module author 117
module_custom directory 284
module_custom/moduleame/templates directory 286
module data
   providing, to CMS Site Search 287-292
module_db_tpl:module_name;template_name 110
module dependencies
   about 141
   specifying 136-140
module directory
   tips, for naming 117
module file
   tips, for naming 117
module_file_tpl:module_name;template_ filename 110
module installation method
   database table, creating 144-147
ModuleMaker module
   about 121
   module stub, creating 122-125
Module Manager
   module dependencies 141
ModuleManager module 244
ModuleOperations object 75
module output
   embedding, in different page 191-193
module release
   publishing 211-214
modules/modulename/templates directory 286
module-specific preference
   creating 257-260
module stub
   creating, ModuleMaker module used 122-125
   creating, Skeleton module used 118-121
module uninstallation
   database table, cleaning up 166-168
Movies.module.php file 229
multiple content blocks
   creating, on page 60-62
multiple files
   module, breaking into 125-127
multiple tabs
   creating, for admin module 228-231

MyModule directory 116
MySQL 146

N

name
  registered trademark symbols, adding to 107, 109
name field 146
namespaces 21
naming conventions, for images 45
NCleanBlue 51
NewDataDictionary 146
NewDataDictionary class 151, 165
NewDataDictionary object 165
News module 284, 287
News Module
  article, posting to 100-103
NotifyAllAdmins() method 281

O

OnVoteFormSubmitted event 274
Open Source community 199
Open Source project 199
Open Source software 199

P

page
  displaying, in CMS Admin 238-241
  multiple content blocks, creating on 60-62
page_attr
  attributes, getting 75, 76
Page Content object
  accessing, via CmsObject in UDT 73, 74
page_counter tag 81
page number
  displaying, UDT used 80-82
parameters
  restricting, to module 179-182
permissions
  about 253
  creating, for module administration 233-237
  enforcing, for module administration 233-237
personnel directory
  creating, Menu Manager used 39-44
phishers 83

play_count field 146
post-compile filter 107, 110
PostSave event
  versus PreSave event 282
pre-compile filter 107, 111
preg_match() method 99
PreSave event
  versus PostSave event 282
Pretty URLs
  about 300
  using, in module 300-305
primary function 20
print_r() function 185
print_r modifier 67
priority attribute 49, 50
ProblemSolver module 119
ProcessTemplateFromDatabase() method 135
ProcessTemplateFromData() method 110, 135
ProcessTemplate() method 177
process_whole_template variable 79
production module 141
project
  importing, into SVN 204, 206

Q

qualifying questions, for module 13, 14
qualifying questions, for tag 13
  criteria, for using 11
qualifying questions, for UDT 9

R

RapidSVN 206
registered trademark symbols
  adding, to name automatically 107, 109
RegisterModulePlugin() method 156, 298
RegisterRoute() method 305, 306
relational database management systems 149
release notes 214
remote command 216
RenameColumnSQL() method 166
RenameTableSQL() method 166
reporter_name field 176

reporter_name parameter 177
RestrictUnknownParams() method 182

S

Save() method 103
screen scraping technique 99
SearchCompleted event 267
Search Engine Optimization (SEO) 50, 283
Search module 291
SearchReindex() method 291
SearchResult() method
  about 292
  parameters 292
SendEvent() method 273, 274
sequences 161
SetInitialValues() method 103
setlist tag 55
SetParameters() method 121, 156, 175, 182, 195, 298, 305, 306
SetParameterType() method 182, 183
SetPreference() method 259
SetTabHeader() method 231
showtemplate parameter 242
simple voting module
  event, generating from 270-274
sitemap attributes
  changefreq 50
  priority 50
sizes
  computing, in stylesheet 32-35
Skeleton module
  module stub, creating 118-121
Smarty
  color set, creating in stylesheet 28-31
  complex comparisons 59, 60
  sizes, computing, in stylesheet 32-35
  variable, exporting from UDT 78
  variable, making available to 76-78
smarty_cms_function_helloworld 20
smarty_cms_modifier_reverse 106
smarty_cms_postfilter_registeredtrademarker 109
Smarty filter 107
smarty_function_helloworld 20
Smarty loops
  stylesheet constructs, generating 53-55

Smarty Modifier
  string, reversing 104, 106
Smarty object 75
Smarty tag 12
Smarty values
  using, as inputs in UDT 87, 88
Smarty variables
  about 59, 89
  using, in JavaScript 52
  using, with module 132-135
  using, with template 132-135
Smarty variables, availability 63, 64, 65
software re-use 120
spammers 83
standard module directory structure
  creating 114-116
StartTabContent() method 231
StartTabHeaders() method 231
StartTab() method 231
status command 207, 208, 218
stock prices, Yahoo
  displaying, with UDT 89-92
stock quote URL format, Yahoo 94
StoreInventory.module.php file 261
string
  reversing, Smarty Modifier used 104, 106
strings
  overriding, of CMS module 284-286
str_replace() method 92
strrev() function 106
Structured Query Language (SQL) 146
stylesheet
  color set, creating in 28-31
  sizes, computing in 32-35
stylesheet constructs
  generating, Smarty loops used 53-55
StylesheetOperations object 75
Subversion. *See* also SVN
  access, maintaining to different revisions 210, 211
  changes, merging 209
  commands 210
  documentation 206
  module, developing with 206, 208
  versus Git 222, 223
Subversion repository
  about 204

creating 205, 206
superglobals 73
SuppressAdminOutput() method 241, 297
SVN
  project, importing into 204, 206
svn commit command 209
svn copy command 210
svn log command 210, 214
svn merge command 210
svn mkdir command 205
svn mv command 210
svn revert command 210
svn rm command 210
svn update command 208

T

tab_headers variable 232
tab_message parameter 232
tab system
  methods, for creating 231, 232
tag
  about 8, 12, 19
  creating 17-20
  criteria, for using 11
  disqualifying questions 12
  functions 19
  qualifying questions 11, 13
  versus UDT 13
tag, functions
  about 19
  about text 20
  help text 20
  primary 20
tag names 21
template
  JavaScript, embedding in 51, 52
  Smarty variables 63-65
  Smarty variables, using with 132-135
template engine 70
TemplateOperations object 75
temporary stylesheet 110
thumbnail attribute 45
TortoiseSVN 130, 206
tpl_body:X 110
tpl_head:X 110
tpl_top:X 110

track feature requests (FRs) 200
track_id field 146
tracking systems 200
translation, of current page
  displaying, Babelfish used 95-98

U

UDT
  about 8, 9, 70, 265
  attaching, to event 266, 267
  CmsObject, using in 73, 74
  ContentOperations object, using in 74
  creating 14-16
  disqualifying questions 10
  Page Content object, accessing via CmsObject 73, 74
  page number, displaying 80-82
  qualifying questions 9
  Smarty values, using as inputs in 87, 88
  stock prices, displaying from Yahoo 89-92
  URL parameters, using in 83-86
  user's IP address, displaying from 71, 72
  variables, exporting from 76-78
  versus tag 13
  working 16
UFOTracker.module.php file 175
Uninstall() method 126
UninstallPostMessage() method 245
UninstallPreMessage() method 245
Upgrade() method 126
  about 127
  parameters 127
URL parameters
  using, in UDT 83-86
urlset attribute 48
User-Defined Tag. *See* **UDT**
UserOperations object 75
user's IP address
  displaying, from UDT 71, 72
UserTagOperations object 75
UTF-8 encoding 50

V

ValidateContentBlockValue() method 252
value parameter 55
var_dump() function 185

variable
    providing, to Smarty 76-78
var parameter 55
victories field 151
VisibleToAdminUser() method 256

W

What You Get Is What You Actually Meant. *See*
        WYGIWYAM
where clause 86
word_id parameter 292
World Wide Web 89
WYGIWYAM 205
WYSIWYG editor 143

X

XSS 104

Y

Yahoo
    stock quote URL format 94

[PACKT] open source
PUBLISHING
community experience distilled

Thank you for buying
CMS Made Simple Development Cookbook

About Packt Publishing

Packt, pronounced 'packed', published its first book "*Mastering phpMyAdmin for Effective MySQL Management*" in April 2004 and subsequently continued to specialize in publishing highly focused books on specific technologies and solutions.

Our books and publications share the experiences of your fellow IT professionals in adapting and customizing today's systems, applications, and frameworks. Our solution based books give you the knowledge and power to customize the software and technologies you're using to get the job done. Packt books are more specific and less general than the IT books you have seen in the past. Our unique business model allows us to bring you more focused information, giving you more of what you need to know, and less of what you don't.

Packt is a modern, yet unique publishing company, which focuses on producing quality, cutting-edge books for communities of developers, administrators, and newbies alike. For more information, please visit our website: `www.packtpub.com`.

About Packt Open Source

In 2010, Packt launched two new brands, Packt Open Source and Packt Enterprise, in order to continue its focus on specialization. This book is part of the Packt Open Source brand, home to books published on software built around Open Source licences, and offering information to anybody from advanced developers to budding web designers. The Open Source brand also runs Packt's Open Source Royalty Scheme, by which Packt gives a royalty to each Open Source project about whose software a book is sold.

Writing for Packt

We welcome all inquiries from people who are interested in authoring. Book proposals should be sent to author@packtpub.com. If your book idea is still at an early stage and you would like to discuss it first before writing a formal book proposal, contact us; one of our commissioning editors will get in touch with you.

We're not just looking for published authors; if you have strong technical skills but no writing experience, our experienced editors can help you develop a writing career, or simply get some additional reward for your expertise.

CMS Made Simple 1.6: Beginner's Guide

ISBN: 978-1-847198-20-4　　　Paperback: 364 pages

Create a fully functional and professional website using CMS Made Simple

1. Learn everything there is to know about setting up a professional website in CMS Made Simple
2. Implement your own design into CMS Made Simple with the help of the easy-to-use template engine
3. Create photo galleries with LightBox and implement many other JQuery effects like interactive navigation in your website

Liferay User Interface Development

ISBN: 978-1-84951-262-6　　　Paperback: 388 pages

Develop a powerful and rich user interface with Liferay Portal 6.0

1. Design usable and great-looking user interfaces for Liferay portals
2. Get familiar with major theme development tools to help you create a striking new look for your Liferay portal
3. Learn the techniques and tools to help you improve the look and feel of any Liferay portal

Please check **www.PacktPub.com** for information on our titles

[PACKT] open source
community experience distilled
PUBLISHING

WordPress 3 Plugin Development Essentials

ISBN: 978-1-84951-352-4   Paperback: 300 pages

Create your own powerful, interactive plugins to extend and add features to your WordPress site

1. Everything you need to know to develop your own plugins for WordPress
2. Walk through the development of five plugins from ground up
3. Prepare and release your plugins to the WordPress community

Science Teaching with Moodle 2.0

ISBN: 978-1-84951-148-3   Paperback: 296 pages

Create interactive lessons and activities in Moodle to enhance your students' understanding and enjoyment of science

1. Follow a sample course to see how lessons, groups, and forums are created
2. Make your student's homework more exciting by enabling them to watch videos, participate in group discussions, and complete quizzes from home
3. Simplify the teaching of difficult scientific notation using animations

Please check www.PacktPub.com for information on our titles